# Aid and Technical Cooperation as a Foreign Policy Tool for Emerging Donors



The question of why countries give aid and assistance to other countries has long been a topic of debate – is it altruism, or selfishness? The assumption is sometimes made that donors from developing countries might be more motivated by altruism than 'traditional' western donors. This book demonstrates that on the contrary, the provision of development assistance can be used to serve national interests, allowing so-called 'emerging' donors to gain soft power in the international sphere by improving their image and global influence.

Technical cooperation, or the transfer of knowledge, is an area of particular interest, as it can enable donors to position themselves as a global leader in a given field, with a unique set of skills and expertise in a knowledge area. This book uses the Brazilian case to demonstrate how a country such as Brazil can seek power and influence by providing no-strings-attached technical assistance. The empirical analysis unpicks the motivations behind development assistance, and how it can be used as a foreign policy tool. In doing so, the book sheds light upon the similarities and variations in the provision of technical cooperation as a foreign policy tool by China, India, and Brazil. This book will be of interest to researchers of International Development, South-South Cooperation, International Relations, and those working on Brazil specifically.

**Déborah Barros Leal Farias** is a Lecturer at the University of New South Wales, Australia.

## Routledge Explorations in Development Studies

This Development Studies series features innovative and original research at the regional and global scale. It promotes interdisciplinary scholarly works drawing on a wide spectrum of subject areas, in particular politics, health, economics, rural and urban studies, sociology, environment, anthropology, and conflict studies.

Topics of particular interest are globalization; emerging powers; children and youth; cities; education; media and communication; technology development; and climate change.

In terms of theory and method, rather than basing itself on any orthodoxy, the series draws broadly on the tool kit of the social sciences in general, emphasizing comparison, the analysis of the structure and processes, and the application of qualitative and quantitative methods.

**United States Assistance Policy in Africa**
Exceptional Power
*Shai A. Divon and Bill Derman*

**Chinese Hydropower Development in Africa and Asia**
Challenges and Opportunities for Sustainable Global Dam-Building
*Edited by Giuseppina Siciliano and Frauke Urban*

**Youth, Gender and the Capabilities Approach to Development**
Rethinking Opportunities and Agency from a Human Development Perspective
*Edited by Aurora Lopez-Fogues and Firdevs Melis Cin*

**Democratic Rural Organizations**
Thresholds for Evolution in Africa and Asia
*Esbern Friis-Hansen, Janki Andharia and Godfrey Suubi*

**Aid and Technical Cooperation as a Foreign Policy Tool for Emerging Donors**
The Case of Brazil
*Déborah Barros Leal Farias*

# Aid and Technical Cooperation as a Foreign Policy Tool for Emerging Donors

## The Case of Brazil

**Déborah Barros Leal Farias**

Routledge
Taylor & Francis Group
LONDON AND NEW YORK

First published 2018
by Routledge
2 Park Square, Milton Park, Abingdon, Oxon OX14 4RN

and by Routledge
52 Vanderbilt Avenue, New York, NY 10017, USA

First issued in paperback 2020

*Routledge is an imprint of the Taylor & Francis Group, an informa business*



*British Library Cataloguing-in-Publication Data*
A catalogue record for this book is available from the British Library

*Library of Congress Cataloging-in-Publication Data*
A catalog record has been requested for this book

ISBN 13: 978-0-367-66654-5 (pbk)
ISBN 13: 978-0-8153-6262-3 (hbk)

Typeset in Times New Roman
by codeMantra

**To my family,**
**you are my past, my present, my future**

# Contents

# Figures

# Tables

# Acknowledgements

The list of those who have helped me directly and indirectly write this book is not small. As I think of everyone who gave me a piece of their time to help me reach this milestone, one word comes to mind: gratitude.

I am grateful for the advice and patience of Prof. Peter Dauvergne. More than a great supervisor, a great person. You have always believed and pushed me to seek higher goals with confidence. It has been a true privilege to have your guidance in this process. I am grateful for the assistance and helpful advice from Prof. Brian Job and Prof. Kathryn Harrison. Together with so many great teachers I had the opportunity to interact with at UBC, you've taught me a lot. Thank you for giving me the opportunity to learn new things from you and with you. I am grateful for the warmth from Josephine Calazan, Dory Urbano, and so many others in that Department that have made this place feel like home.

I am grateful for all of those who helped me conduct my fieldwork. The trust from IDRC, whose grant was essential for conducting the research in Brazil. The support from so many who so kindly provided me with such unique insights and opened so many doors, notably: from the Brazilian Consulate General in Vancouver, Ambassador Sergio Florêncio and Conselheira Maria Cristina dos Anjos; at ENAP, Luis Henrique D'Andrea and Rafael Pinto Duarte; at IPEA, Rodrigo Pires Campos and João Brígido; at the University of Brasilia, Profs. Eiiti Sato, Flavio Sombra Saraiva, Cristina Inoue, Antonio Carlos Lessa, and Eduardo Viola; Nelson Bessa Maia, at the Ministry of Finance, among so many others. The generous welcome from João Marcelo BL Carvalho and my dear aunt Ruth Farias (and Laud), who made me feel at home.

I am grateful for the opportunity to learn from each and every one of those which I had the privilege to interview. This book would not have been possible if it wasn't for you.

I am grateful for the patience and support from so many friends. You've helped me keep my spirits up, and showed me I wasn't alone. Regiane, amiga, our weekly coffees were the best therapy one could ask for – cheers to many more to come! Aim, Anastacia, Jen, Beth, Carla, Katrina... you and so many others have made my time in Vancover simply awesome. Coach Paulie, you and so many great people at Lions MMA, thanks for helping me find a way of unwinding through punches, kicks, and lots of laughs. Margaret, Zoe, Amelie, Daphne, Kepler, Melissa, Jeff, thank you for being there for me and my loved ones.

I am grateful for my family and their unwavering support. You inspire me every day to keep moving and do my best. Thank you for always reminding me of what really is valuable in life. Mami e Papi, Ruizinho-Milla-Lara-Benjamin-Bernardo, Iago and Luna – you are my blood, my heart, my home. Mô, I could not have done this without your daily support and patience. This book is here because of your character as a husband, father, and friend. There are no words to capture how much I love and admire you. Thank you all for helping me make this dream come true.

# Abbreviations

| | |
|---|---|
| ABC | *Agência Brasileira de Cooperação* (Brazilian Cooperation Agency) |
| ARF | African Renaissance Fund |
| BRICS | Brazil, Russia, India, China and South Africa |
| CIS | Commonwealth of Independent States |
| CNAT | *Comissão Nacional de Assistência Técnica* (National Commission for Technical Assistance) |
| COMECOM | Council for Mutual Economic Assistance |
| DAC | Development Assistance Committee |
| EMBRAPA | Empresa Brasileira de Pesquisa Agropecuária (*Brazilian Enterprise for Agricultural Research*) |
| FAO | Food and Agricultural Organization |
| FDI | Foreign Direct Investment |
| FIDES | *Fonds d'Investissements pour le dévelopement économique et social* (Investment Funds for Economic and Social Development) |
| FIOCRUZ | *Fundação Oswaldo Cruz* (Oswalso Cruz Foundation) |
| FTC | Free Standing Technical Cooperation |
| FPA | Foreign Policy Analysis |
| GDP | Gross National Product |
| IADB | Inter–American Development Bank |
| IDA | International Development Association |
| IMF | International Monetary Fund |
| IR | International Relations (discipline) |
| IRTC | Investment–Related Technical Cooperation |
| ITEC | Indian Technical and Economic Cooperation Program |
| LDC | Least Developed Country |
| MENA | Middle East & North African |
| MERCOSUL | *Mercado Comum do Sul* (Southern Common Market) |
| MOFCOM | Ministry of Commerce of the People's Republic of China |
| MRE | *Ministério das Relações Exteriores* (Brazil's Ministry of Foreign Affairs) |
| ODA | Official Development Assistance |

| | |
|---|---|
| OECD | Organization for Economic Co–operation and Development |
| OEEC | Organization for European Economic Co–operation |
| OPEC | Organization of the Petroleum Exporting Countries |
| PALAMA | Public Administration Leadership and Management Academy |
| PPP | Purchasing power parity |
| SADPA | South African Development Partnership Agency |
| SEBRAE | *Serviço Brasileiro de Apoio às Micro e Pequenas Empresas* (Brazilian Micro and Small Business Support Service) |
| SENAI | *Serviço Nacional de Aprendizagem Industrial* (National Service for Industrial Training) |
| SSC | South–South Cooperation |
| SUBIN | *Subsecretaria de Cooperação Econômica e Técnica Internacional* (Sub-Secretary of International Economic and Technical Cooperation) |
| TCDC | Technical Cooperation among Developing Countries |
| UN | United Nations |
| UN-GA | United Nations General Assembly |
| UN-SC | United Nations Security Council |
| UNCTAD | United Nations Conference on Trade and Development |
| UNDP | United Nations Development Programme |
| USAID | United States' Agency for International Development |
| WFP | World Food Programme |
| WTO | World Trade Organization |

OECD Organisation for Economic Co-operation and Development

[illegible]

# 1 Introduction

> Knowledge is Power.
>
> *Francis Bacon (1561–1626)*

This book revolves around the connections that exist between foreign policy motivations and the provision of development assistance (a.k.a. 'foreign aid'). It seeks to understand countries' choices to give aid in light of their foreign policy goals. The main puzzle this research is concerned with is why a country would choose to emphasize *technical cooperation* – essentially the exchange of knowledge and know-how – in its provision of development assistance, particularly through *unconditional* and *untied* agreements. Simply put: *what is the (foreign policy) logic behind giving knowledge with no strings attached?* To answer this question, it looks at Brazil and its provision of development assistance mostly through unconditional and united technical cooperation agreements.

Technical cooperation has a fundamental place in the realm of development assistance. Initially known as 'technical *assistance*',[1] it was the very first instrument used for the explicit purpose of helping other countries develop. Compared to grants and loans, a sustained policy of providing technical cooperation is relatively easier, and viable to a greater number of (potential) donor countries. Because every country has *some* unique knowledge (particular experience or ingenious solution) to share, and many countries face similar issues, it is safe to say most countries in the world – both developed and developing – have provided some type of knowledge to another country via technical cooperation at least at some point in their history.

While there has been more visibility of the technical cooperation flowing from developed countries to developing countries, there is a plethora of under-reported and understudied technical cooperation agreements that occur *between* developing countries themselves. There is growing assurance that developing countries, as a group, have an entire range of modern technical competencies. Centres of excellence in key areas have increased national and collective self-reliance, and there is concrete 'South-grown' expertise to be shared (World Bank, 2008; UN-GA, 2009).

Most developing countries tend to deal with similar problems (e.g., poverty; inequality; high child mortality rates), and some might 'bond' over particular situations, such as: countries that share related environmental characteristics or concerns, like rising sea levels; neighbouring countries handling trans-border problems (e.g., drug trafficking); or countries dealing with delicate issues related to a particular cultural or historical background, such as post-conflict reconstruction, etc. Existing examples of this South-South Cooperation (SSC) include: the agreement between Costa Rica, Bhutan, and Benin to share knowledge over sustainable tropical forest management; Kenya's help to South Sudan in developing technical capacity to run the new government; and not to mention the immense volume of initiatives undertaken in the past decade by Brazil, China, and India with other 'Southern' countries. Because of these features, technical cooperation can be seen as a ubiquitous feature in the provision of development assistance.

Paradoxically though, technical cooperation is not a topic of great investigation in the literature concerning development assistance. Most of the academic attention goes to money-based mechanisms, such as grants, loans, debt forgiveness, etc. Some elements inherent to technical cooperation might be at fault for this, with two of them deserving special attention. First, these agreements tend to be characterized by small scope, breadth, and budget. When compared to financial assistance mechanisms, technical cooperation is poised to have a much more limited capacity to effectively help a country *develop*. So, while these agreements can be useful for helping to overcome *some* specific problem, or fill a knowledge gap in *some* area, they (typically) have a narrow capacity to leverage broad transformations. Second, technical cooperation agreements generally involve non-controversial topics, which tend to fly under the radar of most political debates, media coverage, or public interest. Hence, by themselves, each agreement generally has little reach, limited potential for structural changes in the recipient's development, and low visibility.

But despite these 'weaknesses', technical cooperation agreements still continue to be part of almost all countries' foreign policy mechanisms for providing development assistance. There are four main possibilities for why technical cooperation is such a ubiquitous part of development assistance. While the motives are non-exclusionary, it is common that some (or one) reason will be more prevalent than the others in guiding a country's decision to offer technical cooperation. First, due to its continuous use as a mechanism for providing 'foreign aid', offering technical cooperation has become intrinsic to the idea of providing development assistance itself: it is used because 'everyone who is a donor offers it' and 'it's always been done'. Second, for most developing countries that want to provide development assistance, technical cooperation is probably the *only* option available for nations with few resources, which simply *can't* offer much else to others even if they wanted to (except for an occasional help in emergency situations): 'we can *only* offer technical cooperation'. Third, technical cooperation might be used because it *develops*. Under this logic, sharing knowledge promotes best practices and real solutions. In this case, there is an underlying altruistic bent: 'it is offered because it works' and 'it helps the recipient's development'. The fourth reason – the one which will be explored in depth in this research – is providing technical cooperation *to gain something in return.*

The first two motives only concern the donor, as it asks itself 'what can I provide [in the context of development assistance]'? The next two involve thinking about the nature of the relationship with the recipient: 'what do I, as a donor, *expect* from providing technical cooperation?' – the question this book is most interested in. There is a great deal of academic debate over the broad theme of why give 'foreign aid' in the first place (which will be explored in Chapter 2). The present accepts that countries might be motivated to offer technical cooperation for purely altruistic reasons. However, it assumes that most donors' initiatives are attached to *some interest*: donors do in fact seek to gain something from recipients when they agree to provide technical cooperation (even if it is not publicly admitted).

The idea that countries' foreign policies are motivated by 'gaining power' and that they seek to support 'the national interest' is not new (Morgenthau, 1962; Hook, 1995). But countries can want different things out of their development initiatives, so these answers are not sufficient. Therefore, the question becomes 'if donors want to gain something, *what kind* of gain are they looking for'? Assuming there are different types of gains which could be accrued, allows for a yet deeper layer of analysis: '*what leads* donors to tend to prioritize one type of gain over other(s)'? These two questions are original and relevant, and follow Wendt's (1999:133) call for more empirical research be done to investigate "what kinds of interests state actors actually have".

This book begins by positing a parsimonious approach towards self-interests sought from providing development assistance in general and technical cooperation in particular, dividing it into two basic categories: ***commercial*** and ***diplomatic gains***. The former is straightforward: the primacy is to accrue profits for the donor country. Thus, 'commercial gains' involve seeking concrete returns – *making money* – through the process of selling/buying goods and services. 'Diplomatic gains', on the other hand, will be the term used to designate a broad range of gains that are mostly intangible (albeit very much real and sought-after in foreign policy), and harder to be secured (as they are usually based upon a social element of gratitude and/or recognition). As Chapter 2 will detail, they are related to the concepts of 'soft power' (Nye, 1990a, 1990b, 2004, 2011) and 'middle power diplomacy' (Evans, 1989, 2011; Evans & Grant, 1991, 1995; Cooper et al., 1993). Examples of diplomatic gains to the donor State include:

- recipient's votes and/or implicit support for the donor in international *fora*;
- donor's improved regional/international image as a 'do-gooder';
- strengthened bilateral/regional relations between donor and recipient(s);
- donor's increased regional/international legitimacy as a *necessary* voice regarding a certain topic, etc.

It is important to highlight an important boundary: the present analysis is concerned mainly about gains for *the State*, not for the individual actor engaged in the policy. This means it consciously brackets the analysis of policymakers motivated by *personal* monetary gains (in the form of bribes or side-payments). Also, the word 'diplomatic' has been chosen over '*political* [gains]' in order to highlight the focus on the State, foreign policy, and the international context. Nonetheless, significant connections between national and international politics are taken into consideration, as domestic normative and institutional factors inform foreign policymaking in a "two-level" process decision-makers are simultaneously engaged (Putnam, 1988).

For this book, it is assumed that (1) donors would like to accrue *both* diplomatic and commercial gains from their initiatives; but (2) in each agreement, the donor can give primacy to *only one* of these gains, which concurrently lowers the chances of the other.[2] This does not mean that the donor does not value both diplomatic and commercial gains, nor that these gains are mutually exclusive – it just means the donor must opt between what it wants *more*. The argument posited is that the optimal way to achieve *diplomatic gains* through technical cooperation is by proposing agreements that have *no-strings-attached.*

Development assistance instruments, in general, can be provided with or without certain characteristics: 'conditionalities' and/or 'tied' agreements. To the first point, donors can *condition* their provision of development assistance by demanding that the recipient promote specific institutional changes so that the aid can be provided. Conditionalities can be of political nature (like related to democracy or strengthening institutions) or have an economic focus (such as macroeconomic reforms or trade concessions), and do not need to be directly related to the effectiveness or the goal of a specific development initiative. To the second item, when donors 'tie' the assistance it means the recipient must purchase – exclusively from the donor – certain goods and services related to the projects. 'Tying' an agreement means placing clear commercial provisions that benefit the donor over a specific development-based initiative.

Each one of these 'attachments' is independent from one another. Each donor can choose how it wants to provide its development assistance: (1) conditional and tied; (2) unconditional and tied; (3) conditional and untied; or (4) unconditional and untied. This last combination is the one which will be detailed, and serve as a synonym for what is meant by 'no-strings-attached' technical cooperation.

In sum, development assistance is one out of the many foreign policy initiatives a country has to achieve its goals. Development assistance can be provided by various mechanisms – one of which is technical cooperation. And technical cooperation can be arranged through different combinations: with/without conditionalities and with/without ties. This book is interested in why countries choose to provide technical cooperation agreements that have no conditionalities and no ties in the context of their foreign policy goals (Figure 1.1).

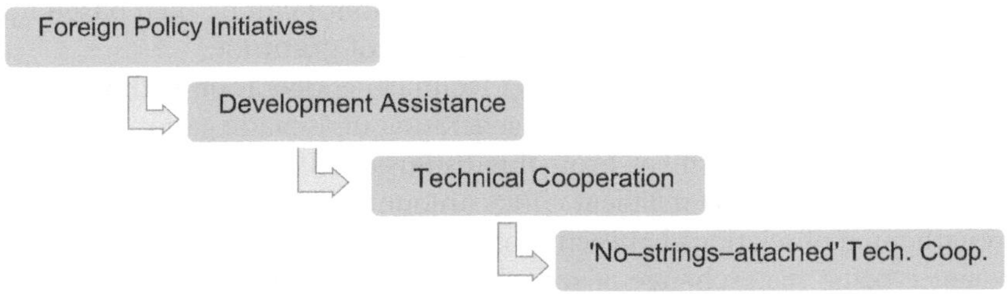


*Figure 1.1* Foreign policy goals through no-strings-attached technical cooperation.

## 'No-strings-attached' technical cooperation

Conditionalities and ties always take away some level of the recipient's autonomy, since they limit the recipient's options. This book assumes that, *ceteris paribus*, recipients will tend towards a no-strings-attached arrangement. This derives from the understanding that placing conditionalities and ties onto technical cooperation agreements will reduce (although not necessarily eliminate) diplomatic gains for the donor from its interaction with the recipient.

In the case of unconditional and untied technical cooperation agreements, donors' expectations of gains (whether commercial or diplomatic) are not formalized. This means they are not written in the agreements, and consequently they are not legally binding under International Law.[3] After all, if they were binding, they would not be *un*conditional or *un*tied. Of course, behind-the-scenes *quid pro quo* 'commitments' might be established. But what matters the most here is that, in these cases, there are no formal commitments made by the State, as they rely solely upon vows made between the individuals involved in the negotiation. Hence, they are *not* legally binding, and a recipient's compliance cannot be explicitly demanded by the donor. This is certainly one of the reasons for the unattractiveness of a no-strings-attached arrangement – it has no 'teeth'. It is not an ideal path for donors who seek guarantees in achieving foreign policy goals embedded in their provision of development assistance. If a donor wants the recipient to assure it will open its markets or promote democracy, having the opportunity to place conditionalities but not doing so might seem nonsensical. If the immediate gain sought by the donor through technical cooperation is a commercial one – such as selling equipment or a specific service – then untied technical cooperation is a missed opportunity.

Nonetheless, even if the donor does not *ask* for anything, donors generally still *expect* to gain something from the recipient even if nothing is openly expressed. This related to the notion that social norms regarding 'gift' retributions (Mauss, 1966[1923]) and reciprocity (Keohane, 1986) can prompt the receiver to 'pay back' the donor (in some way) under the implicit assumption that it is the right thing to do – an idea which will be explored in greater depth in Chapter 2. Diplomatic gains for the donor can be then based upon the *social expectation* of the recipient's feeling of gratitude.

Still, even if a strategy of proposing technical cooperation with no-strings-attached can be deemed rational for generating diplomatic gains, it can be argued to be a weak mechanism. From this disillusioned view, such an agreement – even if satisfying for the recipient – may amount to little more than a nominal strengthening of relations between those involved, with the only practical consequence being the exchange of some technicians or bureaucrats, and thus, a limited impact. In a worst-case scenario, no exchange even occurs, with the agreement serving as just a symbolic piece of paper stating that cooperation *can* occur at some point, with no assurance that it even will.

However, this logic overlooks a long-term, broader dynamic. It appears fair to say that *one* technical cooperation agreement will probably not impact substantially the relationship among two countries. Nonetheless, this is a narrow way of seeing things. A scenario in which two countries sign several technical cooperation agreements (all arranged without conditions or ties) over many themes, and which the recipient believes are helping its development, can have an enormous potential to strengthen bilateral relations. If donor and recipient are neighbouring countries, this can generate even more resonance. A sustained policy of helping-thy-neighbour can mean less problems for both: less illegal trafficking of drugs, people, stolen goods, weapons, etc.; lower potential for conflict among border communities; better management of the bordering natural environment; and/or (potentially) more commerce between the two. Promoting solid relationships with several neighbours can generate diplomatic gains for a donor in an entire region. This dynamic could also be extended to outside of the donor's immediate geographic location: crafting positive relations with several recipients in another region can indirectly improve the donor's status with that entire region.

In this same line of thought, a donor which executes many agreements in a single niche area – like hunger, poverty, health, technological innovation, or post-conflict rebuilding – can also generate considerable diplomatic gains. Such strategy can make/help the donor be perceived as a legitimate voice in that area, potentially leading to a perception that it is a *necessary* actor in international negotiations over that theme. Of course, there are no guarantees that any of these gains will happen because of a series of unconditional and untied technical cooperation agreements. Still, it is logically reasonable to state that there is an increased chance that they will. This bigger picture naturally calls for an ampler timeframe. There is an inherent lag between negotiating an agreement, signing it, putting it into practice, and being able to measure its success. So, an agreement signed today most likely will not generate immediate diplomatic gains for the donor. Then again, building an image – whether it is of a 'do-gooder', 'legitimate actor', 'trustworthy partner', or 'benevolent regional leader' – is not something that typically emerges from a single action or that happens in a short timeframe.

This bigger picture reveals that commercial gains can be sought in tandem with diplomatic gains. However, in this scenario they are a consequence of giving unconditional and untied technical cooperation. In this proposed win-win scenario, the recipient would obtain knowledge with no-strings-attached, and 'thank' the donor out of its own volition and in its own terms and timeframe. While this could come through support for the donor's position in an international organization, it could also mean favouring the purchase of goods and services from the donor – whether in relation to the agreement itself or in other areas – because it *wants to*, as opposed to because it *has to*.

A donor's best chance at securing commercial gains via technical cooperation is to prompt agreements that are conditional to macroeconomic changes and lock-in the recipient's purchases. On the other hand, a donor's best chance at reaping diplomatic gains is by not demanding anything back from the recipient. A visual representation could be depicted as the following: in Scenario I, commercial gains for the donor can be seen as guaranteed, and conceived with a rather short-term timeframe; in Scenario II, diplomatic gains are expected and commercial gains are possible, but the timeframe is longer (Figure 1.2).

A synthesis of the argument is that a country that is committed to providing unconditional and untied technical cooperation as part of its development assistance framework is strategically prioritizing (mid/long term) diplomatic over (short term) commercial gains, counting on the expectation of reciprocity from its recipients. Assuming this assertion is correct, there is yet another question to be answered: *what leads a donor to prioritize diplomatic over commercial gains*? After all, if countries would want both diplomatic *and* commercial gains to accrue from their foreign policy interactions, what drives them to choose to emphasize one over the other? Attaching 'strings' (or not) to technical cooperation reflects different preferences, as it improves the odds for one type of gain but lowers the odds for the other. Assuming this is not a haphazard decision, there are important dynamics which deserve investigation.

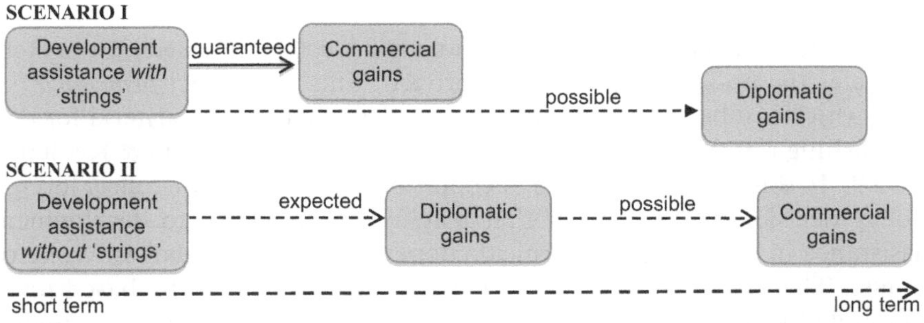


*Figure 1.2* Scenarios: development assistance, commercial, and diplomatic gains.

## Forces shaping foreign policy priorities

This book looks at foreign policy decision-making as a process that reflects and interacts with both domestic and international elements, based on the (no longer controversial) understanding that domestic politics and international relations interact in a profound manner (Gourevitch, 2002:309). There is no single theory of domestic politics to explain international cooperation (Milner, 1992:494). The one that makes more sense for the argument put forth is related to institutional theories of the state, such as bureaucratic and organizational politics, which focus on domestic decision-making structures (*idem*). As posited by Milner (1992:494), "the character of domestic political institutions may condition both the preferences of a state and its ability to negotiate internationally", in which case the national interest "depends on how political institutions shape actors' preferences and condition their access to decision-making forums".

Following Lancaster (2006:4), "the purposes of foreign aid are frequently as much the result of what happens inside of a donor government's borders as what happens outside them". This research posits that three key forces will impact a country's foreign policy decision to prioritize diplomatic gains (through unconditional and untied technical cooperation agreements) over commercial gains, here labelled: ideational, institutional, and positional forces. While each one alone won't necessarily lead to a specific outcome, the combination of these three is poised to set a specific path. Weber's (1946 [1922–1923]:280) interesting metaphor of ideas serving as switchmen – by determining the tracks along which action will be pushed by the dynamic of interests – serves as a good starting point for understanding 'ideational forces'. Ideas can serve as blinders, reducing the number of conceivable alternatives and obscuring the other tracks from view. Hence, this book abides by Goldstein and Keohane's understanding:

> Like Weber, we do not argue that ideas *rather than* interests (as interpreted by human being) move the world. Instead, we suggest that ideas as well as interests have causal weight in explanations of human action.
> (Goldstein & Keohane, 1993:3–4)

Ideational forces can (consciously or unconsciously) guide decision-makers to prefer the no-strings-attached approach. This can reflect *principled beliefs*, which can be defined as "normative ideas that specify criteria for distinguishing right from wrong and just from unjust" (Goldstein & Keohane, 1993:9). In this case, the absence of conditionalities or ties can reflect foreign policy decision-makers' belief that placing 'attachments' to development assistance in general (and technical cooperation in particular) is wrong or unjust. Then again, a decision to place 'attachments' can be based upon principled beliefs just as well. This can come as a reflection of an understanding from the donor's side that there is nothing problematic about these 'attachments', and that they are normal and accepted practices of providing development assistance. If the basic *ethos* that guides foreign policy decision-makers is one directly connected to promoting the country's trade, then untied agreements would be conceived of as bad policy; if the accepted belief system is one that demanding ties will harm the donor's relationship with the recipient(s), decision-makers will likely prefer the 'no-strings' arrangement. But values alone might not determine the final policy: the role of domestic institutions is of great significance, especially the bureaucratic dynamics related to foreign policy decision-making.

If many institutions have a voice in foreign policy making but they all hold similar values for deciding over 'attachments' in technical cooperation (e.g., 'there is nothing wrong with tied aid'), their shared vision will lead to a rather clear path (such as 'tied agreements'). But in most cases, this congruence among interests is not present. As foreign policy tends to interface with many domestic policies, this means institutional tensions and conflicts are common. In many countries, for instance, the lines between which bureaucracy should have the main voice in the decision-making process over a specific topic can be quite blurred. Not all actors who see themselves connected to foreign policymaking will necessarily hold the same view (or even have a clear opinion) of what is 'the right thing' to do when it comes to providing assistance to other countries. While they can all claim to be committed to making decisions based on their country's 'national interest', in practice this can mean significantly different choices – if not opposing strategies.

Foreign policymaking regarding the provision of development assistance can involve (sometimes fierce) competition between two or more institutions, each one holding their own understandings of which priorities the country should have in mind when providing help to other countries. Compounding to different belief systems, some institutions embody projects and visions that call for a longer timeframe than others; some are more pressured by interest groups; some seek decisions based primarily on 'technical' analyses; not to mention that when it comes to giving aid, some would want to help the country's own poor before helping others abroad, or even not provide aid at all.

The bottom line is that usually there are internal forces that concurrently advocate for their vision, either to *push towards* or *pull away from* prioritizing diplomatic gains vis-à-vis commercial gains. The final decision will most likely follow the ideas of whoever has the strongest voice over this matter. So, if the 'winner' happens to be a bureaucratic institution directly concerned on, for example, trade promotion, technical cooperation agreements will most likely be tied. If in a country only one bureaucratic institution is the locus for foreign policymaking and is relatively isolated from outside pressure, the institution's normative understanding over how to provide development assistance will most likely set the path to be followed and repeated over time. So, if 'the' foreign policymaking institution pushes for diplomatic gains, and it has no real challengers to this position, this will probably be the outcome.[4]

> Every organization has a culture, that is, a persistent, patterned way of thinking about the central task of and human relationships within an organization. (...) Like human culture generally, it is passed from one generation to the next. It changes slowly, if at all.
>
> (Wilson, 1989:91)

The final decision on how to provide development assistance (and technical cooperation) can also be very influenced by the country leader's role in determining foreign policy. While some presidents/prime ministers actively exert a prominent role in crafting their own vision of foreign policy, others can be aloof towards international relations, embracing what is recommended by their most trusted source on the issue. Most commonly, this tends to be the Ministry of Foreign Affairs (or its equivalent), although in practice it is not unusual to have this institution be overrun by other voices – which could be the Ministry of Trade, the leader's political party, the Senate, or a 'kitchen cabinet' of close advisers. This highlights the assertion that certain normative and institutional elements inside of each country are deeply interconnected and essential for understanding each one's final foreign policy decisions. At the same time, in democratic settings, policymakers are limited by the law. Therefore, legal directives – such as the Constitution – can constrain interested actors' range of available options.

The third key element to understanding what influences foreign policy decision-makers to opt for (un)conditional or (un)tied technical cooperation is what this book will call 'positional forces'. Here, this will refer to (1) the idea that actors (e.g., countries, firms, individuals) belonging to a specific social structure have a *position* within this arrangement; and (2) it is assumed that all actors seek to either maintain or improve their position. This book argues that where countries see themselves (i.e., their 'position') within the international system, and – more importantly – how they react to this position, can contribute to the decisions made about giving preference to diplomatic or commercial gains. For example, a country might seek to improve its 'international position' through a more prominent role in international organizations, or place itself in a key position within a 'network' of countries interested in the same theme. In most cases, the support from other countries is required to achieve these goals.

Positioning can also imply behavioural expectations from others. As Chapter 4 will show, 'Southern'/developing countries tend to frame conditionalities as something 'traditional' donors do. Thus, if 'rich' developing countries – such as Brazil, China, and India – wish to maintain their legitimacy as part of the 'South', they will be expected to provide development assistance with no conditionalities. In this context, unconditionality is a strategy to mitigate negative impressions accruing from an asymmetric South-South relationship between 'powerful' and 'powerless' developing countries. Highlighting a 'Southern' identity would allow greater ease for emerging donors to portray their development assistance as different from 'traditional' donors, and an us-versus-them type of discourse. However, the same cannot be said for explaining *untied* development assistance. As it will be shown, South-South Cooperation does not explicitly preclude the use of commercial ties in aid provisions. Unlike unconditionality, untied assistance is not a central part of a 'Southern' identity.

Diplomatic gains from technical cooperation are more likely to be sought by countries who believe they have a better shot at improving their position – *gain power* – in the international system through non-coercive ways, i.e., based upon 'soft power'. This could be because the donor country simply does not *have* coercive power sources (such as nuclear weapons, strong military, significant economic weight). Another possibility is that a non-coercive approach can be adopted as purposeful strategy to establish/strengthen a specific positive image, such as 'good international citizen', non-threatening neighbour, and trustworthy partner. This approach goes hand-in-hand with countries embracing a so-called 'middle power *diplomacy*', whose characteristic method is to build coalitions with 'like-minded' countries usually revolving around 'niche diplomacy', and is typically motivated by 'good international citizenship' (Evans, 1989). As Chapter 2 will detail, 'niche diplomacy' refers to the concentration of foreign policy resources in specific issue areas best able to generate returns, rather than trying to cover the field (Evans & Grant, 1991:323); and 'good international citizenship' involves the pursuit of national interests through cooperation and involvement addressing international problems. This specialization in specific areas is expected to improve a country's power as it becomes a go-to reference – i.e., a *necessary* player – in international debates over the theme, resembling a hub-and-spoke model (Figure 1.3), or at least enhance its position among the network of those interested in the subject (Figure 1.4).

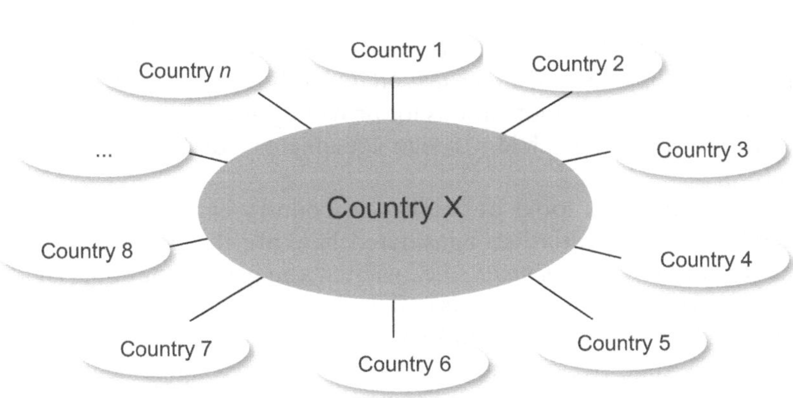


*Figure 1.3* Hub-and-spoke network model.

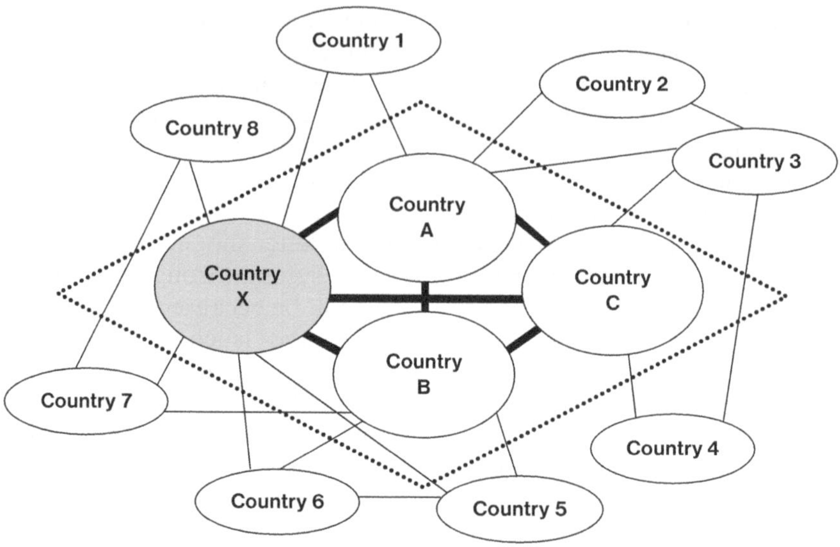


*Figure 1.4* Network model, key-players.

In sum, countries that choose to provide unconditional and untied technical cooperation agreements are prioritizing diplomatic gains over commercial gains. There are usually few – if any – *guarantees* that these gains will occur, with donors relying on *social norms of reciprocity* as a motivation for the recipients to 'pay back'.

## Basic boundaries and definitions

This research looks specifically at development initiatives undertaken by countries.[5] The rationale behind is simple: development assistance will be studied *within the context of foreign policy*, an area where countries are the only actors to have legitimacy and legal capacity to act upon. Other actors engaged in development assistance (ex: NGOs, sub-national actors) might have their own interests and motivations for providing aid, but none has the innate authority to speak – much less to sign agreements – on behalf of a sovereign country.

Because this book looks at country-to-country engagements, the development assistance initiatives considered here are those provided through some sort of *formal agreement* – i.e., written and generating some legal consequences for its signatories. This makes them *treaties* according to International Law: Article 2.1 (a) of the Vienna Convention on the Law of Treaties (1969) states that "treaty" means "an international agreement concluded between States in written form and governed by international law, whether embodied in a single instrument or in two or more related instruments and whatever its particular designation". The term 'agreement' can have both a generic and specific meaning. When used as a specific term (such as in 'technical cooperation agreement'), it designates a particular name given to a treaty that has a somewhat narrow scope of subject matter. Commonly, it is used to designate instruments of a technical, administrative, cultural, and educational character; they may or may not be subject to ratification by countries, depending on each one's domestic legislation and the legal structure of the agreement itself. Not all international arrangements between parties that materially focus on technical cooperation are officially *named* 'technical cooperation *agreements*'. The title assigned to international instruments has normally no overriding legal effects, as it "may follow habitual uses or may relate to the particular character or importance sought to be attributed to the instrument by its parties" (*UN Treaty Collection*, undated).

### *Providing development assistance*

Development assistance can be provided in many ways. Technical cooperation, grants, and loans are traditional mechanisms for this purpose. However, there is no unified legal or academic definition regarding whether *other* initiatives can also count as development assistance or not. Some countries see development assistance (grants + loans + technical cooperation) as a separate category from debt pardons, humanitarian aid, and military assistance. Other donors embrace a broader definition do development assistance, and include many (or all) of the latter initiatives under *their* unique interpretation (Figure 1.5), an issue that will be detailed in Chapters 3 and 4.

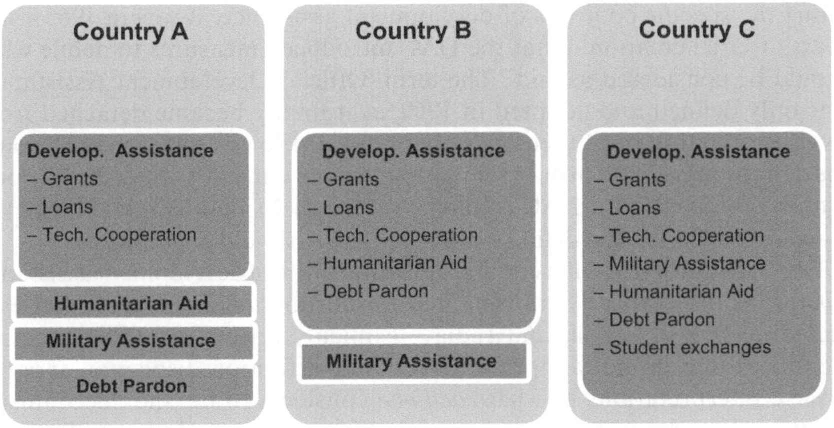


*Figure 1.5* Example of donor's interpretation of development assistance mechanisms.

A good starting point for a definition comes from the OECD's Development Assistance Committee (DAC) and its definition of what it calls 'Official Development Assistance' (ODA):

> *Grants or loans* to countries and territories on the DAC List of ODA Recipients (developing countries) and to multilateral agencies which are: (a) undertaken by the official sector; (b) with promotion of economic development and welfare as the main objective; (c) at concessional financial terms (if a loan, having a grant element of at least 25 per cent). In addition to financial flows, *technical co-operation* is included in aid. Grants, loans and credits for military purposes are excluded. Transfer payments to private individuals (e.g., pensions, reparations or insurance pay-outs) are in general not counted.
>
> (*OECD DAC Glossary*, undated; emphases added)

This definition is helpful since it is the agreed upon definition used by DAC's member-countries and non-member-countries who choose to report their development assistance activities to DAC. The numbers and characteristics of Official Development Assistance matter for at least two very important reasons. First, it captures what traditional donors do, which is still the bulk of worldwide international development activities. Second, having a single template used by so many important countries undoubtedly facilitates comparative and historical analysis by researchers, inasmuch as it identifies qualitative standards of aid transfers, establishes guidelines for reporting and monitoring ODA flows, and compiles these data in annual tables that provide a statistical basis for cross-national comparison (Hook, 1995:xiii).

However, while the definition for what should be counted as development assistance is now rather straightforward for these countries, it was not an easy one to arrive to in the first place. In a testament to the difficulty of defining the specific contours of development assistance, it was in 1965 – five years after its creation – that the DAC introduced measures to define what should be considered as 'aid'. The term 'Official Development Assistance' was only defined and adopted in 1969, as it finally became detached from its categorization until then of "Other Official Flows". Only in 1972 would the definition become firmer, remaining the one currently used. Simply put: it took *twelve* years for DAC countries (not even 20 members at the time) to come up with a unified definition of what ODA should encompass.

DAC's definition of what counts under the rubric of development assistance *cannot* be automatically transplanted for all donors, as many countries – including Brazil, China, and India – explicitly reject this understanding. Countries that do not adopt the DAC/ODA definition display an array of diverse interpretations to what *each one* considers to be 'the' mechanisms for providing development assistance. While the core elements that constitute ODA – grants, loans, and technical cooperation – seem to always be included in every non-DAC countries' definition, other categories that are treated separately for DAC countries are frequently built-in within the measurement and evaluation of development assistance by non-DAC donors.[6] These might include initiatives such as: humanitarian aid; debt relief; provision of goods (i.e., medications, food, clothing) or services (i.e., doctors, technicians); country contributions to international development organizations (i.e., UNDP, FAO) and regional banks (i.e., IADB); scientific and technological cooperation; and scholarships for foreign students. Adding to the complexity, the concept of SSC, adopted by the UNDP and by many developing countries (to be discussed in depth in Chapter 4), calls for an even *wider* net of activities that represent international cooperation towards development:

> South-South Cooperation is a broad framework for collaboration among countries of the South in the political, economic, social, cultural, environmental and technical domains. Involving two or more developing countries, it can take place on a bilateral, regional, subregional or interregional basis. Developing countries share knowledge, skills, expertise and resources to meet their development goals through concerted efforts. Recent developments in South-South Cooperation have taken the form of increased volume of South-South trade, South-South flows of foreign direct investment, movements towards regional integration, technology transfers, sharing of solutions and experts, and other forms of exchanges.
>
> (UNDP What is SSC?; undated)

Different countries have different thoughts regarding what is or should be categorized as 'mechanisms of providing development assistance'. This issue highlights the reality that large-*N* direct comparisons – or even small-*N* comparisons between non-DAC members – of the total volume of countries' reported engagements in 'international development' can be very misleading if the definitional discrepancies are not dealt with in the data analysis. This study does not aim to compare all variations that exist, or investigate why particular items are included or not included in countries' definitions, but rather aims to conceptualize why a country will *privilege* one (or a few) mechanisms over others.

### *Technical cooperation*

Defining technical cooperation as an instrument of international development is not a straightforward task. As well posited by Arndt (2000:158), "technical co-operation is a bit like poverty: difficult to define precisely; but one knows it when one sees it". There is no shortage of definitions employed by different agencies and individuals. The working definition of technical cooperation for this research looks at *agreements between states that are focused upon exchanges of (existing) knowledge aimed at fostering development*, as this covers the core of existing definitions (Burnell, 1997; Arndt, 2000; Browne, 2002; IMF, 2003; DFID, 2012; UNDP, *What is SSC?*; *OECD DAC Glossary*). So, while financial aid – such as grants and loans – can be seen as a mechanism to close resource gaps of developing countries, technical cooperation is a way to compensate for skills (Browne, 2002:1). There is no consensus on what is the precise boundaries or relationship between 'technical' and 'scientific/technological' cooperation. This book uses the term 'technical cooperation' to identity exchanges of *existing* knowledge, whilst the latter used for partnerships to *create new* knowledge. Hence, the expression *technical cooperation agreement* will from herein designate formal (written) understandings between States, whose content is centred upon the exchange of knowledge, i.e., the main goal is to transfer knowledge.

Some international organizations (such as the IMF and the OECD) specifically divide technical cooperation in two categories: (1) free-standing technical cooperation (FTC); and (2) investment-related technical cooperation (IRTC). FTC is "the provision of resources aimed at the transfer of technical and managerial skills or of technology for building up general national capacity without reference to the implementation of any specific investment projects"; IRTC "denotes the provision of technical services required for the implementation of specific investment projects" (IMF, 2003). This research will only deal with the free-standing kind. Ajayi and Jerome (2002:23) go further and propose a detailed categorization of technical cooperation, divided in eight types. While this research will not use these subdivisions, they open opportunities for future research.

The actual training and know-how exchange can be done by specialists and consultants hired for that specific purpose, or rely on public servants with first-hand experience. Pragmatically, technical cooperation aimed at promoting development involves initiatives such as: sharing innovative technologies; providing details and helping to reproduce and adapt successful public policy projects; or offering training and capacity building for public servants. In many cases, for a knowledge exchange to effectively occur, the recipient might have to purchase some type of equipment or good (such as machinery, software, or laboratory equipment) deemed necessary for the project. Also, these agreements typically include details over financial matters related to covering costs and expenses associated with the provision of the knowledge transfer, with the money coming from the donor alone (quite common), both the donor and the recipient (less common), or from third parties (less common). Therefore, the volume of money involved can vary dramatically: it can be very small, such as just enough to cover travel and accommodation expenses for a few public servants for some days abroad; or involve very large sums, as in the case of projects involving large-scale training, a long-term timeframe, and with broad national reach.

## Book outline

This book is divided in seven chapters. Following the introductory chapter, Chapter 2 provides a theoretical overview of development assistance in general and the provision of technical cooperation in particular. The focus is on understanding these topics within the context of foreign policy. Studies over countries' power – e.g., how it is gained, sought, exerted – are brought into the analysis, with attention to the concepts of 'soft power', 'middle power diplomacy' and 'niche diplomacy'. Finally, because attention is given to technical cooperation provided with no conditions or no ties, a logical structure is presented to investigate possible gains from this strategy.

Almost all donors provide development assistance (and technical cooperation) within one of two frameworks: Chapter 3 looks at 'traditional' donors and the OECD's DAC model, while Chapter 4 focuses on SSC. Both chapters present a historical account of the rise of development assistance – focusing on technical cooperation – within each of these frameworks. The goal is to understand the different backgrounds, how these have evolved over the years, and how countries abiding to these models have provided development assistance and technical cooperation. As the chapters show, abiding to a specific framework indicates general patterns, but does not determine behaviour – i.e., technical cooperation is provided in different ways – with/without conditionalities or ties – among countries within the same 'block'.

Chapter 5 extends the previous chapter's analysis of donors abiding to the SSC framework by focusing on a subcategory: so-called 'emerging' donors, with attention to Brazil, China, India, and South Africa. These nations – particularly the first three – are responsible for blurring (even more) the tenuous line between developed and developing countries. Despite the term 'emerging', these countries have a significant history of providing development assistance. What is relatively new is their prominent political and economic importance in the international system, and their unprecedented expansion in partnerships and initiatives. The chapter details China, India, and South Africa's histories and current overall patterns as providers of development assistance. The main goals are: (1) reinforce the point that there are similarities and differences in donors' choices within each aid provision framework; and (2) compare how each of these countries deals with the provision of technical cooperation in particular – and their positions over conditionalities and commercial ties in their provision of technical cooperation.

Chapter 6 deals specifically with the case study: Brazil as a donor. The chapter investigates Brazil's motivations for such a choice, beginning with the broad contours of Brazil's path to becoming an 'emerging donor'. It then moves on to explain the country's decision to (1) focus on technical cooperation in its development assistance strategy, and (2) provide such technical cooperation with no conditionalities or commercial ties. Finally, Chapter 7 concludes the book, providing a summary of the main arguments and findings related to the use of technical cooperation as a foreign policy tool, with great attention to the Brazilian case. The chapter reflects upon what this means for the literature in the fields covered, and proposes areas for further exploration.

## Notes

1 In 1959, there was a change in the official UN nomenclature, as the UN General Assembly expressed the wish that the term be replaced by the term 'technical cooperation' (UN-GA, 1959), with most countries following suit. While it is not incorrect to use 'technical *assistance*' (a few countries still do), it can be seen as an anachronous choice.
2 These assumptions have been derived from academic literature and interviews on recipients' general perceptions of development assistance.
3 Under the rules of the International Court of Justice, customary law and principles of International Law – both unwritten – are not only considered sources of International Law, they have (*a priori*) the same status as treaties. However, the two former sources don't seem applicable to cases involving development assistance (or technical cooperation).
4 Authors who focus on US foreign aid (such as Lancaster, 2006) highlight the important role private business interest groups have in the country's foreign policy in general, particularly foreign aid. This model does reflect the reality of some other countries as well, but it is not a general rule as it will be seen in throughout this research.
5 Some minor attention is given to the actions of international organizations, but only as they represent the result of its *member-countries'* interests.
6 This book follows Mawdsley's concern that as a 'residual' category, the concept of *non-DAC members/donors* might erroneously "promote the normative centrality of DAC, while suggesting a peripheral location, or unfulfilled aspiration for the remainder" (2012:257). For the sake of parsimony, the term 'non-DAC' will be used through this book with the clear understanding that it does *not* signal some sort of subcategory vis-à-vis DAC membership.

## Bibliography

Ajayi, S. I., & Jerome, A. (2002). Opportunity costs and effective markets. *Development Policy Journal, 2*, 23–46.
Arndt, C. (2000). Technical co-operation. In F. Tarp (Ed.), *Foreign aid and development: Lessons learnt and directions for the future* (pp. 154–177). London: Routledge.
Browne, S. (2002). Introduction. In S. Browne (Ed.), *Developing capacity through technical cooperation country experiences* (pp. 1–14). London: Earthscan.
Burnell, P. (1997). *Foreign aid in a changing world.* Buckingham: Open University Press.
Cooper, A. F., Higgott, R. A., & Nossal, K. R. (Eds.). (1993). *Relocating middle powers: Australia and Canada in a changing world order* (Vol. 6). Vancouver: UBC Press.
DFID – Department for International Development. (2012). *Statistics on International Development 2012, Annex 2: Glossary.* www.dfid.gov.uk/Documents/publications1/sid2012/SID-2012.pdf.
Evans, G. (1989). *Making Australian foreign policy.* Australian Fabian Society Pamphlet, no. 50, p. 42.

Evans, G. (2011, June 29). *'Middle power' diplomacy.* Inaugural Edgardo Boeninger Memorial Lecture, Chile Pacific Foundation, Santiago. www.gevans.org/speeches/speech441.html.

Evans, G., & Grant, B. (1991; 1995 2nd edition). *Australia's Foreign Relations in the worlds of the 1990s.* Melbourne: Melbourne University Press.

Goldstein, J., & Keohane, R. (1993). Ideas and foreign policy: An Analytical Framework. In J. Goldstein, & R. O. Keohane (Eds.), *Ideas and foreign policy: Beliefs, institutions, and political change* (pp. 3–30). Ithaca, IL: Cornell University Press.

Gourevitch, P. (2002). Domestic politics and international relations. In W. Carlsnaes, T. Risse-Kappen, & B. A. Simmons (Eds.), *Handbook of International Relations* (pp. 309–328). London: Sage.

Hook, S. W. (1995). *National interest and foreign aid.* Boulder, CO: L. Rienner Publishers.

IMF – International Monetary Fund. (2003). *External debt statistics: Guide for compilers and users – Appendix III, Glossary.* Washington, DC: IMF.

Keohane, R. (1986). Reciprocity in international relations. *International organization, 40*(1), 1–27.

Lancaster, C. (2006). *Foreign aid: Diplomacy, development, domestic politics.* Chicago, IL: University of Chicago Press.

Mauss, M. (1923). Essai sur le don forme et raison de l'échange dans les sociétés archaïques. *L'Année sociologique (1896/1897–1924/1925), Nouvelle série, T. 1,* 30–186.

Mauss, M. (1966). *The gift – Forms and functions of exchange in Archaic societies.* London: Cohen & West.

Mawdsley, E. (2012). *From recipients to donors: Emerging powers and the changing development landscape.* London: ZED books.

Milner, H. (1992). International theories of cooperation among nations: Strengths and weaknesses. *World Politics, 44*(3), 466–496.

Morgenthau, H. (1962). A political theory of foreign aid. *The American Political Science Review, 56*(2), 301–309.

Nye, J. S. (1990a). Soft power. *Foreign policy, 80(Special edition, 20th anniversary*), 153–171.

Nye, J. S. (1990b). *Bound to lead: The changing nature of American power.* New York: Basic Books.

Nye, J. S. (2004). *Soft power: The means to success in world politics.* New York: Public Affairs Store.

Nye, J. S. (2011). *The future of power.* New York: Public Affairs.

OECD – Organisation for Economic Co-operation and Development. *Glossary.* www.oecd.org/site/dacsmpd11/glossary.htm#T.

Putnam, R. D. (1988). Diplomacy and domestic politics: The logic of two-level games. *International organization, 42*(3), 427–460.

UN – United Nations. (undated). *Treaty collection.* Definition of key terms used in the UN Treaty Collection. http://treaties.un.org/Pages/Overview.aspx?path=overview/definition/page1_en.xml.

UNDP – United Nations Development Programme. (undated). *What is South-South Cooperation?* www.unsouthsouth.org/about/about-sstc/.

UN-GA – United Nations General Assembly. (1959, November 20). *Resolution 1383 – Expanded programme of technical assistance.*

UN-GA – United Nations General Assembly. (2009, October 27). *Promotion of South-South Cooperation for development: A thirty-year perspective*. Report of the Secretary-General, A/64/504.

Weber, M. (1946 [1922–1923]). The social psychology of the world religions. In H. H. Gerth & C. W. Mills (Eds.), *From Max Weber: Essays in sociology* (pp. 267–301). New York: Oxford University Press.

Wendt, A. (1999). *Social theory of international politics*. Cambridge: Cambridge University Press.

Wilson, J. Q. (1989). *Bureaucracy: What government agencies do and why they do it*. New York: Basic Books.

World Bank. (2008). *Aid architecture – An overview of the main trends in official development flows*. http://siteresources.worldbank.org/IDA/Resources/Aid_Architecture-May2008.pdf.

# 2 Development assistance and technical cooperation

## A theoretical overview

Writing in the early 1960s, Hans Morgenthau stated: "of the seeming and real innovations which the modern age has introduced into the practice of foreign policy, none has proven more baffling to both understanding and action than foreign aid" (Morgenthau, 1962:301). The goal of this chapter is not to solve this puzzle by attempting to answer the thorny question 'why countries provide foreign aid'? Nonetheless, it is feasible to conceptualize the possible logic(s) that might drive countries to engage as donors, and what they might seek to gain from their actions.

This book's broad interest is to understand why countries choose to provide unconditional and untied technical cooperation in their development assistance programmes. The answer is sought in the context of the donor's foreign policy interests. This chapter's goal is to provide a literature review of links between foreign policy and development assistance, as well as highlight the conceptual framework adopted for explaining why a country – such as Brazil – would choose to give no-strings-attached technical cooperation under the expectation of accruing diplomatic gains. The analysis' main theoretical reference relates to the concept of *power*, drawing mostly from academic debates in the field of International Relations (IR).

In order to conduct this analysis, this chapter is divided into three sections. The initial section looks at the existing theories that deal with the question of *why* countries provide development assistance, focusing on debates from four major viewpoints: Realism, Structuralist/Dependency Theory, Idealism/Liberalism, and Constructivism. The second section deals with relevant connections between power and development assistance, particularly non-coercive sources and uses of power ('soft power'), and foreign policy behaviours linked to 'middle power diplomacy' and 'niche diplomacy'. The third section discusses how power can be attained under the logic of gift-giving (i.e., giving without demanding anything in return) using Mauss' *The Gift* (1966[1923]) as a theoretical reference. Finally, the section ends with an analysis of what kind of gains can be accrued from giving technical cooperation.

### IR theories on development assistance

The literature in the field of IR brings varied explanations as to why countries choose to provide development assistance. While scholars from each of

IR's major schools of thought present their own interpretation for answering this question from a conceptual framework, when it comes to explaining a concrete scenario, each one might only be able to provide a *partial* explanation.

### *Realism*

The general sense from Realist scholars is that foreign aid is essentially a tool to enhance the donor's national power and security. Simply put: decisions regarding development assistance are fundamentally based upon the giver's self-interests, with the recipient's development not being a priority. In this light, "foreign assistance should primarily, if not exclusively, be designed to facilitate donor's interests", and are appropriate only to advance donor interests (Hook, 1995:34–35). The provision of 'tied' aid is understood as an undisputed act of self-interest, as it seeks to increase donor's exports and protect its balance of payments (Hoadley, 1980). Using the United States in the first decade of the Cold War period as a reference point, Liska (1960:14) posited: "Foreign aid is today and will remain for some time an instrument of political power". For him, politics was the governing factor, not an incidental factor which could be dispensed with: foreign aid was all about facilitating donors' interests, with humanitarian goals being de-emphasized. It was "not something to be done, as a Government enterprise, for its own sake for the sake of others", because the United States Government was "not a charitable institution, nor is it an appropriate outlet for the charitable spirit of the American people" (Liska, 1960:127). Regarding the specific role of foreign aid as a source of power, Morgenthau (1962:301) stated: "[The] United States has interests abroad which cannot be secured by military means and for the support of which the traditional methods of diplomacy are only in part appropriate". He then provided his own typology for foreign aid: "[H]umanitarian foreign aid, subsistence foreign aid, military foreign aid, *bribery*, prestige foreign aid, and foreign aid for economic development"; more importantly, he added that "of these distinct types, *only humanitarian foreign aid is per se non-political*" (Morgenthau, 1962:301; emphasis added). Later, and following the same line of thought, Gilpin added that even if some humanitarian values were present, "the primary motives for official aid by governments have been political, military, and commercial", as the "donor's desire to establish spheres of political influence, to bolster military security or to obtain economic advantage has influenced the nature and patterns of aid" (Gilpin, 1987: 311–312).

### *Structuralist/Dependency Theory*

After the 1950s, a series of international talks and negotiations between developing countries questioning their position in the international system began to take place, including the Bandung Conference, New International

Economic Order, and the G-77. In tandem emerged an academic literature providing analytical support for a position which perceived the world as divided by the haves and have-nots. It became especially in vogue with developing countries, serving as the theoretical base for 'South-South Cooperation' (detailed in Chapter 4). The Structuralist/Dependency Theory approach, similar with Realists, suggests the State's self-interests determine characteristics of foreign aid. But unlike Realists, Structuralists argue that development assistance is a consequence of *capitalism*, not simply each individual country's 'national interest'. Aid is yet another capitalist tool used by elites/the core to exploit the marginalized/periphery. The perception that the world's economic structure is framed around a problematic 'North-South' productive system developed at length by the academic literature on Dependency Theory (e.g., Prebisch, 1949; Frank, 1966; Cardoso & Faletto, 1971; Galtung, 1971; Wallerstein, 1974). Strongly influenced by Marxist historical structuralism, their worldview is based upon the concepts of metropolis and periphery, with the latter being subjugated by the former (Abdenur, 2002:63).

### *Idealism/Liberalism*

Idealist/Liberal interpretations tend to look towards the altruistic side of countries' decision to provide development assistance. Some authors explicitly highlight the moral 'paradigm' of helping others being the main driver for actions undertaken. For Zinkin (1978:272), "aid is charity; if it is not charity, it is not aid". Lumsdaine (1993:3), in similar lines, argued "humanitarian concern in the donor countries formed the *main basis* of support for aid" (emphasis added). Under this view, once aid policies of more numerous smaller donors were considered, the altruistic dimensions of global foreign aid could be revealed (Hook, 1995:36). Another line of interpretation within the Idealist/Liberal approach emphasizes the process of international *cooperation* and interdependency to solve 'global public goods',[1] while not dismissing some level of donor self-interest. This angle tends to be frequently highlighted in material produced by International Organizations involved in international development, such as the United Nations Development Programme (UNDP): "International aid [can be seen as] an investment in public goods; (…) *International aid is the point at which moral values and enlightened self-interest intersect.* The moral imperative behind aid is reflected in many value-based systems of thought" (UNDP, 2005:78; emphasis added). However, even if countries frequently give to others out of what appears to be moral and ethical beliefs (such as following natural disasters), there is still room for debate as to (1) if these actions should be categorized as '*humanitarian*' assistance (not *development* assistance); (2) what relationship is there between humanitarian and development assistance (i.e., is humanitarian aid a *type* of development assistance or do they belong in separate categories?); or even (3) when countries decide to help other nations in dire need, if are they doing so out of 'true' ethical and moral concerns or because of calculated gains/losses of *inaction* (expectation from voters, international image, influx of immigrants, geopolitical concerns, etc.). Hence, the assertion that 'a donor is motivated to provide development assistance with no strings attached due to moral/ethical reasons: *it is the right thing to do*' is difficult to evaluate as it hinges on a series of definitions that are also hard to define and measure: what is precisely meant by 'aid', 'humanitarian assistance', or 'development assistance'; how does one measure altruism; whose moral/ethical values, etc.?

### *Constructivism*

There are many forms of defining Constructivism, but its essence lies upon the *social construction of identities and interests* (see Adler, 2002). Unlike other '-*isms*' (such as Realism, Structuralism, or Liberalism) constructivism is not a *theory* of International Relations. It is an *approach* which looks at processes, rather than a substantive outcome (Hopf, 1998:196). The socially constructed nature of world politics is now broadly accepted, and what remains contestable between Constructivists and others is *how* (not 'whether') this insight affects the study of world politics, both in its methodology and in its substance (Hurd, 2008:301–302). Wendt (1999:1–2) conceptualizes a 'thin' version of constructivism, conceding that international reality is a product of *both* socially constructed and material elements. A 'thin constructivist' lens makes sense of material and ideational factors, which co-inform a country's own approach towards providing foreign aid. One fundamental fact highlights why adopting a 'thick' constructivist approach ('ideas all the way down') to explain countries' decisions over foreign aid is not recommended: there are undeniable material constraints to providing foreign aid. Countries' calculations are inescapably based upon what they *can* give, not simply what they *would like to* give. As said, most countries in the world do not have the means to structure a policy of giving grants or loans to other countries simply because they don't have the money to do it or the knowledge to share. Just as South Sudan can't have a structured policy for being a provider of grants and loans to other countries (they don't have the means), Iceland is very unlikely to provide technical cooperation over the production of tropical fruits in semi-arid climates (they don't have the knowledge). These realities can surely change in the future, but at this moment in time, these material constraints exist and are incontestable.

Once material limitations are considered, the next step is to comprehend the ways in which a country provides development assistance. For this, it is necessary to understand the ideas, concepts, and values that form its foreign policy. This entails (1) comprehending the values and political forces that shape its diplomatic contours to find out *what* it wants, and out of these, which one(s) are prioritized; as well as (2) considering how the country's decision-makers see their country's position within the international scenario and the tools available to decide *how* to act. While the first point is finding out 'what do we [as a country] want *more*', the second is '*how* can we get what we that'? A constructivist approach is extremely helpful in finding these answers, as "by making interests a central variable, constructivism explores not only how particular interests come to be, but also why many interests do not" (Hopf, 1998:176).

Realist theory and constructivist epistemology are not incompatible. When constructivism is understood as a set of assumptions about "*how to study* politics"–rather than assumptions about "how politics *work*"–it is clearly compatible with a variety of paradigms, including Realism (Barkin, 2003:338).[2] A State's interests cannot be mechanically deduced from international anarchy and the distribution of material resources (Adler, 2002:102). Policies are made based on inferences about each other's intentions (pessimistic or optimistic), which are tested and revised against of what those intentions really were in a continuous process of interacting with reality (Wendt, 1999:108). This points to the Foreign Policy Analysis (FPA) literature, whose most important contribution to IR theory – according to Hudson (2007:7) – "is to identify the point of theoretical intersection between the most important determinants of State behaviour: material and ideational factors", with this point of intersection being human decision-makers (and not the state). Social constructions like culture, domestic institutions and bureaucracy are essential to fully understand what informs countries policy*makers'* foreign *policymaking* processes.

Numerous Realist scholars share the understanding that non-material factors play a key role in shaping states' interest. These include Thucydides, Clausewitz, and Morgenthau, for whom "identities and values were more important determinants of policy than the constraints and opportunities of the external environment" (Lebow, 2004:345). Morgenthau's point on what constitutes a state's specific interest and *how* this is pursued is of great significance:

> [Realism] does not endow its key concept of interest defined as power with a meaning that is fixed once and for all. (…) [T]he kind of interest determining political action in a particular period of history depends upon the political and cultural context within which foreign policy is formulated. The goals that might be pursued by nations in their foreign policy can run the whole gamut of objectives any nation has ever pursued or might possibly pursue.
>
> (Morgenthau, 1960[1948]:11; emphases added)

A nuanced understanding of how States' interest is crafted also concedes that a donor can gain *through* cooperation, i.e., giving with no-strings-attached can be a form of achieving the donor's self-interest. The existence of payoffs to cooperation does not disprove the idea that state behaviour is egoistic (Lumsdaine, 1993:17). While the main driver to provide development assistance can be to gain something, it is very well possible that this 'something' be better obtained through a strategy of cooperation (as opposed to coercion). There is no *a priori* reason to suppose that transfers cannot assist the recipients just because they are offered on grounds that include self-interest (Burnell, 1997:3), because egotistic ends may be achieved by means that benefit larger collectivities, from the community and State levels to the entire global population (Hook, 1995:184). Hence, the provision of development assistance and the goal of gaining power are intrinsically intertwined, as expected by Realists. But *how* donors seek power and for *what purpose* begs a contextual understanding, at which point a constructivist approach is essential.

## Power through development assistance

The study of power within the discipline of International Relations is marked by an extensive and rich literature. Power is a ubiquitous element in the study of the relationship between nations. It is also a highly contested topic of inquiry and subject to a myriad of analyses. It is more than a variable or a process to be accounted for; it is a *question* to be investigated (Mattern, 2004:345). This section looks at two ways in which the quest for power intersects with development assistance. First, the use of development assistance as a non-coercive ('soft') mechanism to gain power. Second, as a strategy to gain power in a determined *locus* by becoming a prominent actor in a specific group (e.g., regional, 'Southern' countries, francophone nations) or theme (e.g., water management in semi-arid climates, peacekeeping missions, climate change). This latter use of development assistance to strategically gain power in discrete areas can be conceptualized as 'niche diplomacy', and is closely related to the concepts of 'middle powers' and 'middle power diplomacy', both of which will be briefly investigated. 'Niche diplomacy' bears great resonance to Brazil's approach towards technical cooperation, and will be discussed with greater depth in Chapter 6.

### *Non-coercive ('soft') power*

Realism has many times been described as a theory whose focus is not only entirely upon power, but one where power is narrowly conceived. Realists' would value the issues related to the politics *of force* – a.k.a. 'power politics' (*Machtpolitik*). As stressed by Baldwin (2002) and Barnett and Duvall (2005), during the Cold War many in the field of International Relations neglected other forms of power besides coercive power. Power was conceptualized not merely upon material elements (tangible 'things'), but primarily those of military value, such as tanks and bombs. This occurred under a scenario where the conduct of international relations would take place "by force, or the threat of force, without consideration of right and justice" (Wight, 2002[1946]:29). In this context, States would be mainly (if not solely) concerned about the military capabilities necessary to maximize their security.

While it is true that some realists' writing – such as Neo-Realists Stephen Waltz and John Mearsheimer – are overwhelmingly dedicated to these issues, it would be incorrect to state that all Realists see power from this perspective.

So-called Classical and Neoclassical Realists generally see State power as being comprised of a larger gamut of sources. Military capabilities matter, but they are not the only expression of a nation's power; the ability to impose and coerce are important, but so are a country's capacity to attract and co-operate. For these scholars, power comes "in a multiplicity of forms – such as moral authority, force, and even care – and can be expressed in a multiplicity of fashions – for instance through material, ideational, symbolic, and linguistic means", with each of these forms affecting "the conduct and dynamics of international politics differently" (Mattern, 2004:345). Thus, notwithstanding the undeniable importance of coercive instruments and practices for foreign affairs, to understand a country's power and use of power in its foreign policy choices requires going beyond a narrow conception of power and the incorporation of other sources and mechanisms. Many self-described Realists have pointed out how complex and multi-faceted power analysis can be (Barkin, 2003). In 1945, Albert Hirschman stressed the importance of economic dynamism and *influence* as a source of power. Lasswell and Kaplan (1950:77) talked about power as being defined relationally, not as a simple property: "to have power is to be taken into account in others' acts (policies)". For them, "it is of crucial importance to recognize that power may rest on various bases, differing not only from culture to culture, but also within a culture from one power structure to another" (Lasswell & Kaplan, 1950:85). Around the same period, Morgenthau, described power as comprising "*anything* that establishes and maintains the power of man over man", thus covering "*all* social relationships which serve that end, from physical violence *to the most subtle psychological ties by which one mind controls another*" (Morgenthau, 1960[1948]:11; emphases added). In his preface to *Politics Among Nations'* 1960 edition, his disagreement over a reductionist interpretation of power was very clear:

> Against the misunderstanding of the central element of power, which, after having been underrated to the point of total neglect, now tends to be equated with material strength, especially of a military nature, I have stressed more than before its immaterial aspects, especially in the form of charismatic power, and have elaborated the discussion of political ideologies.
>
> (Morgenthau, 1960[1948]: ix)

Still around the same time, Bachrach and Baratz's (1962, 1963) and Wolfers (1962) wrote about the need for a more nuanced understanding of power. Bachrach and Baratz (1962:952) highlighted "the power to limit the scope of negotiations", which they saw as the 'second face of power'. Wolfers (1962) contested the constant evocation to only the *coercive* side power when one discussed the common usage of the term 'power' in International Relations. For him, trying to influence friendly countries with promises or benefits was often a more effective instrument than making threats.

> It is appropriate, therefore, to distinguish between *power* and *influence*, the first to mean the ability to move others by the threat of infliction of deprivations, the latter to mean the ability to do so through promises or grants of benefits. The distinction between power and influence or 'power politics' and 'influence politics' does not mean that the two can be clearly separated in practice; as a rule, they will be found to go hand in hand. (...) *[Influence's] usefulness as an instrument of foreign policy is far from negligible and in some situations, especially where demands are to be made on friendly nations, it outstrips power.*
>
> (Wolfers, 1962:104–105/108, emphasis added)

In 1985, Baldwin emphasized the need to observe both positive sanctions (actual or promised rewards) and negative sanctions (actual or threatened punishments) as means to exercise power, as the first were often overlooked as sources of power. He classified the means of exercising power ('influence') in the international system in four categories: symbolic, economic, military, and diplomatic. For him, power did not have to be necessarily understood as a zero-sum game. This works well with the idea of giving technical cooperation with no-strings-attached: the giver's power is enhanced *through* – and not *taken from* – the recipient.

In the context of the Cold War's aftermath, Joseph Nye (1990a, 1990b) coined a two-fold categorization of power: 'hard power' and 'soft power'. This distinction has transcended academia and became incorporated into mainstream language – "soft power is everywhere" (Kearn, 2011:65). Nye's most thorough definition of soft power is "the ability to affect others through the cooptive means of framing the agenda, persuading, and eliciting positive attraction to obtain preferred outcomes" (Nye, 2011:20–21). While military power and economic power were used to *command* ('hard power'), 'soft power' served to *co-opt*. This process involves the attractiveness of a country's culture, political ideals, policies, and the ability to establish a set of favourable rules and institutions that govern areas of international activity – these are all considered critical sources of soft power (Nye, 1990a, 1990b, 2004).

The concept of 'soft power' resonates with some important aspects of the provision of no-strings-attached development assistance. Soft power uses "a different type of currency (not force, not money) to engender cooperation – an attraction to shared values and the justness and duty of contributing to the achievement of those values" (Nye, 2004:7). The provision of knowledge through technical cooperation can easily be framed as an example of 'a different type of currency to engender cooperation', especially if done by a developing country under the banner of shared 'South' values. Nonetheless, there

*Table 2.1* Hard/Soft power behaviours and resources, according to Nye (2004)

| | *Hard Power* | | *Soft Power* | |
|---|---|---|---|---|
| Spectrum of Behaviours | Command Coercion | Inducement | Agenda Setting | Attraction Co-opt |
| | ◄ | | | ► |
| Most likely Resources | Force<br>Sanctions | Payments<br>Bribes | Institutions | Values<br>Culture<br>Policies |

*Source*: Reproduced from Nye (2004:8).

are some important distinctions which makes the strategy of giving technical cooperation with no conditions or ties strongly connected but not identical to the Nye's definition of 'soft power' resources/behaviour. For Nye, 'soft power' would be at work when a country is persuaded to go along with another "*without any explicit* threat *or exchange* taking place", and the behaviour being determined by "and observable but *intangible* attraction" (*idem*). While command power ("the ability to *change* what other *do*") rests on coercion or inducement, co-optive power ("the ability to *shape* what others *want*") is based upon the attractiveness of a country's culture and values, or the ability to manipulate the agenda (Nye, 2004:7), as presented in Table 2.1.

Given Nye's definitions, using the provision of 'no-strings-attached technical cooperation' as a synonym for 'soft power behaviour' leads to some conceptual caveats. Giving knowledge without demands is certainly not a coercive practice. However, it can be easily categorized as an *explicit exchange* meant to *induce* the recipient to (somehow) return the 'gift'. According to the table above, this would fall under the label 'Inducement', hence an exercise of 'hard power' (even if in a mild version). Also, the provision of any kind of bilateral development assistance is an observable and *tangible* resource. While knowledge is an intangible good, the actual exchange of knowledge between two countries can only take place if certain concrete things occur: a signed agreement between States and individuals have to be designated to transmit the knowledge – not to mention the typical need for material goods (e.g., lab facilities, software, computers). If tangible resources are an expression of 'hard power', then technical cooperation agreements (even if unconditional and untied) can be placed under Nye's definition of 'command-seeking behaviour'.

Many scholars have criticized Nye's choice to link hard power behaviour (seeking command) with tangible resources; and attaching soft power behaviour (seeking to co-opt) with intangible resources. Examples of why Nye's categorization can be conceptually problematic are not hard to find. For instance, values and norms are intangible, but a country can try to impose them; also, norms are commonly used in the international system in name-and-shame campaigns to explicitly – and forcefully – discourage a country's specific activity or policy. On the other hand, countries can use many 'hard' resources (including weapons and money) to attract, whether by providing humanitarian aid, interest-free grants, or military cooperation against common threats such as illegal drug or weapons trafficking. To be fair, Nye has shown his awareness to this "imperfect relationship" since the beginning, but has maintained "the association is strong enough to allow for the useful shorthand reference to hard and soft power" (Nye, 1990a:182).

This has not been enough to dispel the confusion generated from the frequent amalgamation of discussions over defining characteristics of soft power with empirical observations (Baldwin, 2013:289). The hard/soft power division ultimately reflects ideal types; in practice, soft and hard power techniques are frequently mixed (Haugaard, 2011:6). To make the term 'soft power' explicitly connected to the provision of 'diplomatic gains from unconditional and untied technical cooperation', one possibility would be for the present book to propose a particular use of the term. Rothman (2011:50) correctly states that other scholars have defined 'soft power' using a variety of resources: the use of information (Armistead, 2004), philanthropy (Jenkins, 2007), or diplomacy (Kurlantzick, 2007), although this could lead to a debate over 'conceptual stretching' (Collier & Mahon, 1993) by reducing the usefulness of the concept in analytical and policy research.

The bottom line is that using Nye's original categorization of hard/soft power can be problematic for understanding the behaviours and resources donors seek through bilateral (unconditional and untied) technical cooperation agreements. Nonetheless, the concept is still useful for this research for at least two points. First, it highlights the non-coercive nature of seeking power through 'gifts'. Second, 'soft power' (under Nye's understanding) is very adequate for 'diplomatic gains' accrued *diffusely*. Diffuse diplomatic gains relate to the spill over effects of a donor's actions in country 'X' to other countries – whether in the same region or globally. These gains can mean increasing legitimacy over a particular issue or being recognized as an informal leader to speak in behalf of a group of countries (such as 'developing countries'). In this case, the concept of 'soft power' – with its intangible resources and attraction through values – makes sense. As an example, it is worth quoting Celso Amorim, Brazil's former Minister of Foreign Affairs (2003–2010), who once said that "*Brazil's great skill is to be friends with everyone*" (BBC, 2010; emphasis added).

## 'Niche diplomacy' and 'middle power diplomacy'

The origin of the term 'niche diplomacy' can be traced to former Australian foreign minister Gareth Evans, who defined it as the concentration of "resources in specific issue areas best able to generate returns worth having, rather than trying to cover the field" (Evans & Grant, 1991:323). It refers to specialization, somewhat echoing classic economists Adam Smith and David Ricardo's idea of 'comparative advantage'. 'Niche diplomacy' can be pursued by any country, but it has a characteristic generally associated with small and 'middle powers':

> Niche diplomacy, though often associated with very small countries, has in fact been more fully developed by countries that have sufficient size and capacity to play notable roles on the international stage, but are not strong enough to impose their positions or solutions... Very large powers too may develop niche diplomatic and other particular capabilities. The difference is that great powers, unlike small or middle-sized countries, lack either the necessity or the incentive to do so. They usually can exert influence, as well as exercise power, across the board.
>
> (Henrikson, 2005:67)

The research on 'niche diplomacy' is strongly connected to academic discussions related to so-called 'middle powers'. This book embraces Evans' (1989; Evans & Grant, 1991, 1995) distinction between 'middle power' and 'middle power diplomacy', situating the analysis on 'niche diplomacy' on the latter concept, i.e., 'niche diplomacy' is a characteristic *method* of 'middle power diplomacy'. But to understand this distinction or address links between 'niche diplomacy' and development assistance, it is necessary to first understand the concept(s) of 'middle power'.

### *Middle powers*

The term 'Great Powers' has been common in diplomatic parlance since at least the mid-18th century (Buzan, 2004:58). At the same time, there was an acknowledgment that even if some countries were not part of '*The* Great Powers', they could still be *some* 'great powers'. Holbraad (1971:78) notes that the German term *Mittelmacht* – literally translated to '*middle power*' – appears in the "political writings of earlier centuries, not least in those of the nineteenth, where German writers in particular used it", but with a different understanding than that of contemporary use. Reaching even further back in time, in 1589 Giovanni Botero wrote in *Ragion di Stato* about countries with sufficient strength and authority to stand on their own without the need of help from others, which could be very well be interpreted as 'middle powers'.

Notwithstanding this history, the academic literature in the field of International Relations regarding 'in between' actors in the international system began to develop in the early post-World War II years. The term 'middle powers' began to appear in academic pieces right after the creation of the United Nations (see Fox, 1946). Glazebrook (1947) appears to have been the first to explicitly analyse this group as a unit.[3] He broadly defined them as those "which make no claim to the title of great power, but have been shown to be capable of exerting a degree of strength and influence not found in the small powers" (Glazebrook, 1947:307). For him, the UN member-countries which would be recognized as 'middle powers' were: in Europe, Belgium, the Netherlands, and Poland; in the Americas, Argentina, Brazil, Canada, and Mexico; and in the Pacific, Australia, and India. As the Cold War progressed in the 1950s and the international system became increasingly centred upon the two super-powers (United States and the Soviet Union), attention to these 'middle' players in the literature somewhat receded.

In the second half of the 1960s, in light of the *détente* and the concomitant 'emergence' of the Third World, the theme would regain a greater academic visibility. For example, Waltz (1964) mentions 'middle powers' in the context of a stable bipolar world; Rothenstein (1968) and Fox (1969) also engage with 'middle powers' considering their attention to small countries. One of the most important pieces to appear in this period was written by Keohane (1969). His definition involves a four-tiered classification, based upon ability to impact the international system: (1) a *Great Power* is a State "whose leaders consider that it can, alone, exercise a large, perhaps decisive, impact on the international system"; (2) a *secondary power* is a country "whose leaders consider that alone it can exercise some impact, although never in itself decisive, on that system";[4] (3) a *'middle power'* is a country "whose leaders consider that it cannot act alone effectively but may be able to have a systemic impact in a small group or through an international institution"; and (4) a *small* power is a nation "whose leaders consider that it can never, acting alone or in a small group, make a significant impact on the system" (Keohane, 1969:296). From then on, 'middle powers' would be researched continuously, gaining an even greater level of attention after the end of the Cold War.

Moving on from terminology, two fundamental challenges remain in this area: (1) which countries should be classified as 'middle powers' (and based on what criteria), and (2) what are the expectations of foreign policy behaviour for 'middle powers'? Beginning with the first challenge, the literature clearly shows there is no agreed upon single template for gauging countries' 'middle power' status, and trying to come up with a list of such "is an exercise fraught with peril" (Evans, 2011). Cooper et al. (1993:17–19), described three approaches for 'middle power' classification, although two of them has not gained much traction. One highlights geography, i.e., a country physically in the middle of the system's great powers. There would be two variants of this approach: one suggesting that 'middle powers' are countries powerful in their (geographic) regions; the other, that these would be the country ideologically 'in the middle' of polarized great powers. The second approach is a normative one, which takes 'middle powers' as potentially more virtuous then those 'above' or 'below' them. The most commonly used approach outlined by Cooper et al. (1993) – one which is still easily seen two decades later – has been to rank countries within some sort of power hierarchy by considering a series of 'objective' measures. Countries would then be placed within a range of very powerful to very powerless – with some literally in the *middle* of the range, with not too much or too little power. While common, this approach has serious drawbacks. To begin, each researcher can choose which variables it finds to be the 'right' ones; even if there is agreement on which variable to use, a different weight could be attributed to each one, leading to different results. Not to mention the obvious problem of defining the 'ideal' cut-off line between big, middle, and small powers.

One visible consequence of this approach is the enormous variation in which countries should be classified as 'middle powers'. It appears that no country identified as such appears has been spared by someone questioning of whether it deserves or not to be called as such. Even the most common examples of 'middle' countries (Australia, Canada, and Norway) have been subject to political or academic scrutiny over their 'middle' status – e.g., "Canada is not a typical middle power" (Potter, 1996/1997:28). And with the criteria for national effectiveness and global influence in such a state of flux, it is difficult to say which nations are the current great powers (Kennedy, 2013). Ultimately, Hurrell (2006) highlights one crucial point about why numbers alone are not enough to determine which countries belong – or not – to the *great* powers tier: the socially 'constructed' facet of being seen *by others* as belonging to this 'group':

> Being a great power has never been solely about the possession of large amounts of crude material power. It has been closely related to notions of legitimacy and authority. A state can claim great power status, but membership of the club of great powers is a social category that depends on recognition by others: by your peers in the club, but also by smaller and weaker states willing to accept the legitimacy and authority of those at the top of the international hierarchy.
>
> (Hurrell, 2006:4)

### *'Middle power diplomacy'*

Given this unclear picture, the use of 'middle power' as a concept for academic purposes is directly contingent to each researcher's chosen definition of what the 'right' boundaries should be. In several occasions since the late 1980s, Evans (e.g., Evans, 1989, 2011; Evans & Grant, 1991, 1995) has suggested moving on from attempting to classify countries as 'middle powers' and looking instead at 'middle power *diplomacy*' (see also Cooper et al., 1993), and for whom the characteristic method of 'middle power diplomacy' is

> coalition building with 'like-minded' countries [and] usually revolves around '*niche diplomacy*'. (…) By definition, middle-powers are not powerful enough in most circumstances to impose their will may be persuasive enough to have like-minded others see their point of view, and act accordingly".
>
> (Evans & Grant, 1991:344; emphasis added)

The same author posits the *characteristic* motivation for 'middle power diplomacy' as one of 'good international citizenship': a belief in the utility, and necessity, of acting cooperatively with others in solving international problems. However, an important qualification is that this characteristic should not be equated to a foreign policy of "boy scouts doing good deeds". Therefore, 'good international citizenship' is not something separate and distinct from the pursuit of national interests. On the contrary, "'being, and being seen to be, a good international citizen' should itself be seen as a third category of national interest, right up there alongside the traditional duo of security and economic interests" (Evans, 1989:42). Under this logic, the end result of being seriously committed to international problem-solving is that national interests are advanced through two paths. First, through reciprocity: a country helping another solve a problem makes the recipient more willing to reciprocate on other issues. Second, through reputational benefits, since "the perception of being a country willing to take principled stands for other than immediately self-interested reasons does no harm at all to one's own commercial and wider political agendas" (Evans, 2011). Ultimately, for 'middle power diplomacy' to be effective, four main factors are involved: (1) real opportunity for potentially effective action; (2) physical capacity to follow through; (3) a degree of intellectual imagination and creativity applied to the issue, and the ability to lead by the force of ideas; and (4) credibility on part of the country applying to avoid the risk of being changed with hypocrisy (Evans, 2011).

An additional element can be added to the logic of 'middle power diplomacy' through 'niche diplomacy': the creation and/or strengthening of networks. Networking can be defined as "a quiet, methodical business. To have a 'niche' – or privileged or protected corner – in diplomacy, as in business or any other activity, requires wide recognition as well as a secured position" (Henrikson, 2005:70). A network structure "provides power to achieve preferred outcomes *with* other players rather than *over* them" (Nye, 2010). The power that flows from networks "is not the power to impose outcomes. Networks are not directed and controlled as much as they are managed and orchestrated" (Slaughter, 2009:99). Networks create power in a manner well suited for specialization. A country which embraces a diplomatic niche is naturally seeking a prominent or leadership power position vis-à-vis all interested in the topic, and particularly regarding other like-minded countries. The ability to make the maximum number of valuable connections is essential, and so is having "the *knowledge and skills* to harness that power to achieve a *common* purpose" (Slaughter, 2009:100; emphases added). Nye's following example is particularly relevant:

> in a hub-and-spokes network, power can derive from being the hub of communications. (…) If the points in the rim are not directly connected to each other, their dependence on communication through the hub can shape the agenda.
>
> (Nye, 2011:17)

Ultimately, moving away from 'middle power' as a *hierarchical* position to a *behavioural* definition allows a better analysis of choices regarding the use of technical cooperation as a foreign policy tool. To begin, it lessens the burden of determining hard boundaries for who would be 'in' or 'out' of the analysis. Of course, this does not mean that determining who behaves as a 'middle power' is a straightforward feat – it is not. But the list of characteristics thought to identify 'middle power' behaviour can be said to be clearer and more well-defined in the literature, thus allowing a relatively easier assessment of which countries fall under this category in a specific moment in time. In tandem, the concept of 'middle power *diplomacy*' (as opposed to 'middle power') creates a smoother path for developing expectations related to the provision of development assistance and technical cooperation. Countries labelled as 'middle powers' (whether developed or developing countries) have used these foreign policy tools with varying interests in mind. But the juxtaposition of 'middle power diplomacy' and 'niche diplomacy' to the use of technical cooperation yields more robust results.

As a rule, it can be assumed that all countries would prefer to have a good reputation among their peers than a bad one. However, this does not mean that all countries will actively seek this positive image. Even among those who do, there will be variance in how important this is for their foreign policy strategy. Thus, countries which place a high priority on their reputation as 'good international citizens' can be seen as being naturally more likely to seek diplomatic rather than commercial gains from technical cooperation agreements. The claim is not that they will *always* frame agreements unconditionally and untied, but that donors will act in a way which increases their image *for the group* they are 'targeting'. At the same time, technical cooperation is inherently well suited for a strategy of 'niche diplomacy'. Technical cooperation is, in its very essence, the exchange of 'unique' knowledge (including practices, experiences, and technologies). A country's home-grown and tested approach which is deemed successful for solving a problem 'without borders' is likely to foster outside interest from countries also facing that same problem. Again, if the donor places a high value on its image as a 'good international citizen' and is strongly interested in becoming the leader (or at least a major reference) in the problem area, then sharing its knowledge with no conditionalities or ties will serve to increase its diplomatic gains from the initiative.

Thus, countries with valuable expertise in specific 'public goods' – e.g., poverty alleviation, access to basic health in remote areas, anti-corruption strategies, post-conflict reconstruction, protection of biodiversity, water management, rural agriculture – can take the opportunity to promote themselves as key players in that particular debate. The more a country invests in providing aid linked to its 'niche', the more it can solidify its international image in that area. The 'effectiveness' of this diplomatic strategy is likely to increase if no direct commercial ties are attached to what is given by helping lower suspicions of hypocrisy.

## The power of 'giving' development assistance and technical cooperation

There is power inherent to the act of giving. In the context of development assistance, this means specific social dynamics are established between the donor and the receiver when the former provides the latter with grants (non-refundable, by definition), builds a stadium, gives medication, or transfers knowledge with no stipulation for compensation. A useful theoretical framework to understand how power can be accrued from providing no-strings-attached technical cooperation starts by looking at the concept from an anthropological and sociological perspective. In *The Gift*, Mauss (1966[1923]) looks at the importance of social reciprocity and exchanges, inasmuch as these demonstrate the existence of "means of expenditure and exchange *other than economic ones*" (Mauss, 1966[1923]:75; emphasis added). His work is considered to be "the first systematic and comparative study of the widespread custom of gift exchange and the first understanding of its function in the articulation of the social order" (Evans-Pritchard, 1966:ix).

While Mauss looked at so-called "archaic" societies and their processes of gift giving, the conclusions he reached have useful resonance for conceiving development 'gift-giving' among countries. His study found that quite often gifts are neither spontaneous nor disinterested, as they are "for the most part counter-prestations made not solely in order to pay for the goods and services, but also to maintain a profitable alliance which it would be unwise to reject" (Mauss, 1966[1923]:71). Hierarchies can be established through the process, since "to give is to show one's superiority, to show that one is something more and higher, that one is *magister* [master]". At the same time, this dynamic can create an interest from the recipient to give back to signal a horizontal relationship, as "to accept without returning or repaying more is to face subordination, to become a client and subservient, to become a *minister* [minor, subservient]" (Mauss, 1966[1923]:72). In other words, the recipient might want to – as opposed to being or feeling forced to – retribute to bring 'balance' to the relationship.

The main difference between gifts and commodity exchanges is that in the former, some element of interpersonal dependence is still present, as the giver remains 'attached' to what is given. Receiving a gift also indicates interest in developing or maintaining a social relationship between the parties involved. An exchange of commodities, on the other hand, does not imply residual obligations or relationships (Gregory, 1982). Gifting is also different from lending since the expectation of the loan's return is explicitly expected "at the very moment of the drawing up of a contract capable of ensuring that the acts it prescribes are predictable and calculable" (Bourdieu, 1977:5). And while there is the expectation of reciprocal gifting, the means and the timing of the reciprocation is uncertain as the relation between giver-recipient is unmediated and un-institutionalized. Giving is then characterized by "strategic ambiguity and the power to transform a relation of domination into one of generosity and gratitude" (Hattori, 2001:637–640).

The issue of whether the recipient interprets the gift as domination or generosity demands attention, for it is not always straightforward. First, there is concern over *debts* disguised as *gifts*. In this case, the latter is used to euphemize the former, with an almost exact correspondence between the debtor-creditor relation of structural adjustment loans and the donor-recipient relation of grant foreign aid (Hattori, 2001:646–648). Second, even if there is no imposition of a gift 'repayment', the attitude towards giving matters as a condescending approach can work against the donor: "unlike solidarity, which is horizontal and takes place between equals, charity is top-down, humiliating those who receive it and never challenging the implicit power relations" (Galeano, 1998:312). Because of these suspicions, sometimes recipients might be hesitant to receive international development 'gifts' from a (potential) donor. They might wish to escape *symbolic domination*, which Bourdieu (1990:127) refers to as "the gentle invisible violence, unrecognized as such, chosen as much as undergone"; or perhaps a potential feeling of inferiority that can be attached to receiving charity (Baldwin, 1985:365; Korf, 2006; Lindner, 2006:82–87; Mawdsley, 2012). This echoes the warning that when nations are involved in (apparently) altruistic acts, "suspicion of hypocrisy will be easily aroused; the self-righteous claims of pure benevolence, by hurting the pride of others, will diminish the desirable effect of greater amity" (Wolfers, 1962:77).

As a final point, it is worth mentioning Keohane's (1986) approach to the issue of reciprocity. For him, reciprocity had a *specific* and a *diffuse* meaning. The typical meaning of reciprocity in economics and game theory would be of 'specific reciprocity'. This refers to situations in which "specified partners exchange items of equivalent value in a strictly delimited sequence. If any obligations exist, they are clearly specified in terms of rights and duties of particular actors" (1986:4). By contrast, in 'diffuse reciprocity' the equivalence is less precise, the sequence of events is less narrowly bounded, and it "involves conforming to generally accepted standards of behaviour" (*idem*). What this means is (1) the notion of reciprocity used by Mauss – and the one here adopted – is mostly related to Keohane's '*diffuse* reciprocity'; and (2) the 'standards of behaviour' would come from unwritten social norms of interaction related to 'gift-giving'. The phenomenon of 'silent understanding' or 'mutual interests' – often based on bilateral relations which go beyond the donor-recipient aid relationship – plays an important role in why countries would choose to *give* to others (Jepma, 1991:19). Recipients are not obliged to 'pay back' the donor, but there is a common social expectation that it should occur.

Milner's (1992:469) analysis of the connections between cooperation and reciprocity is noteworthy. As expected by game theorists, iteration and the prospect of rewards for cooperating matter for this process: "Cooperation arises tacitly; it evolves over time as the actors' expectations converge." For Milner, some authors argue that cooperative behaviour may be more likely when countries pursue a strategy of reciprocity because countries know they will be punished for defecting and rewarded for cooperating. However, in a no-strings-attached provision of development assistance, the diffuse nature of reciprocity makes a recipient's 'defection' much harder to establish. Donor sanctions are also much less likely given that nothing was *formally* demanded. Even if an informal deal exists, sanctions would be hard to impose; the donor is probably limited to foot-dragging in ongoing agreements or signing less agreements with the recipient in the future.

### *Gains from conditional, unconditional, tied, and untied aid*

The combined approach of unconditional *and* untied provision of international development deserves a closer look since it is a somewhat 'unique' combination for donors, and it is the one adopted by Brazil. This arrangement is the weakest in securing immediate commercial profits and the most optimistic about the likelihood of 'soft-power' resources, like a better image or strengthened bilateral relationships, being transformed into some sort of concrete gains in the mid/long-term. Pure altruism could be the possible explanation for the choice of giving development assistance with no conditionalities or ties. But this research assumes that in the context of foreign policymaking, donors do take into consideration potential gains they could obtain from giving aid.

Choices produce intended and unintended consequences; and some choices are more likely to produce certain gains than others. Whether the unintended effects of the actions (or inactions) of donors tends to be beneficial or detrimental to the interest of those affected is an empirical question (Baldwin, 2002:279). Confronted by the need to choose, "nations, like individuals, must weigh the costs and benefits that seem likely to attend each path. Whether the issues are economic or military, they must pick the strategy that seems best to serve their interests" (Stein, 1990:20). Given the complexity of what is being analysed, this research bundles up donors' gains into simply two categories: commercial and diplomatic gains (this one subdivided in bilateral and diffuse). This research follows the understanding that not all national purposes are mutually incompatible; that is, it is not necessary that one nation's purposes be accomplished at the expense of another set of national purposes (Snyder et al., 1954). Hence, commercial and diplomatic gains should not be seen as either/or categories, but more as within a range of more or less important priorities that the donor has regarding its foreign policy goals, with a stronger/weaker likelihood of yielding gains (Table 2.2).

### *'Giving' technical cooperation*

As any development assistance mechanism, in principle, technical cooperation can be conditional or unconditional, and tied or untied. From the donor's perspective, the provision of *unconditional* and *untied* development assistance shows the best prospects for fostering diplomatic gains. Commercial gains are

*Table 2.2* Potential for commercial and diplomatic gains

| | | | *Characteristic* | | | | |
|---|---|---|---|---|---|---|---|
| | | | *Conditionalities* | | | *Ties* | |
| | | | Conditional | | Unconditional | *Tied* | *Untied* |
| | | | Market C. | Political C. | | | |
| Likelihood of Gains | *Commercial Gains* | | Strong | Weak | Weak | Very strong | Weak |
| | *Diplomatic Gains* | *Bilateral* | Weak | Weak | Strong | Weak | Very strong |
| | | *Diffuse* | Weak | Unclear | Unclear | Weak | Strong |

possible as well, but unlike conditional/tied agreements, the process is indirect, subtle, and has weak guarantees (if any at all). The likelihood of gains from providing unconditional and untied technical cooperation agreements increases with certain conditions: (1) the *volume* of initiatives undertaken; (2) the *diversity* of recipients, and (3) the 'desirability' of the knowledge shared. A donor which has several agreements with each one of its many recipients (in many areas of the world), regarding knowledge considered to be 'exclusive' or 'the most efficient' can be expected to generate diplomatic gains much more easily (and with greater certainty) when compared to a donor with few agreements with a couple of recipients regarding a theme which many donors know about.

A significant and systematic provision of no-strings-attached technical cooperation with a variety of recipients is poised to generate/strengthen the donor's positive image with each one of the recipients, as well as with others. Still, giving without asking for anything in return can easily have recipients become suspicious of the donor's 'real' intentions. Using Arvin and Baum's (1997) terminology, a donor which claims to operate – or wishes to be *seen* as operating – a 'diplomacy of good-will' will only be credible if recognized by the recipient(s) as such. For this to happen, there must be consistency in how the donor *continuously* gives without demanding payback to *all* recipients, regardless of their potential for valuable 'retributions'. A collection of technical cooperation agreements promoted by a single actor with many partners can also alter collective dynamics in the international sphere: it can create a 'hub-and-spoke' interaction model. Here, the International Relations debates on network analysis are helpful. Network analysis concerns relationships defined by links among nodes, which can be individuals or corporate actors (such as organizations and States), and addresses the associations among nodes, rather than the attributes of specific nodes. Ties between nodes can be channels for transmission of both material and non-material products – such as information, beliefs, and norms – where persistent patterns of association among nodes create structures that can define, enable, or restrict the behaviour of nodes. More importantly, the relationship between networks and *power* are of great importance, since:

> The perspective of network analysis suggests that *countries skilled at building and exploiting their position in multiple networks* – particularly mid-level, open, and connected powers – *may gain in influence vis-à-vis poorer countries with less central network positions.*
>
> (Hafner-Burton et al., 2009: 574; emphases added)

Providing technical cooperation with no-strings-attached over the same issue establishes and reinforces the donor country's position as a central node in a network based upon a unique knowledge. The power related to *what* is being transmitted cannot be understated. It would be a mistake to overlook Foucault's (1977) call for attentiveness to the exercise of power, where to 'put something in its place' means limiting what will be an adequate or proper knowledge of it. This brings back Chapter 1's reference to Weber (1946[1922–1923]:280) and metaphor of ideas serving as switchmen, acting as blinders which reduce the number of conceivable alternatives. Also relevant is Goldstein and Keohane's (1993) point of how knowledge influences policy when (1) the causal beliefs that they embody provide road maps that increase actors' clarity about goals and means-end relationships; (2) they affect outcomes of situations in which there is no unique equilibrium; and (3) they become embedded in political institutions. Hence, a country that provides the same knowledge to a significant number of recipients is in a better position to, over time, *frame* the international debate over that issue (on the concept of framing, see Entman, 1993). Table 2.3 summarizes the possibilities for diplomatic gains from unconditional and untied technical cooperation.

One final point relates to the potential for *domestic* gains from fostering a high volume of agreements, resonating with Putnam's (1988) domestic/international dynamic. As pointed out by an academic interviewee, these initiatives can serve as a way of "externally validating domestic policies". It would allow government officials to claim: "look at all these countries interested in what we are doing", thereby strengthening domestic legitimacy and allowing it more room to mute the opposition – i.e., "who are *you* to question our domestic strategies [when everyone else wants to follow us]"?

The following chapters will address concrete cases of development assistance (and technical cooperation) provision. Many of the theoretical elements presented in this chapter will be both implicitly and explicitly present throughout the analyses to come. As it will be shown, even if countries provide development assistance with 'national interest', their actual policies will vary. This will be very clear in how different nations have chosen to address technical cooperation.

*Table 2.3* Donor's perspective for diplomatic gains from technical cooperation

| | *Single Receiver* | *Multiple Receivers* | *International Scenario* |
|---|---|---|---|
| **Short run** ↓ | Perception of benevolent action from the giver's part | Formation/ strengthening of giver's regional presence | Increased awareness from other countries of potential for partnership with giver |
| | Formation and/or strengthening of: bilateral relationship; increased chances of economic gains; common discourse on issue area (centred on giver's discourse); mutual understanding over "good practice" on issue area | Formation and/ or strengthening of: network over theme (centred on giver's interests) in international fora; increased number of players with common discourse on issue area (centred on giver's discourse); increased number of players with mutual understanding over "good practice" on issue area (centred on giver's practice) | Formation/ strengthening of: network of likeminded actors; international recognition of giver's power/expertise in issue area; giver seen as 'indispensable' actor on issue; giver's discourse becomes reference (sole or one of the most relevant) for international debates elevation of country's international status; formation and/or strengthening of bargaining power of those 'within' the network vis-à-vis those outside |
| **Long run** | | Strong opportunity to frame the debate over a specific theme with all recipients | Increased opportunity to frame international debate over a specific subject |

## Notes

1 Global public goods can be defined in the following way:

> Global public goods must meet two criteria. The first is that their benefits have strong qualities of 'publicness' – that is, they are marked by non–rivalry in consumption and non–excludability. These features place them in the general category of public goods. The second criterion is that their benefits are quasi universal in terms of countries (covering more than one group of countries), people (accruing to several, preferably all, population groups), and generations (extending to both current and future generations, or at least meeting the needs of current generations without foreclosing development options for future generations).
>
> (Kaul et al., 1999:2–3)

2 Wendt explicitly self-identified as a Realist, while adding "interests should not be seen as an exclusively 'Realist' variable. What matters is how interests are thought to be constituted" (Wendt, 1999:113–114).
3 Wolfers mentions the term in a 1945 article, but only briefly (Wolfers, 1945).
4 The '*secondary* powers' category was used by Keohane (1969) and Holbraad (1971), but never gained mainstream popularity.

## Bibliography

Abdenur, A. (2002). Tilting the north-south axis: The legitimation of southern development knowledge and its implications for comparative education research. *Current Issues in Comparative Education, 4*(2), 57–69.

Adler, E. (2002). Constructivism and international relations. In: W. Carlsnaes & T. Risse, & B. A. Simmons (Eds.), *Handbook of international relations* (pp. 95–119). London: SAGE.

Armistead, L., (2004). *Information operations: Warfare and the hard reality of soft power*. Washington, DC: Brassey's.

Arvin, B. M., & C. Baum. (1997). Tied and untied foreign aid: A theoretical and empirical analysis. *Keio Economic Studies, 34*(2), 71–79.

Axelrod, R. (1992). How to promote cooperation. *Current Contents, 44,* 10.

Bachrach, P., & Baratz, M. (1962, December). Two faces of power. *American Political Science Review, 56*(4), 947–952.

Bachrach, P., & Baratz, M. (1963, September). Decisions and non-decisions: An analytical framework. *American Political Science Review, 57*(3), 632–642.

Baldwin, D. (1985). *Economic statecraft*. Princeton, NJ: Princeton University Press.

Baldwin, D. (2002). Power in international relations. In W. Carlsnaes & B. A. Simmons (Eds.), *Handbook of international relations* (pp. 177–191). London: Sage Publications.

Baldwin, D. (2013). Power in international relations. In W. Carlsnaes & B. A. Simmons (Eds.), *Handbook of international relations* (pp. 273–297). London: Sage Publications.

Barkin, J. S. (2003). Realist constructivism. *International Studies Review, 5*(3), 325–342.

Barkin, J. S. (2010). *Realist constructivism: Rethinking international relations theory*. Cambridge: Cambridge University Press.

Barnett, M., & Duvall, R. (2005). "Power in international politics". *International Organization, 59*(1), 39–75.

Bauer, P. (1981). *Equality, the third world, and economic delusion*. Cambridge, MA: Harvard University Press.

*BBC News*. (2001, March 23). *Brazil emerges as a leading exponent of 'soft power'*. http://news.bbc.co.uk/2/hi/americas/8580560.stm.

Bourdieu, P. (1977). *Outline of a theory of practice*. New York: Cambridge University Press.

Bourdieu, P. (1990). *The logic of practice*. Stanford, CA: Stanford University Press.

Burnell, P. (1997). *Foreign aid in a changing world*. Buckingham: Open University Press.

Buzan, B. (2004). *The United States and the great powers: World politics in the twenty-first century*. Cambridge: Polity.

Cardoso, F. H., & Faletto, E. (1971). *Dependencia Y Desarrollo en América*. Mexico: Siglo Veintiuno.

Collier, D., & Mahon, Jr., J. E. (1993). Conceptual "stretching" revisited: Adapting categories in comparative analysis. *The American Political Science Review, 87*(4), 845–855.

Cooper, A. F., Higgott, R. A., & Nossal, K. R. (Eds.). (1993). *Relocating middle powers: Australia and Canada in a changing world order* (Vol. 6). Vancouver: UBC Press.

Cox, R. (1989). Middlepowermanship, Japan, and future world order. *International Journal, 44*(4), 823–862.

*Economist, The*. (2006, September 14). *The new titans*. Special section, 3–8.

Entman, R. M. (1993). Framing: Toward clarification of a fractured paradigm. *Journal of communication, 43*(4), 51–58.

Evans, G. (1989). *Making Australian foreign policy*. Australian Fabian Society, Pamphlet 50, p. 42.

Evans, G. (2011, 29 June). *'Middle power' diplomacy*. Inaugural Edgardo Boeninger Memorial Lecture, Chile Pacific Foundation, Santiago. www.gevans.org/speeches/speech441.html.

Evans, G., & Grant, B. (1991; 1995 2nd edition). *Australia's foreign relations in the worlds of the 1990s*. Melbourne: Melbourne University Press.

Evans-Pritchard, E. E. (1966). Introduction. In M. Maus (Ed.), *The gift – Forms and functions of exchange in Archaic societies* (pp. v–x). London: Cohen & West.

Foucault, M. (1977). *Discipline and punish: The birth of the prison*. London: Penguin Books.

Fox, A. B. (1969). The small states in the international system, 1919–1969. *International Journal, 24*(4), 751–764.

Fox, W. (1946). The super-powers at San Francisco. *The Review of Politics, 8*(1), 115–127.

Frank, A. G. (1966). *The development of underdevelopment*. Boston, MA: New England Free Press.

Frank, C., & Baird, M. (1975). Foreign aid: Its speckled past and future prospects. *International Organization, 29*(1), 133–167.

Galeano, E. (1998). *Upside down: A primer for the looking-glass world*. New York: Henry Holt & Co.

Galtung, J. (1971). A structural theory of imperialism. *Journal of Peace Research, 8*(2), 81–117.

Gilpin, R. (1987). *The political economy of international relations*. Princeton, NJ: Princeton University Press.

Glazebrook, G. (1947). The 'middle powers' in the United Nations system. *International Organization, 1*(2), 307–318.

Goldstein, J., & Keohane, R. (1993). Ideas and foreign policy. In J. Goldstein & R. O. Keohane (Eds.), *Ideas and foreign policy: Beliefs, institutions, and political change*. Ithaca, NY: Cornell University Press.

Gregory, C. A. (1982). *Gifts and commodities*. London: Academic Press.

Guimarães, S. P. (1999) *500 anos de Periferia – Uma contribuição ao estudo da política internacional*. Porto Alegre: UFRGS.

Hafner-Burton, E. M., Kahler, M., & Montgomery, A. H. (2009). Network analysis for international relations. *International Organization, 63*(3), 559–592.

Hattori, T. (2001). Reconceptualizing foreign aid. *Review of International Political Economy, 8*(4), 633–660.

Haugaard, M. (2011). Editorial. *Journal of Political Power, 4*(1), 1–8.

Henrikson, A. K. (2005). Niche diplomacy in the world public arena: The global 'corners' of Canada and Norway. In J. Melissen (Ed.), *The new public diplomacy: Soft power in international relations* (chapter 4, pp. 67–87). Den Haag, Netherlands: Netherlands Institute of International Relations.

Hirst, M. (2006). Intermediate states, multilateralism and international security. In A. Costa Vaz (Ed.), *Intermediate states, regional leadership and security: India, Brazil and South Africa* (pp. 165–194). Brasilia, Brazil: Editora UnB.

Hoadley, S. (1980). Small states as aid donors. *International Organization, 34*(1), 121–137.

Holbraad, C. (1971). The role of middle powers. *Cooperation and Conflict, 6*, 177–190.

Holbraad, C. (1984). 'Middle powers' in international politics. London: Macmillan.

Hook, S. W. (1995). *National interest and foreign aid.* Boulder, CO: L. Rienner Publishers.

Hopf, T. (1998). The promise of constructivism in international relations theory. *International security, 23*(1), 171–200.

Hudson, V. (2007). *Foreign policy analysis: Classic and contemporary theory.* Plymouth: Rowman & Littlefield Publishers.

Hurd, I. (2008). Constructivism. In C. Reus-Smit & D. Snidal (Eds.), *The Oxford handbook of international relations* (pp. 298–316). Oxford: Oxford University Press.

Hurrell, A. (2000). *Some reflections on the role of intermediate powers in international institutions.* Working Paper N° 244. Paths to Power: Foreign Policy Strategies of Intermediate States (pp. 23–41). Washington DC: Woodrow Wilson International Centre.

Hurrell, A. (2006). Hegemony, liberalism and global order: What space for would-be great powers? *International Affairs, 82*(1), 1–19.

Jenkins, G. (2007). Soft power, strategic security, and international philanthropy. *North Carolina Law Review, 85*, 775.

Jepma, C. J. (1991). *The tying of aid.* Paris: OECD.

Kaul, I., Grunberg, I., & Stern, M. A. (1999). Defining global public goods. In I. Kaul, I. Grunberg & M. A. Stern (Eds.), *International cooperation in the 21st century* (chapter 2, pp. 2–19). New York: UNDP.

Kearn, D. W. (2011). The hard truths about soft power. *Journal of Political Power, 4*(1), 65–85.

Kennedy, P. (2013, August 13). The great powers, then and now. *New York Times.* www.nytimes.com/2013/08/14/opinion/global/the-great-powers-then-and-now.html?pagewanted=all&_r=0.

Keohane. R. (1969). Lilliputians' dilemmas: small states in international politics. *International Organization, 23*(2), 291–310.

Keohane, R. (1986). Reciprocity in international relations. *International organization, 40*(1), 1–27.

Khanna, P. (2008). *The second world – Empires and influence in the new global order.* New York: Random House.

Knoke, D., & Yang, S. (2008). *Social network analysis.* London: Sage publications.

Korf, B. (2006). Antinomies of generosity: Moral geographies and post-tsunami aid in Southeast Asia. *Geoforum, 38*(2), 366–378.

Kurlantzick, J. (2007). *Charm offensive: How China's soft power is transforming the world.* New Haven, CT: Yale University Press.

Lasswell, H. D., & Kaplan, A. (1950). *Power and society: A framework for political inquiry.* New Haven, CT: Yale University Press.

Lebow, R. N. (2004). Constructive realism. *International Studies Review, 6*(2), 346–347.

Lindner, E. (2006). *Making enemies: Humiliation and international conflict.* Westport, CT: Praeger Security International.

Liska, G. (1960). *The new statecraft: Foreign aid in American foreign policy*. Chicago, IL: University of Chicago Press.

Lumsdaine, D. H. (1993). *Moral vision in international politics: The foreign aid regime, 1949–1989*. Princeton, NJ: Princeton University Press.

Mattern, J. B. (2004). Power in realist-constructivist research. *International Studies Review*, *6*(2), 343–346.

Mauss, M. (1923). Essai sur le don forme et raison de l'échange dans les sociétés archaïques. *L'Année sociologique (1896/1897–1924/1925), Nouvelle série, T. 1*, 30–186.

Mauss, M. (1966). *The gift – Forms and functions of exchange in Archaic societies*. London: Cohen & West.

Mawdsley, E. (2012). The changing geographies of foreign aid and development co-operation: Contributions from gift theory. *Transactions of the Institute of British Geographers*, *37*(2), 256–272.

Milner, H. (1992). International theories of cooperation among nations: Strengths and weaknesses. *World Politics*, *44*(3), 466–496.

Morgenthau, H. (1960[1948]). *Politics among nations* (3rd ed.). New York: Alfred A. Knopf.

Morgenthau, H. (1962). A political theory of foreign aid. *The American Political Science Review*, *56* (2), 301–309.

Nye, J. S. (1990a). Soft power. *Foreign policy, 80(Special edition, 20th anniversary)*, 153–171.

Nye, J. S. (1990b). *Bound to lead: The changing nature of American Power*. New York: Basic Books.

Nye, J. S. (2004). *Soft power: The means to success in world politics*. New York: Public Affairs Store.

Nye, J. S. (2009). International relations: The relevance of theory to practice. In C. Reus-Smit & D. Snidal (Eds.), *The Oxford handbook of international relations*. New York: Oxford University Press.

Nye, J. S. (2010, October 08). The future of power. *Project Syndicate*. www.project-syndicate.org/commentary/the-future-of-power#yXzsXIHAU6gb3fvc.99.

Nye, J. S. (2011). *The future of power*. New York: Public Affairs.

Potter, E. (1996/1997). Niche diplomacy as a Canadian foreign policy. *International Journal*, *52*(1), 25–38.

Prebisch, R. (1949). *The economic development of Latin America*. CEPAL. http://archivo.cepal.org/pdfs/cdPrebisch/002.pdf.

Putnam, Robert D. (1988) Diplomacy and domestic politics: the logic of two-level games. *International organization*, *42*(3), 427–460.

Rothenstein, R. L. (1968). *Alliances and small powers*. New York: Columbia University Press.

Rothman, S. B. (2011). Revising the soft power concept: What are the means and mechanisms of soft power? *Journal of Political Power*, *4*(1), 49–64.

Simonds, F., & Emeny, B. (1937). *The great powers in world politics: International relations and economic nationalism*. New York: American Book Co.

Slaughter, A. M. (2009). America's edge: Power in the networked century. *Foreign Affairs*, *88*(1), 94–113.

Snyder, R. C., Bruck, H. W., & Sapin, B. (1954). *The decision-making approach to the study of international politics*. Foreign Policy Analysis Project Series No. 3. Princeton, NJ: Princeton University Press.

Stein, A. (1990). *Why nations cooperate? Circumstance and choice in international relations*. Ithaca, NY: Cornell University Press.

UNDP – United Nations Development Programme. (2005). *Human development report 2005 – International cooperation at a crossroads – Aid, trade and security in an unequal world*. New York: United Nations.

Vandenbosch, A. (1964). The small states in international politics and organization. *The Journal of Politics*, *26*(2), 293–312.

Wallerstein, I. (1974). *The modern world systems*. New York and London: Academic Press.

Waltz, K. (1964). The stability of a bipolar world. *Daedalus*, *93*(3), 881–909.

Wasserman, S., & Faust, K. (1994). *Social network analysis: Methods and applications*. Cambridge: Cambridge University Press.

Weber, M. (1946 [1922–1923]). The social psychology of the world religions. In H. H. Gerth & C. W. Mills (Eds.), *From Max Weber: Essays in sociology* (pp. 267–301). New York: Oxford University Press.

Wendt, A. (1999). *Social theory of international politics*. Cambridge: Cambridge University Press.

Wight, M. (Ed.). (1946/2002) *Power politics*. London: Continuum.

Wolfers, A. (1945). The role of the small states in the enforcement of international peace. *Proceedings of the Academy of Political Science*, *21*(3), 24–31.

Wolfers, A. (1962). *Discord and collaboration – Essays on international relations*. Baltimore, MD: John Hopkins Press.

Zakaria, F. (1997). The rise of illiberal democracy. *Foreign Affairs*, *76*(6), 22–43.

Zinkin, M. (1978). Aid and morals: Addressing the aspirations of the poor countries. *The Round Table: The Commonwealth Journal of International Affairs*, *68*(271), 222–228.

# 3 International development and technical cooperation

## "Traditional" donors

The provision of technical cooperation has taken place since the early days of international development initiatives.[1] Nonetheless, there have been many important variations in this provision, such as: the importance of technical cooperation, vis-à-vis other mechanisms, within a donor's overall international development policy; the gains sought to be obtained through technical cooperation; the characteristics of the technical cooperation agreements (conditional, unconditional, tied, or untied); and the effectiveness of the technical assistance provided. This chapter argues that to understand these differences, one must contextualize donors' attitudes towards providing international development in its entirety, since technical cooperation is one mechanism within this broader framework. So, the characteristics of a specific donor's provision of technical cooperation must be seen as part of a bigger picture of what its interests and values are towards being a development donor in the first place.

When it comes to the norms around the provision of international development, donors have almost always embedded their approach within one of two 'frameworks': (1) DAC/ODA and (2) South-South Cooperation (SSC). The DAC/ODA paradigm refers to Official Development Assistance (ODA), the term used by the Development Assistance Committee (DAC), which has been the *locus* of convergence between traditional aid providers in the Organization for Economic Co-operation and Development (OECD). Notwithstanding the polyphony among non-DAC donors, SSC has been the most significant counterpoint to the rules and values adopted by DAC/ODA donors. As it will be shown in this and the following chapter, States' interests in providing development assistance have never been identical among all countries under each paradigm. In many cases, countries' *own* interests and approaches have changed – sometimes significantly – over time. Still, a general rule has been that donors do not tend to switch *frameworks*.[2]

DAC/ODA was chosen as a shorthand reference to *developed* countries' general approach to development assistance, while SSC will be used to designate *developing* countries' general approach to development assistance. Working with these broad and complex definitions is not an easy task, and there are important grey areas to consider. The main reasoning behind juxtaposing DAC members to developed countries/donors' rests upon the fact that *all* of DAC's 25 member-countries are considered high-income countries (i.e., 'developed countries') by the World Bank. Hence, referencing 'developed countries' in the context of development assistance as 'DAC members' has a substantially solid base, and will be used in this research.

To address these issues and develop the argument proposed, this chapter focuses on the empirical dynamics of development assistance provided first by DAC members, while the following one deals with the SSC context. Both chapters build upon the theories and abstractions presented in Chapter 2, incorporating 'real-life' evolution of international development. The goal is to look at why and how countries have provided international development – with a continuous focus on technical cooperation. It details the international development model that traditional donors have adopted for their provision of development assistance, and provides empirical knowledge to better understand how they have used technical cooperation.

## Development Assistance Committee (DAC)

This section will begin by exploring the history and reasoning behind development assistance of some of the member countries to the DAC, then focus on the DAC itself. Created in 1961, the DAC was a reconstituted version of the 1960 Development Assistance Group (DAG). DAC's goal was to create a forum for consultations among providers of development assistance, which at the time were almost all members of the OECD. For over 50 years now, the DAC has grouped the world's main donors, defining and monitoring global standards in key areas of development (OECD, 2010:3). While the DAC was never *absolute* in the power to direct donor activity, it has played an undeniable key role in many aspects:

> [It has been] instrumental in defining terms and concepts in development assistance, identifying best practices, and providing a framework within which bilateral donors can interact with a higher degree of synergy than if they had been left to their own devices.
>
> (Rowlands, 2008:4)

Official Development Assistance – the term used by DAC members for the provision of development assistance – is done through grants, loans, and technical cooperation.[3] Total DAC flows of ODA rose steadily from 1960 to 1990, with a decrease "due to fiscal consolidation in donor countries after the recession of the early 1990s", and peak moments in 2005 and 2006, due to exceptional debt relief operations for Iraq and Nigeria (OECD, 2010:71–72). Statistics suggest that funding specifically for technical cooperation has fluctuated around one quarter of overall ODA over the last 50 years, but with major variations among donors. In absolute terms, it represents a significant expenditure, nowadays plausibly in the $25 billion/year range (OECD, 2011b:10–11).

It is possible to group DAC countries' approach to technical cooperation into three 'generations' (Morgan, 2010; *apud* OECD, 2011a:5). The first took place from the 1960s until the early 1980s, characterized mostly as: heavily donor driven, gap filling at the level of individuals, use of industrialized world's concept of 'good practice', and highly tied to commercial gains. The very first debates regarding untying development aid began already in the early 1960s: in 1962 the DAC's chairman called for "joint efforts to reverse the trend towards more tying of aid", and the next year it adopted a "Resolution on the Terms and Conditions of Aid" recommending "appropriate terms" for aid (World Bank, 2008:33). In 1969, the "Pearson Report" came out against tying aid or at least limiting it to the identifiable external expenditure of projects receiving assistance (Caine, 1970). However, the first set of rules for DAC members concerning tied aid was only reached in 1974, when 10 members subscribed to a "Memorandum of Understanding on Untying of Bilateral Development Loans in Favour of Procurement in Developing Countries". One explanation for why not all DAC members engaged in this agreement was that in the 1970s, public support for development cooperation was widely different among donor countries. And

> where public support was low, tying was seen as an essential rationale for providing aid, while where public support for aid was strong, tying increased the risk of using aid to gain commercial advantage to the detriment of development effectiveness.
>
> (World Bank, 2008:33–34)

Yet, the agreement never became fully operational "as the oil crises diverted attention to more pressing issues" (OECD, 2001:4). In a broad sense, progress on untying aid would prove to be difficult until the end of the Cold War. Most importantly, for the present research, efforts towards untying development aid did *not* include technical cooperation agreements, but exclusively grants and loans.

In the second generation, from the 1980s until the 2000s, the DAC (and most donors individually) began to focus more on the ideas of ownership, efficiency, capacity development, and a call for untied agreements. One result was that between the turn of the century and 2008, the proportion of untied bilateral aid rose progressively from 46% to 82% (OECD, 2010). Once again, the untying of *technical cooperation* was left as an exception, with most aspects of it becoming increasingly managed and implemented by 'outside' (i.e., non-government) contractors. In 2001, the DAC reached an agreement on a recommendation to untie ODA to the *least* developed countries by 2002 and to non-LDC Highly Indebted Poor Countries by 2008. Yet, this was reached only "after intensive discussions", as there were some activities "*notably technical co-operation* and food aid, where it [was] recognized that untying would pose more delicate problems for some donors than for others" (OECD, 2001:5; emphasis added). Thus, DAC donors can *opt* to untie their technical cooperation agreements (OECD, 2008:5).

Another important characteristic of this period is that after the end of the Cold War, the idea of conditioning development assistance to 'good governance' goals became a common feature among DAC donors. One of the first milestones in this regard came already in 1991 when the OECD Ministerial and the DAC High-Level produced a document emphasizing the "importance OECD countries attach to promoting human rights, democratization, open and accountable government institutions and the rule of law and reduction of excessive military expenditures." (OECD, 2006:24). This characteristic would go on through the next decades, remaining present in most DAC donors' current development assistance projects.

The ability of traditional donors to condition aid on the adoption of reforms increased with the demise of the Soviet Union (Dunning, 2004:419). With the end of the Cold War, 'national security' no longer served as a justification for spending on foreign aid. The rationale behind international assistance had to be reconceived to focus on 'new' issues if it was to continue to be funded – hence the focus on promoting economic and political transitions, addressing global problems, furthering democracy, and managing conflict (Lancaster, 2006:48). Nonetheless, from the early post-Cold War days, some scholars already began to question the 'true' intentions behind good governance conditionalities. Time would show that many times donors would not follow through on imposing the execution of conditionalities for development aid transfers. An analysis of DAC donors' approach reveals that many times donors would ignore good governance factors, if not provide even *more* aid to recipients with known 'bad governance' records (Zanger, 2000:311), depending on the recipient's overall strategic importance for the donor.

With the new millennium, the criticism over what development assistance was achieving in practice – as opposed to achieving on paper – grew significantly. The gap between 'real' aid – i.e., "resources transferred aimed at creating long-term sustainable development" (Stokke, 1996:56) – and 'formal' aid (i.e., everything formally labelled as 'foreign aid') reached the forefront of the debates over development assistance. Donors' incentives would increasingly become more structured to favour support for – or at least favour the *appearance* of support for – certain development goals, while still shy of actually achieving them, with "little oversight either by domestic actors within donor states or internationally to monitor the congruence of actual policy with the rhetorical statements" (Breuning, 2002:375).

The third (and current) generation in traditional donors' approach to development assistance would come about in the early 2000s – and can be seen still as an *emerging* process (Morgan, 2010). Two very important issues characterize the contemporary reality of traditional donors' development aid: (1) concerns over 'aid effectiveness', and (2) the undeniable importance of non-traditional donors to the development aid 'governance'. The topic of effectiveness began to be addressed in 2003 with the 'Rome Declaration', which established commitments for donors and focused on harmonizing donors' procedures and practices to reduce transaction costs for recipient countries. Then in 2005, *the Paris Declaration on Aid Effectiveness* was signed, containing a long list of commitments to implement monitorable actions to increase effectiveness. Other commitments would be made later – particularly the Accra Agenda for Action (2008) and the Busan Partnership for Effective Development Cooperation (*Busan*, 2011) – all focusing on improving aid effectiveness.

Looking specifically at the contemporary broad structure of technical cooperation agreements within DAC donors, it appears that there has been little change over the decades, especially when compared to the explicit changes to terms and principles linked to providing development-oriented grants and loans. Technical cooperation remains more tied than aid in general: in 2009, 64% of all bilateral technical cooperation was reported untied, 22% tied, and 14% not reported, which "significantly undermines transparency and leads to increased lack of trust regarding the real extent of untied aid" (OECD, 2012b:54). Since reporting expenses on technical cooperation is optional for DAC donors, these numbers cannot be taken at face value – the expectation is of tied technical cooperation being much higher in practice. In any case, notwithstanding calls for untying all bilateral aid, including technical cooperation and food aid, as called for by recipient countries and NGOs, these exceptions remain within the DAC framework.[4]

Recipients complain about this opaqueness of donors' practices in relation to technical cooperation, arguing that the system of 'bundling' technical cooperation within a package of foreign aid prevents recipients from being able to make informed choices and identifying the different types of costs related with different types of technical cooperation (Ajayi & Jerome, 2002; Wangwe & Madete, 2002; ECDPM, 2006; Watson et al., 2007; Scott, 2009). A common perception among recipients is that most of DAC donors' technical cooperation still leads to a supply-driven structure that is frequently "poorly aligned with partner government priorities" (OECD, 2012a:54; see also Browne, 2002:8–9). Adding to this scenario, studies have shown that tying aid increases the costs of goods and services by 15–30% on average (and up to 40% for food aid) reducing the overall effectiveness of aid flows (Tarnoff & Lawson, 2011:19).

Another related issue raised by the many recipients of traditional donors' technical cooperation is its tendency to rely (or *over*-rely) upon consultants – almost always exclusively from the donor country – and often poor alignment with the recipients' needs and domestic realities. These two elements have been deemed responsible for the failure to properly translate technical cooperation into an adequate instrument for capacity-building (Berg, 1993). As stated in a World Bank (2000:244) report, technical assistance displaced local expertise and drew away civil servants to administer aid-funded programmes – precisely the opposite of the capacity-building intentions of donors and recipients. Even if well intentioned, the critiques to 'expatriate' expertise are many. It is frequently seen as insensitive to local realities; generating little domestic learning, memory, or capacity building; and in many occasions, serving more the donor's than the recipient's development interests (Helleiner, 2000:15). More critical assessments reported the frustration of expatriate consultants not only taking jobs from nationals, but sometimes "being paid 20 to 30 times the national salary" (Singh, 2002:64); or simply being deemed incompetent, usually being "too young, inexperienced, culturally insensitive and completely lacking in knowledge of the local context in which they have arrived" (Scott, 2009:3). Despite criticism and various policy commitments to reform technical cooperation practice among DAC donors, the bottom line is that there appears to be little evidence of meaningful change, and technical cooperation has been highly tied in practice.

Still, it is essential to keep in mind that analyses of the DAC numbers, principles, and actions are not enough to capture each member's individual approach towards development aid or technical cooperation. As already alluded to, just because countries are members to the DAC and follow their guidelines does not mean that they have been a block in terms of interests and actions. There is significant deviation, with nation-states' varying sometimes widely in practice, reflecting the independent prerogatives of each one, revealing much about national interest and its role in guiding foreign policy behaviour (Hook, 1995:4). Because this research is focused on the use of technical cooperation as a *foreign policy* tool, the next section will explore aspects of individual 'traditional' donors' approach towards development assistance and technical cooperation.

## Traditional donors: technical cooperation and foreign policy

The conception and the practice of development assistance and technical cooperation precede the creation of the DAC by almost 20 years. Moreover, in the decades after its creation, countries within the DAC's 'umbrella' have made different choices, such as: to *if* and *how* to characterize their development aid regarding conditions and ties; their level of commitment and financial engagement; the 'preferred' recipient countries; as well as in their most used mechanism of ODA. This section will explore these variations in three parts. The first one covers what can be seen as 'the early years,' pre-DAC; the second between the 1960s until the end of the Cold War; and the last covers between the post-Cold War and contemporary period.

### *Early years: from World War II to the 1950s*

The phenomenon of development assistance in its modern day understanding – essentially countries helping other countries to develop – had its first steps at the end of World War II. Short term-relief aid to mitigate human suffering and palliative actions based on religious beliefs both have more extensive histories. However, direct actions to overcome other countries' 'structural' impediments to growing were only introduced during the second half of the 1940s – most notably with the Marshall Plan (1947) and the Point Four (1949). Nonetheless, some important moves towards *rationalizing* international aid-for-development can be found during World War II. According to Elliot Roosevelt (1946:36), his father – US President Franklin Delano Roosevelt (FDR) – had the following conversation with United Kingdom's Prime Minister Winston Churchill during the Atlantic Conference, in August of 1941:

FDR: I am firmly of the belief that if we are to arrive at a stable peace it must involve the development of backward countries. Backward peoples. How can this be done? It can't be done, obviously, by eighteenth-century methods. Now

CHURCHILL: Who's talking eighteenth-century methods?

FDR: Whichever of your ministers recommends a policy which takes wealth in raw materials out of a colonial country, but which returns nothing to the people of that country in consideration. *Twentieth*-century methods involve bringing industry to these colonies. *Twentieth*-century methods include increasing the wealth of a people by increasing their standard of living, by educating them, by bringing them sanitation-by making sure that they get a return for the raw wealth of their community.

Whether or not this conversation took place in these words, the result of the Conference did reflect something very close to it. The two leaders agreed to abide by certain common principles, such as: to endeavour to further the enjoyment by all states "of access, on equal terms, to the trade and to the raw materials of the world which *are needed for their economic prosperity*"; the "desire to bring about the fullest collaboration between all nations in the economic field with the objector securing, for all, *improved labour standards, economic advancement and social security*"; and that after the final destruction of the Nazi tyranny, they hoped to see established a peace which would "afford assurance that all the men in all the lands may live out their lives in *freedom* from fear and *want*" (Atlantic Conference, 1941; emphases added). Elements of this same spirit would also appear in the United Nations' Charter (1945), whose Preamble called for the employment of "the international machinery for the promotion of the economic and social advancement of all peoples". While no significant action was directly derived from any of these documents immediately, they still represent an important signal of how this idea began to appear formally in the international stage – and how it was initially pushed by the United States. By the end of the 1940s came the Marshall Plan, a milestone in the history of development assistance. As stated by Frank and Baird (1975:135), "the use of public funds on subsidized terms to assist in the development and growth of sovereign nations has no significant precedent before the Marshall Plan".[5] Aiming specifically for *economic* recovery and development, it was officially called the "European Recovery Program". The Plan was approved in 1948 by the United States' Congress, and would in the end provide approximately $13 billion in financial aid (mostly grants) for several countries in Western Europe until 1951.

There is no shortage of diverging explanations of what was the 'real' cause behind the United States' decision to help these countries. The variation in accounts for "*why* the Marshall Plan?" alone underscores the complexity of understanding and dissecting which forces matter to motivate development assistance in theory and in practice. There is a consensus that altruism was not the Plan's purpose, but authors still debate whether the main reasons were of mostly economic or political interests; and even when one of these is considered the most prominent, there is no agreement over which economic or political interest was the most important one. A few examples of the literature regarding this theme are useful to help understand these diverging interpretations. Making the case for economic drivers, Gimbel (1976:04) argued that the Plan originated as a "crash program to dovetail German economic recovery with a general European recovery program to make German economic recovery politically acceptable in Europe and in the United States" and was *not* conceived by long-range planners "as a response to the Soviet Union or as an element in the Cold War". Hogan (1987:xii) saw the Plan as an "international projection of the corporative political economy that had evolved in the United States", whose forces had been present long before the second post-war era. Wood (1986:36) also dates the origins of the Plan to before 1947, but highlighted how the fear of post-war Depression was pervasive among US policymakers during the war, reaffirming that "the case of the Marshall Plan was first made in economic terms, before the emergence of the Cold War fears that were to secure the plan's passage through Congress". On the other hand, the diplomatic driver "hypothesis" also has its strong defenders. Lancaster (2006:5) was blunt in stating that "foreign aid began as temporary expedient of Cold War diplomacy" and that it was *not* driven mainly by commercial interests or a desire to spread capitalism. In the same line, Milner and Tingley (2010:200) argued that "[t]his instrument [foreign aid such as the Marshall Plan] has been a primary way for the United States to engage other nations in pursuit of its foreign policy goals". Perhaps one of the most known assertions in the regards of connecting the Marshall Plan to the beginnings of Cold War actions was made by US President Truman himself, who declared the Marshall Plan and the "Truman Doctrine"[6] to be "two halves of the same walnut" (Offner, 2002:213).

The Marshall Plan became the prelude of many other projects, as it led to a widespread belief that "the combination of capital and technical assistance could transform economies in a very short time" (World Bank, 2008:31). Strengthening this positive view was the realization that from a foreign policy wise perspective the Plan was an initiative that could be packaged in a very positive light: one of altruism, even if it would eventually come under great suspicion and criticism. For Gronemeyer (1992:65), the Marshall

Plan should be regarded as a "political masterstroke", since its designers succeeded in presenting it to the American population and to the recipient countries as a generous offer to help. However, he continues, the "boundaries between giving and taking were blurred to the point of unrecognizably. There were two benefits stemming from this 'help': economic-material and political-legitimizing."

As the Marshall Plan advanced from paper to reality, another milestone in the evolution of international development took place in the turn of the decade. In his 1949 Inaugural Speech, President Harry Truman stated that the United States' programme for "peace and freedom" would emphasize four major courses of action. The fourth point – from thereon in known as "Point Four" – was that the country should "embark on a bold new programme for making the benefits of our scientific advances and industrial progress available for the improvement and growth of underdeveloped areas". The President also added that the material resources the United States could afford to use for the assistance of other peoples was limited, but its *"imponderable resources in technical knowledge are constantly growing and are inexhaustible"* (Truman, 1949a; emphasis added). The United Nations took its first steps into the promotion of technical assistance as a means of development slightly before the Point Four. In 1948, the General Assembly passed Resolution 200, entitled "Technical assistance for Economic Development", where it stated, "the technical assistance furnished shall not be a means of foreign economic and political interference in the internal affairs of the country concerned and shall not be accompanied by any considerations of a political nature". However, Truman's Point Four marked the first time ever that the idea of knowledge transfers was explicitly incorporated into a country's *foreign policy*. Therefore, while the Marshall Plan was a landmark for development assistance in general, Point Four represented the "birth" of technical cooperation as a foreign policy tool in the context of development assistance. Right after the announcement of Point Four, there would be much speculation as to what were the "real" intentions behind the United States' decision to go in this new direction.

Those connected to Truman's administration placed Point Four under a very positive and altruistic light. In 1952, for instance, Secretary of State Dean Acheson summarized Point Four as being about preserving the "American dream" by exporting "the American revolution" (Acheson, 1952). President Truman would declare that there was nothing of imperialism in the concept of Point Four as "we [US] do not propose to dominate other people, or exploit them, or force them to change their ways of life" (Truman, 1952). It could be seen as a declaration regarding the "concept of maintaining the peace of the world through technical assistance to underdeveloped areas" (Raushenbush, 1950:16). However, this was not how most analysts saw the use of technical cooperation in United States foreign policy. Most academic interpretations are similar to Pierce's (2007:256) view: "Truman's primary concern was neither financial nor humanitarian.

His main objective was the expansion of the power (which included the unity) – of the free world". In other words, technical cooperation was conceived as a means of seeking primarily diplomatic-political gains in the context of the Cold War.

The birth of Point Four appears to be much more haphazard than how it was portrayed then by the United States Administration or by political analysts afterwards. Working at the State Department at the time, Louis Halle offered a detailed first-hand account of how the Point Four came to be. He talks about how at some time in November 1948, a routine message from the President's speech-writing assistant requested the State Department to send over any proposals it had for the content of the inaugural address. After three proposals were given, a question was raised: "any more?" which – according to Halle – was followed by the exchange below, worth reproducing in detail (Halle, 1964:15–16):

> There was a pause while everyone searched his mind. The Deputy Director ended the pause by asking: how about technical assistance for underdeveloped countries (...)? That's a good idea, said the Director of Public Affairs.
>
> So "Point Four" was set down without further discussion, and there the meeting adjourned. When the four points proposed for inclusion in the President's address went up through the Department's clearance-machinery, the fourth was discarded. (...) So, the first three points, without the fourth, were sent to the White House.
>
> (...) A few days later, the Director of Public Affairs received a call from the presidential assistance [who said] the President would like to have something in his speech that is just a bit original. At this juncture, without proper time for reflection, the Director of Public Affairs (...) [said] there had been a fourth point, but it had been thrown out.
>
> What was it?
>
> The Director told what it was.
>
> That's great, said the voice from the White House, and "Point Four" went back again.

Therefore, what was initially a "public-relations gimmick, thrown in by a professional speech-writer to give the speech more life" (Halle, 1964:17), ended up being *the* Point Four.[7] To the surprise of the Administration, newspapers dramatized "Point Four" in their headlines – the New York Times called it the "World Fair Deal" (NYT, 1949). The State Department is said to have been "caught flatfooted" as officials simply did not know "what in the hell [*sic*]" President Truman had on his mind; as a matter of fact, even the Secretary of State Dean Acheson first learned about Point Four in the inaugural speech – and was one who "apparently saw no anti-Soviet profit" in it (Beisner, 2006:212–213). Hence, President Truman's explanation, given less than a week after the inaugural speech, explaining that Point Four had been in his and the Government's mind "for the past two of three years, ever since the Marshall Plan was inaugurated" (Truman, 1949b) was simply untrue, as was the claim that the Plan originated with the Greece and Turkey propositions.

The origins of America's technical assistance as a foreign policy tool reveals it was not an immediate product of foreign policy strategic planning. While this is interesting in many ways, it is relevant to the present analysis for at least two important reasons. First, there was no *a priori* definition on how the agreements would be implemented (i.e., conditional, unconditional, tied, untied), which means that in principle they could have gone in any direction. Second, this story matters since presidential diplomacy also played an important role in many countries' approach – such as Brazil's approach during President Lula's tenure – to the use of technical cooperation as a foreign policy tool.

By the early 1950s, America's discourse over aid began to not only be about development but also about communist containment, which is unsurprising given the latter was the most vivid topic in the country's foreign policy at the time. In 1951, US Congress passed the Mutual Security Act, authorizing close to $7.5 billion for foreign military, economic, and technical aid to American allies, and aimed against Soviet 'encroachment', in the words of Secretary of State Dean Acheson.[8] While the focus of this Act was more about providing military rather than economic assistance, it was nonetheless framed as a *development* issue, being essential "to help the free countries of Asia in their struggle to make good their independence *and bring economic and social progress to their people*" (Truman, 1951; emphasis added). The overarching logic was that economic development of 'friendly' nations contributed to a list of politically positive things: democracy, peace, non-communist governments, good will, and international understanding (Packenham, 1973:47–48). In tandem, technical assistance was framed as also promoting economic development which also meant benefits for the United States. For the following decades until the end of the Cold War, numerous United States development initiatives would be embedded within a broad logic of Soviet/communist containment – even if economic interests were many times the (co)main driver of the process. Given the quite clear reality that the United States' promotion of development abroad was not a product of altruism, but of the donor's national interests, in the early days of implementing technical cooperation initiatives, there were those with strong words against technical assistance and Point Four, such as "no policy of the United States in living memory had done more to create suspicions and resentment in Asia and Middle East than Point Four" (Groseclose, 1953:26).

As the 1950s advanced, the United States would not stay for long as the sole donor of development assistance. While from 1946 to 1959 the United States was clearly the biggest donor, accounting for almost 60% of aggregate DAC aid, France represented 22% of all DAC assistance – the largest foreign aid programme at the time in relative terms (vis-à-vis GDP), and the

United Kingdom around 8% (World Bank, 2008:25). Other countries would join the United States as providers of international development initiatives, although not always with the same motivations as the United States. The Soviet Union was one that clearly sought to 'counter' the United States in these early days of the Cold War. Since the Marshall Plan was opened to *all* European countries – including those under the Soviet sphere of control and some did show interested in it – in 1949 the Soviet Union (together with Bulgaria, Czechoslovakia, Hungary, Poland, and Romania) launched the Council for Mutual Economic Assistance (COMECOM). The Council would be an intrinsic part of Soviet aid, with COMECOM historically accounting for 10% of total ODA until the end of the Cold War (World Bank, 2008:26). Most of the Soviet programme of providing aid and technical assistance began in 1953, after the death of Stalin, rising significantly at the end of the decade. Geographically, it was less ambitious than the United States programme, and concentrated mostly on countries in the periphery of the Communist bloc. Between 1957 and 1958, for instance, Egypt, Syria, and Yemen received 97% of the economic aid to the Middle East and Africa; while Afghanistan, India, and Indonesia received 82% of the aid to South and Southeast Asia (Nielsen & Hodjera, 1959:40–41). There was much attention given to technical cooperation within their development assistance actions, with Soviets taking "pride in their training of native technicians" (Goldman, 1965:350). However, as they (and many other developed countries) would soon realize, simply transplanting donors' solutions to solve recipients' problems could not only be extremely ineffective but also do very little in terms of any actual *development*.

As the Cold War took shape as the dominant concern of the bipolar world, foreign aid became intrinsically entangled in it – as would the expanded use of technical assistance as a foreign policy tool. The competition between superpowers for more alliances and influence over as many countries as possible would not only be sought through traditional military partnerships or sheer domination: development assistance would serve as means of attracting and rewarding 'friends'. But how successful this policy was in producing the desired gains is questionable: Goldman (1965:357) concluded that both the United States and the USSR had realized by the early 1960s that a recipient's acceptance of their foreign aid did not assure acquiescence with the donor's policies, friendship, or even gratitude – much less 'eternal' gratitude (as perceived in the USSR-China relationship). By the early 1950s, the seeds of "aid rivalry" had been sown (Hook, 1995:25). Some authors even argue that were it not for the Cold War there would have been no foreign aid programmes, as it would have been impossible to generate the domestic political support in the donor countries necessary to sustain foreign assistance for more than four decades (Griffin, 1991:647). However, this seems to be an overstatement. After all, many other countries would become donors for diverse and 'non-ideological' reasons, even if under the shadow of bipolar rivalry.

France and Britain's motivations for foreign aid appeared to be much more connected to maintaining their presence and influence in their former colonies than anything else. If anything, it can be said that they had, in fact, more reasons to be *concerned* about United States aid and its potential to overtake the former colonizers' 'privileged' space. On the other hand, for most Nordic countries – Norway, Sweden, and Denmark – analysts often point to their shared values and norms, such as sponsoring missionary activities abroad as significant motivations for international development assistance (Lancaster, 2006:30). Moreover, as for Germany[9] and Japan, it can be said that their desire to become donors was in part economically motivated and in part acted as "conscience money", to re-establish their own self-respect and regain the moral approval of the civilized world (Niblock, 1970:553).

France's early foreign aid actions began with a focus on its colonies, before the major wave of decolonization had begun. In 1946 there was the establishment of 10-year development plans for the territories under the Ministry of Overseas through the *Fonds d'intervention pour le dévelopement économique et social* (FIDES). Later in 1959, General Charles de Gaulle created the Ministry of Cooperation, assigned to develop the "countries within its scope", mainly former colonies in Africa, also providing technical and military assistance to these countries (Pacquement, 2010). France would also engage heavily in cultural cooperation, with Niblock (1970:553) arguing, "French aid seems to have been prompted more by the desire to spread French culture than to help the people concerned".

Norway and Sweden both became bilateral foreign aid donors in the early 1950s; Denmark would initially engage through the UN; and Finland only in the next decade. In 1952, Norway created the "Aid Fund for Underdeveloped Countries", also referred to as the 'India Fund' since most resources went to this one country. According to Van der Veen (2011:159), reputation became a prominent frame for the Norwegian government who sought to closely follow and imitate Sweden. Under this interpretation, the great increase in the volume of Norwegian aid in the 1960s happened because "the concern for *reputation* was joined – and even partially displaced – by the *obligation* frame, as aid became accepted as a policy area in which Norway had an international obligation to become more active" (Van der Veen, 2011:159; emphasis added). Sweden's first step was the creation of the Central Committee for Swedish Technical Assistance to Less Developed Countries in 1952; its first programme came to life in 1954: an agreement with Ethiopia, where Swedish missionaries had once settled in the 1860s.

Germany and Japan also began to take their early steps as development providers in this period. As early as 1953, the German government began to provide a small amount of technical assistance, although not immediately as *development* assistance, but as training: at this initial stage, the goal was to help importers of German goods use them effectively (Lancaster, 2006:30). In the mid-1950s, Japan was still in the process of post-war reconstruction and received financial assistance from overseas, including from the World Bank (Hiroki, 2008).[10] However, it began to provide economic assistance to some Asian countries through post-war reparations and *quasi*-reparation grants, as well as (modestly) providing technical assistance through the Colombo Plan.[11] According to the country's Ministry of Foreign Affairs at the time, one of the main reasons behind the initial focus on technical cooperation (along with private cooperation) in Japan's budding development assistance was because "only limited resources were available for government and capital assistance" (Rix, 2013:10).

### *Development assistance as the "New Normal": 1960s–1980s*

Notwithstanding all these events taking place in the 1940s and 1950s, it was in the 1960s that development assistance fully blossomed, with the establishment of the institutional basis for the contemporary aid regime. It was from then on that almost all developed countries began to systematically engage as donors and structure their own bureaucracies to provide this assistance; and that the idea that "rich nations [should accept] a measure of responsibility for the progress of the poor" became the norm (Woods, 1966:207).[12] It was also at this time that several international organizations became big players in providing development as well: the World Bank's International Development Association (IDA); the creation of the United Nations Conference on Trade and Development (UNCTAD); and the already discussed OECD's DAC. Contributing to this *zeitgeist*, in 1961 the United Nations declared the 1960s as the 'Development Decade,' fitting well to the reality of fast-paced decolonization.[13]

The United States would continue to play a major role in the realm of development assistance – both as an individual donor and as a force in the burgeoning multilateral development world. By the early 1960s, provision of foreign aid was very much ingrained in United States foreign policy. Until the end of the Cold War, it would continue embedded within two reinforcing logics: providing aid to developing countries was (1) a mechanism to attract countries to the United States' sphere of influence and (2) generate profits for American companies. Developing countries' prosperity and stability could positively affect the United States' prosperity and stability, and money spent on aid was often viewed as a jobs programme from which many workers and employers could benefit (Hagen & Ruttan, 1988:2). The year of 1961 was particularly meaningful for the United States and development assistance: the United States Agency for International Development (USAID) was created, charged with managing the entire United States bilateral economic assistance. The Alliance for Progress was also presented, conceived as a 10-year plan to aid Latin America; and the Peace Corps was introduced to organize US volunteers interested in participating in development initiatives in the developing world, (hopefully) improving the country's growing negative image abroad. However, while development assistance grew in enormous importance in US foreign policy in the 1960s, US provision of *technical* assistance within this context was confronted with key bureaucratic challenges. Most significantly, in that decade, technical experts and projects within USAID faced a decline in agency leaders' interest in their work, with *capital* assistance being pushed to the forefront, and technical assistance to the margins (Butterfield, 2004:26).

The United States did not limit its interest over development assistance to internal rearrangements and bilateral engagements. For instance, the idea of the UN Decade of Development was proposed to the UN General Assembly by President Kennedy himself. In addition, the United States began a process of engaging with other aid donors through a coordinated effort, as already in the late 1950s it begun to apply pressure on European countries for more substantial development aid contributions (Pharo, 2003:528). In 1961, the Organization for European Economic Co-operation (OEEC) – created under the auspices of the Marshall Plan – was reorganized, becoming the OECD. One important difference between these two was that the OECD now included non-European members – hence the United States would be able to join it, which would provide a direct avenue for influencing the organization. DAC would become the main point of conversion for assistance by developed countries. In this same period, IDA was established as part of the World Bank, and began to provide concessional loans. It was created following the initiative of then US Secretary of the Treasury Robert Anderson, under President Eisenhower's leadership (Kennedy, 1969). One of the most important goals was to "get other developed countries to begin to share more of what had come to be seen as the aid burden", with the United States as by far the most important donors of initial IDA contributions, at 42% of the total (Gwin, 1997:206–207). Hence, there was no shortage of US pressure in having the "aid burden" – a term still used by DAC – shared among other donors (World Bank, 2008:25).

Therefore, a series of factors converged towards the systematic growth in provision of development assistance by developed countries. Not only was the United States 'instigating' developed countries to participate (and with greater volume), but the expectation that all developed countries *should* engage in helping developing countries became 'normal'. By the 1960s, most European countries' economies had recovered from post-war problems, which allowed for further engagement. Moreover, as more and more countries decolonized, more opportunities to 'help' – and seek economic and diplomatic gains – emerged as well. During this decade, most developed countries began to establish specific, in some cases independent, development cooperation structures. Between 1960 and 1963 alone, the UK, France, Canada, Germany, Japan, Sweden, Switzerland, Belgium, Denmark, Norway, and the Netherlands created ministries or agencies to manage their development cooperation programmes (World Bank, 2008: 26–27).[14] In 1961, the United Kingdom created the Department of Technical Cooperation to structure its system of aid in 1961. Apparently, British aid burgeoned only when the Government realized that its former dependencies might need some incentive to remain within the Commonwealth (Niblock, 1970:553). A series of white papers emerged in the 1960s, arguing that the best way to lift poorer nations out of poverty was through economic development, arguing that the UK had a "moral duty" for development, and explicitly supported the idea that aid was both a good in itself, but also as encouragement to trade (Barder, 2005:6). In the same year, both Germany and Japan established their own specific bureaus to deal with development assistance (including *technical* assistance). Germany created the Federal Ministry for Economic Cooperation and Development (*Bundesministerium für wirtschaftliche Zusammenarbeit und Entwicklung* – BMZ), and Japan introduced the Overseas Economic Cooperation Fund.[15]

By the 1970s, development assistance was fully established in almost all developed countries' foreign policies. During this decade and the next, other important changes would take place in the universe of developed country donors. In the 1970s, there was a significant redistribution in the pattern of countries' provisions, with the relative weight of the United States, France, and the UK falling considerably, and the substantial increase in the volume of aid among others Nordic countries and Japan. While the United States, France, and the UK accounted for an average of close to 90% of all ODA provided between 1946 and 1959, their relative weight declined substantially in the 1970s and 1980s, stabilizing at slightly over a third of total net flows by the 2000s (World Bank, 2008:25). Different countries continued to give different priorities to and *within* their development assistance programmes: the United States and France aimed at a variety of diplomatic purposes, Japan pursued commercial and diplomatic interests, and other traditional donors sought a mix of purposes, including humanitarian intentions (Lancaster, 2006:43).

In the case of the United States, the beginning of the (relative) decline in money available for development assistance can be traced to 1971, when the Senate rejected foreign aid funding for the fiscal years 1972 and 1973. At the same time, domestic political debates in Northern European Countries and in Japan led to opposite outcomes, with aid budgets being substantially *increased*. By the mid to late 1970s, Sweden, Netherlands, Norway, and Denmark were already providing over 0.7% of their Gross National Income (GNI) towards developmental aid. The biggest change came in Japan: in 1978, it launched its first 'doubling-of-ODA' plan; by 1984 it was the second largest DAC donor, and would become the largest by 1989 (World Bank, 2008:31).

One important shift that occurred in the 1980s – the so-called 'Lost Decade' for most Latin American countries – was the increased use of macroeconomic conditionalities in bilateral and multilateral development assistance, particularly regarding grants and loans. The World Bank and International Monetary Fund (IMF) "joined forces with major bilateral donors, and 'like-minded' governments (including the Nordic ones) fell in line" by the end of the decade (Stokke, 2009:319); this had great impact upon recipients since they had to agree to IMF conditions before they could receive assistance from bilateral donors. Still, highlighting the variations within donors' choices, until the 1980s, France and the UK "each developed its own quite stable aid policy, an original mixture brewed from its history" (Pacquement, 2010:§63); and did not always follow ideas proposed by the World Bank (Cumming, 2001).

### *Post-Cold War*

Contrary to the widespread expectations that foreign aid flows would weaken or disappear with the demise of the Cold War, the scope and complexity of aid relations increased in the 1990s (Hook, 1995:3); this trend has continued since, with the current international development assistance scenario being even more multidimensional. The end of the Cold War would affect individual DAC donors' structure of development assistance – but not in the same way. While some DAC donors would be more directly affected than others by this phenomenon, the post-Cold War period and its 'new' issues – e.g., calls for democracy, good governance, and globalization – would indirectly impact all donor countries' approaches towards development assistance.

One of the most common features to emerge in the 1990s was traditional donors' incorporation of political conditionalities to their concession of development assistance. According to the OECD's statistic database, there are significant variations in the overall levels of tied aid for DAC donors since the 1990s, especially low levels of tied aid until the early 2000s then a significant increase by mid-decade.[16] By the early 2010s, almost all individual DAC donors appeared to be completely untying their ODA grants and loans. According to the OECD database for 2011, Australia, Norway, and the UK reported to be providing *fully* untied ODA grants and loans; Canada, France, Ireland, Luxembourg, Sweden, and Switzerland all indicated their levels to be above 98%. Still, while the total DAC average for untied ODA was 83%, the United States' was only 65%. So, while most DAC countries are now practically untying all their ODA grants and loans, the United States stands with the minority of 'laggards'. One argument used by many donors to explain why they are not able to commit to higher untying rations is that tying would help maintain public support for aid budgets (especially in periods of budget pressure), or cite unfair competition from non-DAC donors' whose development assistance is also tied (OECD, 2012b:7). In the case of the United States – still the highest overall ODA donor in the world in absolute value – this might be explained as a reflection of the "perception of policymakers that maintaining public and political support for foreign aid programs requires ensuring direct economic benefit" to the country (Tarnoff & Lawson, 2011:19).

One the most intriguing aspects of tied and untied aid from DAC donors is that these numbers explicitly *do not* include technical cooperation (nor food, humanitarian, or military aid). As made clear in the DAC's own statistics regarding Tying Status of Bilateral ODA, "members have agreed that administrative costs and technical co-operation expenditure should be disregarded in assessing the percentages of tied, partially untied and untied aid".[17] Hence, the 'real' level of untied development assistance, broadly understood, is not reflected accurately in the numbers presented above, meaning that a DAC country's level of untied ODA cannot be interpreted as signalling its level of untied technical cooperation. Unsurprisingly, there is great speculation as to what their 'true' level is once tied technical cooperation is added to the picture. After all, if countries have a substantial volume of tied technical cooperation programmes in their overall development aid structure and this tying status is not reported, "donors will appear more untied than they really are, with statistics thus not presenting an accurate, comprehensive and comparable picture of tying status" (OECD, 2012b:8). In the case of the United States, their level of tied technical cooperation appears to be quite significant, although precise figures are difficult to come across. It has been reported that of the top 100 firms used as consultants by USAID in 2000, more than 80 were US companies, accounting for 87% of the contract values, with the remainder being nearly all multinationals with offices in the United States (ActionAid, 2006:37). According to Oxfam America, the bulk of that funding went to US consultants, "whose real expertise is often knowing how to adhere to complex US procurement and administrative procedures rather than having knowledge of context or the focus on long-term poverty reduction orientation" (*Oxfam America*, 2008:24). In addition, it is not uncommon to find strong words from those in recipient countries, such as: "USAID is notorious for using US inputs, especially consultants. 'All the money goes home' is a popular saying with USAID" (*Oxfam America*, 2009:2; see also Rahman, 2003; apud ActionAid, 2003:07).

Adding to the complexity of finding precise numbers on untied aid in general – and untied technical cooperation agreements in particular – is the issue of *informal* tying. As already said, a serious analytical problem is that there is no way of making broad assertions as to the donors' power of *imposing* the purchase of its goods and services to provide technical cooperation. Investigations of formally untied projects have shown that a high proportion of the contracts were still awarded to firms within the donor country (Clay et al., 2009); it is hard to believe that this is simply a coincidence. In 2009, 89% of US untied aid procurement contracts were still awarded to US firms (Brautigam, 2011:2). In Australia, for instance, "while officially adopting an untied aid program, informal aid continued, with Australian companies receiving the majority of aid contracts" (Aid Watch, 2008).

Finally, Nordic countries – particularly Norway – are helpful in highlighting current variations among DAC donors. These countries have commonly been "held up as examples of ideal donors" due to their overall generous levels of ODA and with limited geo-strategic interests to divert their efforts toward narrower self-interested objectives (Rowlands, 2008:5). One explanation has been that because of a lack of colonial heritage, "Nordic countries [have] to rely on more abstract motives for its aid to developing countries during its inception, which in this case [is] 'international solidarity'" (Danielson & Wohlgemuth, 2005:520). However, Nordic countries should not be taken as a block of pure humanitarianism. When talking about Denmark's motivations for development assistance, Olsen (2005) says that even though the country is usually listed as one of the few who focus on being in-tune with what recipients want, this does not mean that there are only altruistic motives guiding its development policy as "quite considerable business interests are present as well" (Olsen, 2005:190). In fact, Denmark and Finland have been found to tie their aid more closely to the interests of their private sectors than in Norway and Sweden. In Denmark, aid untying had a history of being strongly opposed by the business community as well as by the government, and the aid community, even though it did begin a process of untying in the mid-2000s (Selbervik & Nygaard, 2006:3–6).[18] Norway however, by all accounts seems to be in effect driven by a non-commercial logic – even if not necessarily altruistic. As detailed by Selbervik and Nygaard (2006:6), in Norway, it has been difficult to even "gather parliamentary acceptance for endeavors to promote economic interests to any large extent", where "economic self-interest has been perceived to be at variance with humanitarian concerns, and there has been an explicitly expressed fear that this could tarnish Norway's reputation in important circles in poor countries". This can be exemplified by the declaration that this 'style' of development policy "counteracts a picture of Norway as a country where self-interest, materialism and egoism rule the ground" (Proceedings of Parliament, *apud* Stokke, 2005:452). Even more interesting is the following assessment:

> Norway's model is to pick a few global themes on which it has a 'special competence' and expand them globally. (...) In this, it is somewhat like the south-south co-operation that is all the rage at Busan, more of an exchange of knowledge and expertise than a funding of specific large-scale costs. Perhaps Norway's relatively small size enables it to play a more horizontal role in its development partnerships.
>
> (Glennie, 2011)

Curiously, Brazil (as a donor) reveals overlaps in its motivations and strategies with Norway – something quite unexpected, given their significantly different histories, cultures, economic backgrounds, etc. Still, a possible link might be found from the point of view of 'middle power' and 'niche diplomacy' (mentioned in Chapter 2). Both countries can be framed as strategically using their provision of development assistance as a foreign policy tool to craft and improve their international image. In fact, one high-ranked Brazilian diplomat made a specific reference to this overlap, jokingly saying Brazil wanted to be "the dark Scandinavian".

## Traditional donors: an assessment

As already stated, this book's goal is not to present a thorough comparison of various countries' motivations and choices in their provision of development assistance. Nonetheless, it is important to understand the broad scenario to situate what appears to be Brazil's 'uniqueness' as a provider of development assistance, particularly unconditional and untied technical cooperation. Ultimately, some broad patterns emerged over the years of developed countries' approach towards development assistance, which was certainly made more cohesive from their membership in the OECD's DAC. According to Rowlands (2008:5), the emphasis on tied aid and specific patterns of geographic dispersion of aid would be "manifestations of the dominance of strategic and commercial interests as the motivation and operating principles for the assistance programs of traditional donors".

While this does appear to be a quite reasonable interpretation of the broad scenario, important nuances become more apparent once a deeper analysis is undertaken. DAC membership has provided, with time, some degree of harmony in how its member-countries approach development assistance. However, harmony is not a synonym for homogeneity. General assertions can be made for the sake of parsimony, but should not be taken as straightforward depictions of all country's motivations or strategies regarding development assistance.

The findings demonstrate synchronic and diachronic variations among developed countries' use of development assistance (including technical cooperation) as a foreign policy tool. Enough evidence exists to easily state that it is incorrect to claim that all developed countries provided (or continue to provide) development assistance or technical cooperation in the same manner or with the same intentions. Even if DAC countries appear to be comfortable with political conditionalities, and most are on their way to (officially) fully untying their ODA, there appears to be important variations in providing development assistance, which ultimately reflect in their choices regarding how they provide technical cooperation in practice.

The same caution against generalizing all donors' actions based upon their development assistance 'framework' is valid for dealing with countries engaging in SSC, as it will be shown in the next section. This awareness of nuance and variation will be explored with more depth in the following chapters when assessing the choices made by emerging donors (such as Brazil, China, India, and South Africa). These countries are frequently – and problematically – treated as a homogeneous unit, as if all were led by similar logics and interests in what they wish to attain from providing development assistance. Just as there are similarities and variations among DAC donors, the same also occurs among those linked to SSC.

## Notes

1 The act of countries pursuing knowledge abroad from their *own* development has a much longer history though; seeking "modernization", for instance, in the 18th century Russia brought in experts and technology in substantial quantities from Western Europe, as Japan did in the second half of the 19th century (Browne, 2002:7).

2 South Korea is the most prominent exception: it went from having a development programme based on the spirit of SSC in the 1980s (one of the founding members of the G77, and a very active member for most of the time) to becoming a member of the OECD in 1997 and of DAC by 2009.
3 The full definition of technical cooperation used by DAC for accountability purposes can be found in OECD's *Glossary*. www.oecd.org/site/dacsmpd11/glossary.htm#T.
4 According to ActionAid (2003:8), it was the United States government who lobbied the strongest for food aid and technical cooperation exemptions within the current OECD aid untying policy.
5 These authors also reference the overseas capital flow from European countries in the late 19th century and in the first half of the 20th century – but whose destination was limited to their colonial possessions.
6 The "Truman Doctrine" came about as President Truman called for Congress to support efforts in Greece and Turkey to stop authoritarian/communist expansion in Europe.
7 For more, see Hechler (1996:114–120).
8 From the US House of Representatives – Historical Highlights, "The Mutual Security Act of 1951"; retrieved from http://history.house.gov/HistoricalHighlight/Detail/35416.
9 'Germany' will be used here to reference both *West* Germany (Federal Republic of Germany) in the 1949–1990 period and the "unified" Germany (since 1990); the former German Democratic Republic will be referred to explicitly as *East* Germany.
10 For Hiroki, when Japan started to provide ODA to other countries, it did so with the financial support from other donors for implementing aid, and "this was *indeed South-South Cooperation*" (Hiroki, 2008; emphasis added).
11 The Colombo Plan for Cooperative Economic and Social Development in Asia and the Pacific was created in 1950, and now has almost 30 member-countries.
12 George Woods was the president of the World Bank between 1963 and 1968.
13 In 1950, the United Nations had 60 member-countries; 10 years later it would be 99 members (in 1960 alone 17 new countries joined the UN); by 1975 this number would reach close to 150.
14 Among the major donors of the time, only Italy did not have a dedicated agency or a department for development cooperation.
15 In the case of Germany, Lancaster (2006) argues that the creation of a *Ministry* for development had more to do with domestic politics than because development deserved a ministerial level position.
16 However, the changes appear to be mostly attributed by the United States, which did not report its levels between 1997 and 2004.
17 Source: OECD online statistics. http://stats.oecd.org/Index.aspx?datasetcode=TABLE7B#.
18 In the 1990s, the Danish government declared that a certain percentage of its ODA should be returned to Denmark, and the 'return percentage' should be as high as possible (see Olsen, 2005).

## Bibliography

Acheson, D. (1952, April 09). Address before the National Conference on International Economic and Social Development, Near Eastern and African Staff Subject Files 1951–1953, Technical Cooperation Administration, General Records of the Agency for International Development and Predecessor Agencies, 1948–1961, Record Group 469, National Archives.

ActionAid. (2003). *Towards effective partnership – Untie aid.* London: ActionAid International.

ActionAid. (2006). *Real aid 2: Making technical assistance work.* London: ActionAid International.

Aid Watch. (2008, November 16). *Tied aid.* London: ActionAid International.

Ajayi, S. I., & Jerome, A. (2002). Opportunity costs and effective markets. *Development Policy Journal, 2*, 23–46.

*Atlantic Conference: Joint Statement by President Roosevelt and Prime Minister Churchill.* (1941, August 14).

Barder, O. (2005, October). *Reforming development assistance: Lessons from the UK experience.* Washington, DC: Center for Global Development Working Paper No. 70.

Beisner, R. (2006). *Dean Acheson: A life in the Cold War.* New York: Oxford University Press.

Berg, E. (1993). *Rethinking technical cooperation: Reforms for capacity-building in Africa.* New York: UNDP.

Brautigam, D. (2011b). U.S. and Chinese efforts in Africa in global health and foreign aid: Objectives, impact and potential conflicts of interest. In X. Boyton (Ed.), *China's emerging global health and foreign aid engagement in Africa* (pp. 1–12). Washington, DC: Center for Strategic & International Studies (CSIS).

Breuning, M. (2002). Foreign aid, development assistance, or development cooperation: What's in a name? *International Politics, 39*, 369–377.

Browne, S. (2002). Introduction. In S. Browne (Ed.), *Developing capacity through technical cooperation country experiences* (pp. 1–14). London: Earthscan.

*Busan Partnership for Effective Development Co-Operation.* Fourth High Level Forum on Aid Effectiveness, Busan, Republic of Korea, 2011, November 29–December 1.

Butterfield, S. H. (2004). *U. S. development aid – An historic first: Achievements and failures in the twentieth century.* Westport, CT: Praefer Publishers.

Caine, S. (1970). Review: Partners in development. Report of the Commission on International Development. *The Economic Journal, 80*(318), 377–379.

Clay, E. J., Geddes, M., & Natali, L. (2009). *Untying aid: Is it working? An evaluation of the implementation of the Paris Declaration and of the 2001 DAC. Recommendation of untying ODA to the LDCs.* Copenhagen: Danish Institute for International Studies.

Cumming, G. (2001). *Aid to Africa: French and British policies from the Cold War to the new millennium.* Burlington, VT: Ashgate.

Danielson, A., & Wohlgemuth, L. (2005). Swedish development co-operation in perspective. In P. Hoebink & O. Stokke (Eds.), *Perspectives on European development co-operation – Policy and performance of individual donor countries and the EU* (pp. 518–545). London: Routledge.

Dunning, T. (2004). Conditioning the effects of aid: Cold War politics, donor credibility, and democracy in Africa. *International Organization, 58*(2), 409–423.

ECDPM – European Centre for Development Policy Management. (2006). *Changing minds and attitudes: Towards improved Belgian technical assistance.* Belgian Technical Cooperation.

Frank, C., & Baird, M. (1975). Foreign aid: Its speckled past and future prospects. *International Organization, 29*(1), 133–167.

Gimbel, J. (1976). *The origins of the Marshall Plan.* Stanford, CA: Stanford University Press.

Glennie, J. (2011, December 01). Norway's wise ways on aid. *The Guardian – Poverty Matters Blog.*

Goldman, M. (1965). A balance sheet of Soviet foreign aid. *Foreign Affairs, 43*(2), 349–360.
Griffin, K. (1991). Foreign aid after the Cold War. *Development and Change, 22*(4), 645–685.
Gronemeyer, M. (1992). Helping. In W. Sachs (Ed.), *The development dictionary: A guide to knowledge as power.* New York: Zed Books.
Groseclose, E. (1953, October 05). Point four aid discussed. *New York Times*, Letter to the Editors, p. 26.
Gwin, C. (1997). US relations with the World Bank. In D. Kapur, J. Prior Lewis, & R. Charles Webb (Eds.), *The World Bank: Its first half century – Volume 2: Perspectives* (pp. 195–274). Washington, DC: The Brookings Institution.
Hagen, J. M., & Ruttan, V. W. (1988). Development policy under Eisenhower and Kennedy. *The Journal of Developing Areas, 23*(1), 1–30.
Halle, L. J. (1964). On teaching international relations. *Virginia Quarterly Review, 40*(1), 11–25.
Hechler, K. (1996). *Dean Acheson: A life in the Cold War.* Columbia: University of Missouri Press.
Helleiner, G. (2000). *Towards balance in aid relationships: Donor performance monitoring in low-income developing countries.* CIS Working Paper 2000-2.
Hiroki, S. (2008, January 20). Speech given at the UN High-Level Symposium "South-South and Triangular Cooperation: Recent Trends and Progress", Cairo.
Hogan, M. (1987). *The Marshall Plan: America, Britain and the reconstruction of Western Europe, 1947–1952.* Cambridge: Cambridge University Press.
Hook, S. W. (1995). *National interest and foreign aid.* Boulder, CO: L. Rienner Publishers.
Lancaster, C. (2006). *Foreign aid: Diplomacy, development, domestic politics.* Chicago, IL: University of Chicago Press.
Milner, H., & Tingley, D. (2010). The political economy of US foreign aid: American legislators and the domestic politics of aid. *Economics & Politics, 22*(2), 200–232.
Morgan, P. (2010, February). *AusAid's approach to technical assistance: Getting beyond good enough.* Report prepared for AusAid Office of Development Effectiveness.
Niblock, T. (1970). The politics of economic aid motives and objectives. *International Relations, 3*(8), 550–564.
Nielsen, W., & Hodjera, Z. (1959). Sino-Soviet bloc technical assistance-another bilateral approach. *Annals of the American Academy of Political and Social Science, 323,* Partnership for Progress: International Technical Co-Operation, 40–49.
NYT – *New York Times.* (1949, January 23). *World 'Fair Deal'; Truman's four points.* Review of the Week Editorials.
OECD – Organisation for Economic Co-operation and Development. (2001, July). *Untying aid to the least developed countries.* Policy Brief. OECD Observer.
OECD – Organisation for Economic Co-operation and Development. (2006). *The development dimension: The development effectiveness of food aid – Does tying matter?* Paris: OECD.
OECD – Organisation for Economic Co-operation and Development. (2008). *DAC recommendation on untying ODA to the least developed countries and heavily indebted poor countries.*
OECD – Organisation for Economic Co-operation and Development. (2010). *The DAC: 50 years, 50 highlights.*
OECD – Organisation for Economic Co-operation and Development. (2011a). *Perspectives note technical co-operation for capacity development.* 2011, January.

OECD – Organisation for Economic Co-operation and Development. (2011b). *Capacity development: Lessons learned and actions for Busan and beyond – Synthesis report.* Draft for Discussion at the Cairo Workshop on Capacity Development: From concepts to implementation, 2011, March 28–29.

OECD – Organisation for Economic Co-operation and Development). (2012a). *Aid effectiveness 2011: Progress in implementing the Paris Declaration.* Better Aid, OECD Publishing.

OECD – Organisation for Economic Co-operation and Development. (2012b, November 8). *Aid untying: 2012 report.* DCD/DAC (2012)39/REV1.

Offner, A. (2002). *"Another Such Victory": President Truman and the Cold War, 1945–1953.* Stanford, CA: Stanford University Press.

Olsen, G. R. (2005). Danish aid policy in the Post-Cold War period: Increasing resources and minor adjustments. In P. Hoebink & O. Stokke (Eds.), *Perspectives on European development cooperation: Policy and performance of individual donor countries in the EU* (pp. 184–214). New York: Routledge.

*Oxfam America.* (2008, February 11). Smart development: Why US foreign aid demands major reform. Briefing paper. Washington, DC: Oxfam America.

*Oxfam America.* (2009, January 15). Smart development in practice: The tied aid "round trip". Briefing paper. Washington, DC: Oxfam America.

Packenham, R. (1973). *Liberal America and the third world: Political development ideas in foreign aid and social science.* Princeton, NJ: Princeton University Press.

Pacquement, F. (2010). How development assistance from France and the United Kingdom has evolved fifty years on from decolonisation. *Revue internationale de politique de développement. International Development Policy Series, 1,* 51–75.

Pharo, H. (2003). Altruism, security and the impact of oil: Norway's foreign economic assistance policy, 1958–1971. *Contemporary European History, 12*(4), 527–546.

Pierce, A. (2007). *Woodrow Wilson & Harry Truman: Mission and power in American foreign policy.* New Brunswick, NJ: Transaction Publishers.

Rahman, S. (2003). *Case study on USAID's tied assistance in the health sector in Bangladesh.* Dhaka: ActionAid Bangladesh.

Raushenbush, S. (1950). Point four. *Scientific American, 182*(3), 16–19.

Rix, A. (2013). *Japan's economic aid: Policy making and politics.* New York: Routledge.

Roosevelt, E. (1946). *As he saw it.* New York: Duell, Sloan and Pearce.

Rowlands, D. (2008). *Emerging donors in international development assistance: A synthesis report.* International Development Research Center (IDRC), Canada.

Scott, Z. (2009). *Southern perspectives on technical cooperation – Analytical review and annotated bibliography.* Governance and Social Development Resource Centre (GSDRC).

Selbervik, H., & Nygaard, K. (2006). *Nordic exceptionalism in development assistance? Aid policies and the major donors: The Nordic countries.* Chr. Michelsen Institute (CMI) Report (R 2006:8). Bergen: CMI.

Singh, S. (2002). Technical cooperation and stakeholder ownership. *Development Policy Journal,* Special Issue on Technical Cooperation, *2,* 47–71.

Stokke, O. (1996). *Foreign aid towards the year 2000: Experiences and challenges.* New York: Frank Cass & Co. Ltd.

Tarnoff, C., & Lawson, M. L. (2011). *Foreign aid: An introduction to U. S. programs and policy.* CRS Report for Congress. Washington, DC: Congressional Research Service.

Truman, H. (1949a, January 20). *The President's inaugural address.*

Truman, H. (1949b, January 27). *The President's News Conference.*

Truman, H. (1951, May 24). *President Truman's special message to Congress on Mutual Security Program.*

Truman, H. (1952, April 08). *Address before the National Conference on International Economic and Social Development.*

Van der Veen, M. A. (2011). *Ideas, interests and foreign aid.* Cambridge: Cambridge University Press.

Wangwe, S. M., & Madete, L. (2002). *Pooling of technical assistance in the context of sector wide approaches in Tanzania.* Economic and Social Research Foundation – Consultancy conducted for the European Centre for Development Policy Management.

Watson, D., Minh Thong, N., & Zinke, J. (2007). *Provision of technical assistance personnel in Vietnam: Cooking pho, peeling potatoes and abandoning blueprints.* ECDPM Discussion Paper 77. Maastricht: ECDPM.

Wood, R. E. (1986). *From Marshall Plan to debt crisis: Foreign aid and development choices in the world economy.* Berkeley: California University Press.

Woods, G. D. (1966). The development decade in the balance. *Foreign Affairs, 44*(2), 206–215.

World Bank. (2000). *Can Africa claim the twenty-first century?* Washington, DC: World Bank.

World Bank. (2008). *Aid architecture – An overview of the main trends in official development flows.*

Zanger, S. (2000). Good governance and European aid: The impact of political conditionality. *European Union Politics, 1*(3), 293–317.

# 4 International development and technical cooperation

## South-South Cooperation

With the traditional/DAC donors approach towards providing development assistance already covered in the previous chapter, the next step is to look at the other framework for providing development assistance: South-South Cooperation (SSC). As this chapter will detail, the concept of SSC began as a 'response' from a few – and most recently decolonized – developing countries to the foreign aid that was beginning to be provided by developed countries in the mid-1950s.[1]

While the number of developed countries grew only slightly from the end of World War II, the absolute number of new developing countries increased exponentially. As such, this research is especially pertinent considering that the studying of 'traditional' donors' histories, approaches, and values is an easier task than doing the same for the substantially more heterogeneous group of developing-country donors. Using UN membership as a measure for statehood, there are currently 193 countries in the world; given that only 30 are official members of DAC, this means that 163 are *not* DAC-member-countries. Most non-DAC countries embrace the concepts of SSC (although some more emphatically than others), with the most notable exception being non-DAC European donors. There are also some few non-DAC countries in somewhat of a 'twilight' zone: while they have not 'renegaded' their South-South bonds in discourse, they voluntarily choose to report their ODA to the DAC (even if they are not DAC members), such as Kuwait, Saudi Arabia, Thailand, Turkey, and the United Arab Emirates. Ultimately, the non-DAC-donor category embraces under the same roof much more extreme variations in countries' capabilities of providing development assistance than the DAC-donor category.

A first assessment of the real-life scenario is that there are many developing countries that have practically no means of providing any 'assistance', particularly the Least Developed Countries (LDCs).[2] Again, it does not mean they cannot assist in any way. However, when this occurs, the likelihood is of a one-time, small or symbolic initiative, usually related to humanitarian crisis; such was the case for Myanmar's donation of $50,000 USD for Thailand's 2011 devastating floods, and Bolivia's pledge to send food staples and blood to Haiti after the 2010 earthquake.[3] There has also been room for technical cooperation even among the poorest developing countries. An interesting case is the "Knowledge Exchange about Non-Timber Forest Products", involving Bhutan (LDC), Benin (LDC), and Costa Rica, which states:

> Given the expertise of Bhutanese technicians and communities in the cultivation of mushrooms, the expertise of Beninese technicians and communities in the collection and cultivation of insects and the Costa Rican expertise in systematizing traditional ecological knowledge, the three partner institutions saw the opportunity for knowledge exchange and dissemination as relates to the cultivation and/or collection of non-timer forest products.[4]

Moving up the income scale, most developing countries do find themselves able to engage as providers of some kind of development assistance in more than moments of crisis, and have 'niche' expertise capabilities that can be shared – even if the sum of its development initiatives cannot be fully leveraged and amassed into an actual foreign policy strategy. It is in this group that technical cooperation is likely to be significant. After all, providing and exchanging knowledge tends to be much more at reach – if not the *only* real development instrument available – than giving grants or loans for other countries, as most still rely (sometimes heavily) on financial assistance from abroad. Because most technical cooperation initiatives tend to involve small projects with (relatively) minor budgets and little 'projection' outside of those involved, they can easily go unnoticed or be unreported in global databases of development assistance. Nonetheless, many real examples of these initiatives are out there, such as the cooperation between Brunei, Indonesia, and Malaysia towards building a green economy in the Heart of Borneo; and technical cooperation among Small Islands Developing States (SIDS) regarding rising sea-levels, as well as between SIDS and Singapore, to mention a few.

The overall relevance given to technical cooperation under each of the two development assistance paradigms is not the same: the SSC framework places it in a much more prominent position than the DAC/ODA. Still, this does not mean that individual countries within the SSC paradigm have (or have always) given more attention to technical cooperation than DAC donors have. As this chapter will show, there has been significant variation in the importance and characteristics of technical cooperation provided by countries within the SSC paradigm – whether because of their capacity or strategy. This has great relevance given the inadequacy of reducing the analysis of SSC and technical cooperation among developing countries to merely what is done by only some of them, such as equating all SSC to the actions of a few countries (e.g., only China and India).

This chapter begins by exploring the definitional aspect of SSC, as well as a discussion of the concept of 'South' itself. The second section deals with the use and the importance of technical cooperation within this paradigm, starting with a historical overview, followed by the principles and practice of what is known in SSC as Technical Cooperation among Developing Countries (TCDC). The specific case of emerging donors – as a subsection of SSC donors – will be analysed separately in Chapter 5.

## South-South Cooperation (SSC)

A simple working definition of SSC is "the processes, institutions and arrangements designed to promote political, economic and technical cooperation among developing countries in pursuit of common development goals" (UNCTAD, 2010). However, there are many other ways of conceptualizing what SSC is. Not only are there different definitions and usages in academic literature and international organizations, but individual countries also have varying understandings of what it means and specific uses in their foreign policy discourses and actions. While there is 'soft' international law[5] describing what is SSC, it still does not help those who seek a parsimonious definition, as visible in the 2010 *High-Level United Nations Conference on South-South Cooperation* outcome document:

> South-South Cooperation is a common endeavour of peoples and countries of the South, born out of shared experiences and sympathies, based on their common objectives and solidarity, and guided by, *inter alia*, the principles of respect for national sovereignty and ownership, free from any conditionalities. South-South Cooperation should not be seen as official development assistance. It is a partnership among equals based on solidarity. (…) South-South Cooperation embraces a multi-stakeholder approach, including non-governmental organizations, the private sector, civil society, academia and other actors that contribute to meeting development challenges and objectives in line with national development strategies and plans.
>
> (UN-GA, 2009:3)

Hence, in practice, SSC is used in various ways. At times, it is simply expressing a non-contentious interaction between two developing countries, whether through governmental or non-governmental actors. It can serve as little more than an appealing buzzword in political speeches or be the baseline framework for a solid and formalized commitment between two 'Southern' countries. Sometimes its use is directly linked to issues of development, other times only indirectly, since SSC can also be used to indicate trade and investment initiatives with actors (public or private) from developing countries.

Comparing the broad frameworks under which countries place their provision of development assistance – in this case, related to DAC or SSC – can bring along many difficulties. The most important methodological problem is that it is not possible to directly compare DAC/ODA and SSC numbers:

they simply do not measure the same things. First, SSC encompasses more things than DAC's definition of what counts as ODA. SSC can incorporate humanitarian, military, and food aid that is transferred between developing countries, and possibly even include all trade and FDI between non-DAC countries. Even if the classical definition of ODA was applied on 'ODA' from 'Southern' countries (i.e., only grants, loans, and technical cooperation) significant volumes would still be excluded from the final count, as most of the shares of SSC do not have a grant element of 25% (Lengyel & Malacalza, 2011:6–7).[6] Therefore, SSC embraces a broad range of formats and instruments for interaction, where each country's cooperation agenda leads to a choice of its own conception (Lengyel & Malacalza, 2011:18).

A second point is that while ODA refers to the transfers of only public funds (private funding channelled through market mechanisms are not accounted for), SSC usually includes public *and* private funding and partnerships. In the latter case, the logic being that "developing countries see value in creating beneficial environments for trade, investment and development in partner countries using their *full range* of resources" (Zhou, 2010:2; emphasis added). The bottom line is that when a non-DAC country discloses the value on how much it has provided in the context of SSC or 'development-related' initiative, this number cannot be directly compared to ODA. Even if used as a proxy reference, it must be made clear in the analysis that the methodologies are different in several meaningful ways. Adding yet another layer of complexity, SSC can also be seen as having altogether unquantifiable elements, such as the 'spirit of cooperation' between governments and the peoples of developing countries, which can't be put into numbers but can still be very meaningful in the context of foreign policy.

Another important point is related to a deeper discussion over *who is* and *what is* 'South' in the context of *South-South Cooperation*. As already stated, for working purposes the chosen boundaries have been drawn roughly around OECD membership: as simplification, its members are treated as 'developed', while non-members are referred to as 'developing'. However, the most relevant aspect of this issue has to do with the fact that many developing countries, such as Brazil and China (and OECD members like Chile and Mexico), chose to explicitly embrace and highlight this self-identification in their foreign policies. The dichotomy of a world divided between the (industrialized) 'North' and the (underdeveloped) 'South' can be traced back to the early years of the Cold War: the 'North-South' axis signified a reconceptualization of a world then symbolically divided into 'West' *versus* 'East', with Horowitz (1966) being one of the first authors to use this North vs. South vocabulary. The push for the increased connections among developing or 'Southern' countries grew alongside the extensive decolonization process taking place from the late 1940's until the mid-1970's, when around 100 new countries became independent – all of which were developing countries.

The Bandung Conference (1955) symbolically marks the political 'birth' of SSC.[7] It was attended by 29 countries whose combined population was at the time close to 1.5 billion people. It was the first time post-colonial countries came together bound by an identity that combined mutual concerns over their *own* (under) development, desire for deeper integration, formal condemnation of colonialism, as well as dialogue about their place in a world whose most powerful countries were immersed in Cold War concerns. The Conference called strongly for the practical application of many principles contained in the UN Charter (1945), such as self-determination, respect for human rights, peace and peaceful conflict resolutions, etc. But it also embraced new issues, and presented an enormous symbolic value: it was "an act of confident assertion vis-à-vis the ruling elite of international society and not a passive act of seeking acceptance (…) where not a single 'white' or 'Western' state was present" (Shimazu, 2011:5). No textual mention is made to the expressions 'Third World' or 'Non-alignment' in the final document of the Conference. The first noted use of the expression 'Non-alignment' was made by the Head of the Indian delegation to the V.K. Krishna Menon, in a speech given in 1953, and shortly afterwards adopted by India's Prime Minister Nehru, and would become institutionalized in 1961. The first recorded use of the term 'Third World' was in 1952 by French historian, demographer, and anthropologist Alfred Sauvy, when he wrote about how the United States and the Soviets (i.e., the 'First' and 'Second' worlds) were struggling to control the underdeveloped 'Third World', to which he compared to the French Revolutions' Third State (*'Tiers Monde'*). Then, in 1956, Balandier published the first academic piece with the term, entitled *Le "tiers monde": Sous-développement et développement.*

Nonetheless, the ideas related to 'Third World' and 'Non-alignment' were clearly present in the Communiqué's recognition of the "urgency of promoting economic development (…) and the general desire for economic co-operation among the participating countries on the basis of mutual interest and respect for national sovereignty". The document also stated, "all nations should have the right freely to choose their own political and economic systems and their own way of life". It also called for the abstention "from the use of arrangements of collective defence to serve the particular interests of any of the big powers [and] by any country from exerting pressures on other countries" (Final Communiqué, 1955:G). In short, the Bandung Conference represented an early landmark in the emerging *zeitgeist* of numerous explicitly pro-active interactions *by* and *for* 'Southern' countries that would occur in the next decades.

The 1960s and 1970s would be filled with international initiatives explicitly aimed to encourage the relationship between developing countries, and strengthen their collective voice vis-à-vis the interests of developed countries – a passive international role was not acceptable. Dependency Theory embraced the understanding that political independence did not automatically translate to *economic* independence, and SSC appeared "as an alternative to the status quo, an almost subversive strategy to strengthening developing countries both politically and economically" (Jules & Silva,

2008:56). Non-industrialized countries needed to foster their *own* mechanisms for economic development. One of the most important voices for this path was Raul Prebisch, sometimes referred to as the 'J.M. Keynes of Latin America'.[8] He focused on the deterioration of the terms of trade, with one of his main arguments being the value of what non-industrialized (developing) countries exported – i.e., essentially commodities – was bound to follow a downward trend in value when compared to what industrialized (developed) countries traded. Thus, a valid domestic policy strategy was to pursue industrialization through import substitution, adopted by almost all Latin American countries between the 1950s and 1980s.

In parallel, the idea of 'self-reliance' shared strong intellectual roots outside of development dependency theory, as "both Gandhi and Mao Tse-tung stressed similar concepts in their call for development approaches based on self-help and regeneration through one's own efforts" (Bobiash, 1992:9). In the 1970s, "some scholars appropriated the Maoist term collective self-reliance to describe their attempt to break the pattern of dependency, and then shifted to 'softer' terms such as cooperation, assistance, and horizontal cooperation, and – most recently – South-South Cooperation" (Abdenur, 2002:65). It is in this context that the concept of South-South engagement would explode in initiatives. The 1961 *Conference of Heads of State or Government of Non-Aligned Countries* (simply referred to as the *Non-Aligned Movement*) – a continuation of the Bandung Conference's spirit – was a clear political statement from several developing countries that they did not want to be 'forced' to be aligned with either Cold War bloc. In 1964, the United Nations Conference on Trade and Development (UNCTAD) was created, with its focus being to accelerate the economic development of developing countries. During its first session, the Group of 77 (named after the initial number of member-countries) was formed as an "act of South-South Cooperation that opened the way for developing countries to participate actively in international negotiations and global governance" (UN, 2009:19). UNCTAD's mission to improve the position of developing countries in international trade would be strongly reaffirmed in 1974 by the *Declaration for the Establishment of a New International Economic Order*, which should be based on "equity, sovereign equality, interdependence, common interest and cooperation among all States" (UN-GA, 1974).

Several regional South-South initiatives also emerged in this period. The Organization of the Petroleum Exporting Countries (OPEC) came to life in 1960 as an initiative of five major oil-producing nations (Iran, Iraq, Kuwait, Saudi Arabia, and Venezuela), emphasizing the inalienable right of all countries to exercise permanent sovereignty over their natural resources in the interest of their national development (OPEC, 1968). In this same year, seven Latin American countries created the Latin American Free Trade Association (ALALC). The Organization of African Union was formed in 1963, initially with 32 members. In 1967, Indonesia, Malaysia, the Philippines, Singapore, and Thailand formed the Association of Southeast

Asian Nations (ASEAN). In addition, the Organization of the Islamic Conference's Charter was signed in 1969 – just to mention a few of the several international bodies created *by* and *for* developing countries' own interests.

It is in this background that SSC specifically aimed at development initiatives, particularly technical cooperation among developing countries, would gain life. This would take place through bilateral actions, regional institutions, as well as internationally, coordinated mostly by the United Nations Development Programme (UNDP), created in 1965. The path of technical cooperation as a development mechanism within this South-South context would go through various phases in the last decades. However, before conducting this analysis, it is necessary to look closely at the thought of 'South' itself, and – most importantly for this book – what it signals to frame the provision of a technical cooperation development initiative within the context of SSC.

## 'South' or 'Souths'?

The concepts of 'Southern', 'developing', or 'Third-World' countries became part of the lexicon in international debates since the 1950's. Writing in the mid-1970s, Rosenbaum and Tyler (1975:245) talked about how "Third World spokesmen during the past 25 years [i.e. since 1950] have claimed repeatedly that their countries share a common culture, one derived from poverty and exploitation". However, there never has been a homogenized block of 'North' or 'South' – just as there never was a monolith among the 'East' or 'West' blocs (see Bauer & Yamay, 1982; MacFarlane, 2006; Eckl & Weber, 2007). Nor for that matter, have there ever been firm boundaries between similar divisions, such as: First/Second/Third worlds, centre/periphery, developed/developing, or rich/poor countries. To embrace any of these categories or divisions as reified entities, or objective 'facts', would be a mistake. As a quick reminder of why the hemispheric division should be taken only as a symbol (and never as a 'real' geographic depiction), close to 9 out of 10 people in the world live geographically *above* the Equator line. Thus, whichever term is used, all represent a highly diverse group of states, and there is significant debate as to their defining characteristics (Bobiash, 1992:11).

> There is a continuous range of incomes in the world, both between countries and within them, making the line of division between rich and poor countries quite arbitrary. One could say that the world is two-thirds rich and one-third poor, or one-tenth rich and nine-tenths poor, or choose any other two fractions which add up to one. The size of the celebrated gap between rich countries and poor countries (i.e., the difference in their average incomes) depends on the placement of the arbitrary line of division.
>
> (Bauer & Yamay, 1982:54)

Nonetheless, these terms and divisions are relevant political constructions because states *react* to them, consciously choosing to embrace them – or not – as part of their domestic and foreign policy discourses. The term 'North' as reference to developed countries, although past its heyday, can still be found in the specific literature that deals with '*South*'. More importantly though, it was never a term with which 'Northern' countries self-identified. The reverse circumstance can be seen regarding the conception of a world made up of 'civilized' and 'uncivilized' peoples. This division was embraced by most European countries and the United States until (at least) the early 1950s, and (unsurprisingly) never adopted by the 'uncivilized'. Surprisingly, this wording is still present in the International Court of Justice Statute's Article 38, whose text maintains the dated expression as it embraces the "general principles of law *recognized by civilized nations*" (emphasis added).

'South' on the other hand, has been historically embraced by what appears to be the great majority of developing countries. The most noteworthy exception probably are the former communist states in Eastern Europe "whose economic standing and concerns with nation building would naturally bring these states closer to others in the South" did not – and still don't – embrace a 'Southern' identity, but rather one that is tilted towards a European identity (Vieira et al., 2010:2). But as an example of the different interpretations of who is or is not 'South', Jules and Silva (2008:45) defined it as being composed as "all developing countries in Africa, Asia, *Eastern Europe*, Latin America, and the Caribbean" (emphasis added). Another interesting case is that of Arab countries, which do not seem to embrace the 'Southern' identity in policy discourses as strongly as other countries in Latin America or Africa, but certainly do not renege being connected to it. While the general rule in the literature is to see them being labelled as 'Southern' donors, in some instances these countries are in a separate category within non-DAC donors:

> In international forums, the views of Arab donors are often aligned with those held by providers of South-South Co-operation. Indeed, Saudi Arabia was a prominent participant in the Bandung Conference. Aid has been an important instrument to promote solidarity among Arab countries, and religious obligations appear to be an important basis for co-operation.
>
> (Smith et al., 2010:7)

In any case, self-identification matters. A country's choice to embrace this term in foreign policy discourses serves as a signal of where its stands internationally, where it sees itself belonging, and who are its 'natural' peers.[9] There is a particularly meaningful impact for the case of 'emerging' countries self-identifying as 'South'.

> The term 'the South' is meaningful precisely because it forms a source of national and transnational identity [which is] reified through the

> continuing formation of foreign policy within Southern pressure groups. (...) It is an identity that encapsulates the shared experience of colonialism and imperialism [and] the shared dilemmas of developing economies. Finally, the South serves as a mobilizing strategy based upon a profound critique of the contemporary international system
>
> (Vieira et al., 2010:3–4)

A final point about what it means to embrace SSC is that it implies more than just two self-identifying 'Southern' polities involved in some way. To place a provision of development between developing countries under the banner of SSC signals that the parties involved wish to guide the interaction under certain specific *values*. Even if one argues that a similar thing can be said from traditional donors nowadays (e.g., efficiency), the DAC was not conceived to uphold specific *principles*. Its immediate goal was structure and to coordinate actions among existing donors.

The keywords embedded in the concept of SSC are many, with the most important ones being 'horizontality' and 'sovereignty'. Cooperation means all involved give and receive something, in a solidarity process to help one another. In concept, it is expected to be promoted by most developing countries "as a two-way learning experience in which involved parties learn from each other and see the mutual gains that have been or can be achieved" (UNDP, 2008:4). This is directly connected to the idea of a horizontal relationship – as opposed to a vertical (top-bottom) arrangement – where there would not be an active donor and a passive recipient but an understanding that the parties negotiate while having the same 'status'.

Sovereignty is explicitly connected to a collective understanding that conditionalities are an unwelcome intrusion, as they violate each country's right to conduct itself without outside interference, which in context bears great linkage to the 'trauma' of the colonial experience. A current understanding of SSC principles can be found in the 'Guiding Principles of South-South Cooperation', as phrased by the United Nations Office for South-South Cooperation (UNOSSC), housed inside the UNDP:[10]

> South-South Cooperation is a *manifestation of solidarity* among peoples and countries of the South that contributes to their national well-being, their national and collective self-reliance and the attainment of internationally agreed development goals, including the Millennium Development Goals. The South-South Cooperation agenda and South-South Cooperation initiatives must be determined by the countries of the South, guided by the *principles of respect for national sovereignty, national ownership and independence, equality, non-conditionality, non-interference in domestic affairs and mutual benefit*.[11]
>
> (emphases added)

Of course, this does not mean that all such values have always been upheld in countries' *practices* in SSC activities – a situation that certainly is not unique to this case. Solidarity for instance, is difficult to capture in this context. Taking the word's dictionary definition, it represents the "unity (as of a group or class) that produces or is based on community of interests, objectives, and standards".[12] In practice, solidarity in the context of SSC can mean different things to different people/countries, such as: voting in international organizations to support a developing country's position; facilitating trade; investing in another 'Southern' country, or choosing to share knowledge to foster development could all be placed under this vast umbrella. Moreover, there is no easy way – if any at all – of separating 'true' solidarity from self-interest 'disguised' as solidarity.

The question of whether there is 'real' horizontality in South-South relationships is also difficult to answer. After all, differences among countries' capacities cannot be changed simply with wishful thinking. The questions then are *if* and *how* this might affect the way in which developing countries deal with each while embracing SSC principles. It appears that the answers are *probably*, and *it depends.* The main (but certainly not only) variable being how much the 'stronger' partner takes advantage of its position to set the cooperation to its favour. So, while asymmetry is important, it cannot by itself determine if the SSC development initiatives involving, for example, Burundi with South Africa, China, or Tanzania, would be automatically more or less horizontal simply based upon the relative differences between Burundi and the 'stronger' partner in the dyad.

'Southern' countries' active support for sovereignty and non-intervention is arguably its most recognized position in international politics (Vieira et al., 2010:5). Conditionalities, whether political or economic in nature, are indeed practically absent in the broad practice of SSC. The first possible explanation is because these countries *really* value these principles. However, a less normative and more cynical interpretation can focus on the fact that only a handful of developing countries even have the *capacity* to demand conditionalities from others. Then again, the few developing countries that could potentially mandate them from others (in special emerging donors) might not be interested in doing so. Even if the result is quantitatively the same – no conditionalities in SSC actions – there is a qualitative difference between not *wanting to* and not *being able to* demand them.

In the specific case of the SSC position on tying agreements, the situation is more blurred. Although it can be interpreted that the values of SSC oppose it – since one of its core principles is 'national ownership' – practice appears to have been more mixed. Again, it must be made clear that SSC relates to development cooperation initiatives undertaken by over 160 countries, most of which have a limited number of industries, or who, in many cases, rely essentially on commodities. Therefore, it can be implied that countries in this situation who wish to cooperate in development actions are not exactly in the position to tie agreements; after all, agreements are tied to the purchase of materials (or labour) to be used in the development initiative.

Adding to this, tying agreements are more likely to occur when one actor has something the other one really wants (such as money or specific knowledge) and thus is willing to accept a less-than-optimal arrangement: what it obtains from the initiative compensates for the lack of full 'national ownership'. As the case of conditionalities then, countries might not tie their initiatives because of a normative stance or due to material conditions – i.e., there is little that *could* be tied to agreements or what one has to offer is not so valuable for the other party. These are points frequently overlooked in the literature, which many times take what some emerging donors do and extrapolate their actions as a representation of all SSC. Take as an example the assessment that South-South development cooperation regards: "tying is permissible and widely used" (Chandy & Kharas, 2011:743). While looking only at what could be seen as emerging donors, Lengyel and Malacalza (2011:15) fall in the same slip-up of equating the actions of some developing donors with what is done in the context of *all* SSC, such as stating that tied aid (which they call "procedural conditionality") usually precedes SSC agreements or the start of activities. However, as it will be shown in detail in the next chapter, there is significant variation in how emerging countries deal with tying agreements, with some visibly embracing the practice while others are not comfortable with it.

The next section addresses the historical context and evolution behind developing countries joining forces for their collective advancement. This allows for a more refined understanding not only of SSC itself but also of how different countries have connected to it in their foreign policies, which will facilitate a more thorough analysis of the use of technical cooperation within the framework of SSC.

## SSC and technical cooperation

Technical cooperation is an integral part of both the concept and practice of SSC. It has particularly been the focus of many smaller Southern providers of assistance, while also playing a significant role for larger providers (Davies, 2010:12). The prominence of technical cooperation as a mechanism for fostering development has always been much more significant in the context of SSC than in that of the OECD/DAC. As most developing nations have never had 'extra' money to *provide* grants or loans, this has left technical cooperation as one of the prominent tangible instruments available to promote the development of other countries. While the lack of options is of great significance for developing countries "choosing" technical cooperation, this is not the only reason why this tool has been prominent within SSC discourses and practice. At least three positive expectations surrounding the use of technical cooperation between developing countries can be traced.

The first is that technical cooperation from developing countries is expected to be low cost. Most of the knowledge shared comes from public initiatives, typically transmitted by civil servants, not through 'external' consultants. Hence, a developing country can do more with the limited funds it has available for foreign policy actions, undoubtedly an aspect of enormous practical significance to decision-makers. One analysis found that "an expert working from the North in an assistance program in a developing country costs on average one-third of a developed country expert" (Rosseel et al., 2009). In this same line, another study on 'Northern' development assistance argued:

> [T]he domination of technical cooperation initiatives (TCIs) by expatriates can significantly compromise the sustainability of TCIs and raise other problems, among them donor credibility. This often happens when donors prescribe cuts in government expenditure and insist upon greater equity in distributing resources, but send in consultants who are paid 20–30 times the national salary.
>
> (Singh, 2002:64–65)

Second, knowledge shared between developing countries is projected to be *effective* for development. This would be a consequence of two intertwining shared realities. One, developing countries tend to face similar problems. Tested solutions to comparable development challenges faced tend to be more appropriate to the special needs and circumstances of other developing countries given their similarities in environment, background, or development path:

> [M]any kinds of technologies—health, food productivity, environmental management—(...) are very strongly ecologically specific. Advances that come in the rich temperate zone world are not typically directly applicable in the impoverished tropical world, so diffusion of technology, while it works, is a very hard process. It's not automatic because the technologies useful in one part of the world have to be translated to the ecological specificities of a different part of the world.
>
> (Sachs, 2002)

In addition, developing countries tend to have similar social, political, and economic structural contexts: razor thin budgets, problematic infrastructure, large-scale poverty, low-skilled workers, etc. This implies that solutions have to be crafted with great ingenuity to manoeuvre through substantial obstacles, thus offering new sources of ideas, models and practices already tested inside a (relatively) similar environment, facilitating the replication of 'southern solutions' (UN-LDC, 2011). The proximity of experience would then be "a key catalyst in promoting capacity development in developing countries" thereby "accentuating the principles of South-South Cooperation" (UN, 2009:Annex, §17).

The third positive expectation is that technical cooperation can facilitate the promotion of *horizontal* relationships between developing countries – one of the cornerstone principles of SSC. As already stated, unlike the availability of financial assets, every country has unique experiences and accumulated knowledge. This apparently trivial assessment challenges the long-held portrait of the world divided by development providers and development recipients. The idea that all countries have something to teach others and something to learn from others reflects a horizontally conceptualized international system. This is reflected in the language of SSC, where most countries – although not all – are uncomfortable to use terms like 'donor' and 'aid' to describe what they would like to define as cooperation among peers (Smith et al., 2010). The SSC 'spirit' of horizontality would still be present even in agreements with overwhelmingly one-directional structures of knowledge-giver/knowledge-taker, embodied by the logic of *docendo discimus*: the one who teaches also learns through the process.

Conceptualizing the best-case scenario then, technical cooperation in the South-South context would allow developing countries to find appropriate, low-cost, sustainable solutions to their problems in the experiences of other developing nations. The relationship would be horizontal, particularly among partners with similar development levels. Countries would mostly share experiences rather than give solutions. Agreements would always embrace SSC principles such as respect to national sovereignty, no conditionalities, and collective self-reliance. Unfortunately, this idyllic scenario cannot be taken at face value. Some developing countries have in practice adopted top-bottom technical cooperation arrangements, including tying knowledge 'exchanges' to clear commercial gains. The effectiveness of many projects has been subpar, whether due to poor crafting of the agreements themselves; budgets that are too small to impact; inability to follow through with (usually grandiose) promises; or inadequate institutional capabilities to sustain cooperation, among other possibilities.

To better understand the mismatches between theory and practice, the next subsections will explore (1) the historical employment of technical cooperation in the SSC context, and (2) the strengths and weaknesses of its use. The next chapter will detail the case of emerging countries and their relationship with SSC and technical cooperation.

### *Historical evolution of SSC-technical cooperation*

As previously mentioned, the idea of using technical cooperation as a development mechanism began in the post-World War II period, both in the context of the OECD/DAC and SSC. A common milestone between the OECD/DAC and SSC was the United Nations' approval of the "Technical assistance for Economic Development" in 1948. Since then, countries within both frameworks would continue to agree on the *importance* of fostering technical cooperation projects as a development instrument. Nonetheless, there would be great attention given by developing countries to differentiate the *motivations* behind the technical cooperation that they provided each other and that led 'rich' countries to do the same.

From the 1950s until the 1980s, a common interpretation for aid (such as technical cooperation) provided by developed countries for developing countries was that it did not 'really' seek development. For Knorr (1973:166) only a mere "fraction of foreign economic aid [could] be safely attributed to a plain sense of human solidarity or to a sincere feeling that the wealthy [had] the responsibility to share with the destitute two-thirds of mankind". The concept of a 'genuine' partnership between developed and developing countries lacked credibility, as there had "never been any real sense of equality between donors and recipients even when they attend[ed] the same consortium meetings and [sat] around the same table in many other forums" (Patel, 1971:305).

Under this light, development assistance was essentially "a foreign-policy tool used to project economic and political influence in the Third World" or a part of a new relationship pattern between some Western nations and their former colonies (Bobiash, 1992:1). Development experts from 'rich' countries reproduced – consciously or not – a colonial mind-frame, as the idea of promoting development itself was "a product of a long-term relationship between Europe and non-European parts of the world that has for centuries been determined by colonial power relations" (Six, 2009:1103). Aid from developed countries was described as "a concession by the imperialist powers to enable them to continue their exploitation of semi-colonial countries" (Hayter, 1971:9).

The international politics of development assistance in the 1970s should not be underestimated. In the Appendix to Hayter's book (called *Aid as Imperialism*), he explains with detail how the book almost was not published at all.[13] Financed by the World Bank's Overseas Development Institute (ODI), it began as a study of the Bank's activities in Latin America. The Bank did not welcome the author's deeply critical understanding. In the late 1970s, the Bank would commission in what became known as the 'Brandt Reports' – *North-South: A Program for Survival* (1980) and *Common Crisis: North-South Cooperation for World Recovery* (1983). Led by Willy Brandt, the commission was formed by equal representatives of developed and developing countries. It "hoped to produce in North-South economic relations the kind of breakthroughs [Brandt] had in the East-West political arena" (Quilligan, 2002:1). It had hard words for 'Northern' development assistance, but most of what was proposed was not accomplished. Also in the early 1970s, yet another study described the situation in the following manner:

> In a way, the present-day experts have replaced the members of the Colonial Service, which constituted the core of the administration of each African country prior to independence. The privileges which the colonial officers enjoyed were one of the outward symbols of colonial domination. Paradoxically enough, their privileges never reached the level of those enjoyed by the UN technical personnel or even of those accorded to the experts working under development-assistance agreements.
>
> (Widstrand & Ctervenka, 1971:44)

The idea of developing countries helping other developing countries through technical cooperation emerged embedded within SSC's 'ideological' framework. It is mentioned in the Bandung Conference's final document: "The participating countries agreed to provide technical assistance to one another, *to the maximum extent practicable*" (Final Communiqué, 1955; emphasis added). The central role of education in SSC was "closely tied to the role of knowledge as a fundamental tool of development" (Abdenur, 2002:66). It would be in the 1960s and 1970s that the idea of South-South knowledge exchanges via technical cooperation would fully blossom, mostly sponsored by international organizations governed by the interests of *developing* countries.

In the context of the creation of the UNCTAD and G77 (1964), SSC began to be structured around two main paths: Economic Cooperation between Developing Countries (ECDC) and Technical Cooperation among Developing Countries (TCDC).[14] The former was to be embraced by UNCTAD, and the latter to be led by the UNDP, founded in 1965. The formal evolution of TCDC occurred essentially within the UN system. Some developing countries did adopt their own interpretations of why and how to provide technical cooperation for other developing countries. Nonetheless, it is fair to say that *all* have based their approaches upon a common 'Southern' collective vision of TCDC that evolved through the UNDP. It was under the coordination of this programme, that in 1972 the UN General Assembly created a working group on TCDC.[15] Two years later, the UN General Assembly officially endorsed the establishment of a special unit within the UNDP to "promote technical cooperation among developing countries with the objective of integrating this activity of technical co-operation among developing countries fully within the Programme".[16]

The most important step in the institutional and normative structuring over South-South technical cooperation would be the 1978 Buenos Aires Plan of Action (BAPA) for Promoting and Implementing TCDC.[17] The BAPA represents the first and main UN document to systematize the promotion and implementation of this cooperative instrument. According to the document, the values inherent to TCDC are "strict observance of national sovereignty, economic independence, equal rights and non-interference in domestic affairs of nations, irrespective of their size, level of development and social and economic systems" (UN, 1978:Art. 13); and this is its importance:

> [TCDC] is a means of building communication and of promoting wider and more effective co-operation among developing countries. It is a vital force for initiating, designing, organizing and promoting co-operation among developing countries so that they can create, acquire, adapt, transfer and pool knowledge and experience for their mutual benefit and for achieving national and collective self- reliance, which are essential for their social and economic development.
>
> (UN, 1978:Introduction)

The Buenos Aires Conference was presented as part of "a broad effort by developing countries to cooperate in accelerating their economic and social development, and close the gap between themselves and the industrialized countries that had opened up during the colonial period" (UN-GA, 2009:3). It was perceived as a way of fostering 'Southern' countries to better develop their indigenous economy, reflecting "the influence of the dependence school that highlighted the restraining effects that the northern control of the global economy had especially on their former colonies' development schemes" (Lassey, 2010:5). Beginning in 1980, member-countries of the UNDP agreed to meet every two years to monitor the implementation of the BAPA.

Notwithstanding the evolving dynamic of debates of TCDC within the international stage, the actual implementation of these actions certainly did not follow this same pace. While some developing countries did engage in promoting some activities during this time, by no means did the aggregate of activities come close to reaching TCDC's imagined potential or 'revolutionary' power. The actions that took place were almost always bilateral, small in scale, and moved at a slow pace (Puente, 2010:82); and the majority occurred within regional contexts. The more active countries engaged in TCDC at the time included Egypt and Tunisia's exchanges in the Anglophone and Francophone States respectively, as well as in sub-Saharan Africa. In Africa, Nigeria, Senegal, Ethiopia, Ghana, and the United Republic of Tanzania were major supporters of TCDC. China, India, Thailand, Singapore, and Indonesia established bilateral TCDC programmes. And Argentina, Brazil, Chile, Colombia, Mexico, and Venezuela played leading roles in promoting TCDC both through their own independently funded bilateral programmes as well as through sub-regional arrangements (UN, 1995:7–9).

As the 1970s gave way to the 1980s, despite the abovementioned initiatives, TCDC would progressively be relegated to a much less prominent position than that initially envisioned. Technical cooperation among 'Southern' countries never ceased to occur during 1980s.[18] Nevertheless, TCDC in this decade would be thin in volume and timid in ambitions. The most likely explanations were the economic problems affecting most developing countries in this period (in the wake of the two Oil Crises), such as the Latin American's 'Lost Decade' of 1980 (Amador, 2001). Also, the consequence of many developing countries' prioritization of economic interests vis-à-vis ideological or ideational ones (Ekoko & Benn, 2002); and very importantly, the "tendency on the part of many developing countries to view TCDC as a less desirable technical cooperation modality compared with traditional North-South exchanges" (UN, 1995:11). By the turn of the 1980s to the 1990s, the overall impression of SSC – applicable to TCDC – was that "despite frequent rhetorical appeals and the endorsements of the 'action programmes' for South-South co-operation, the success of South-South co-operation [was] mixed" (Bobiash, 1992:7).

The 1990s would witness a 're-launch' of technical cooperation among developing countries. The end of the Cold War, the more stable political situation and economic growth of many developing countries, and the changes in the international policy agenda to focus (once more) on 'low politics' themes, such as development were some of the elements that contributed to a more favourable scenario to SSC in general, particularly TCDC. In 1994, UN's General Assembly called for the High-level Committee on the Review of Technical Cooperation among Developing Countries to produce a report regarding the "New directions for technical cooperation among developing countries".[19] The full report was released the following year, and one of its main conclusions was:

> despite unmet needs and the fact that TCDC is still not optimally integrated within the operational activities of the United Nations system, *the concept remains valid and indeed is likely to assume increased importance in the future in the light of the changes occurring in the international system and their impact on the traditional structure of multilateral technical cooperation.*
>
> (UN, 1995:1; emphasis added)[20]

Since then, many international initiatives – particularly within the UN system – have taken place explicitly towards strengthening the use, effectiveness, and visibility of SSC and TCDC.[21] Several high-level UN meetings on SSC/TCDC have continually highlighted the belief that cooperation among developing countries is "a fundamental component of international efforts to deliver development results".[22] The increased international attention on SSC/TCDC has occurred in tandem to the amplified involvement of developing countries in these activities, particularly regarding 'emerging' donors (to be explored in the next chapter).

Developing countries as a group now have an entire range of modern technical competencies, with centres of excellence in key areas that have increased their national and collective self-reliance (UN, 2009). It is fair to say that technical cooperation among developing countries has been embraced like never before. Tangible advances by developing countries include new technologies, technical know-how, and competencies in many areas including renewable energy, genetic engineering and biotechnology, electronics and semiconductors, information and communication technology; all of which could be "transferred to, and replicated in, other developing countries" (UN-LDC, 2011:7). On the 'intangible' side, there are also actions involving a large array of initiatives, like improving crop yields of tropical fruits; decreasing the spread of AIDS; collaborating in research and practices related to combating tropical diseases (such as dengue fever, Chagas disease, malaria, etc.); successful mechanisms in fighting corruption; water management in semi-arid climates; strategies for low-cost internet and phone access; and microcredit experiences, among a myriad of possibilities. Despite all the promotion of technical cooperation among developing countries, it would be naïve to assume that it is devoid of problems. The next subsection deals with issues surrounding its practice.

### *Principles and practice of SSC/TCDC*

There is little question that the increased use of technical cooperation among developing nations has been welcomed – especially by these countries. The substantial volume of these initiatives (undertaken particularly since the early 2000s) and the easier access to information over them has prompted a growing number of in-depth analyses of SSC in 'real' life. In this context, important questions have been raised regarding how close the practice of TCDC has been to the discourse. This has been particularly the case in consideration of its 'true' level of horizontality, 'Southern identity', sovereignty and non-intervention, and effectiveness. As posited by Betancourt and Schulz (2009:3),

> a more honest debate is needed on whether South-South Cooperation risks following the same vertical dynamic found in North-South cooperation, especially when it takes place between countries at different levels of development. This debate should also consider the possibility that the characteristics which distinguish SSC from conventional aid might not be detected in its foundations, but rather in its mechanisms and operative modalities.

Questions over the translation of SSC 'values' into policy practices are not exactly novel. Amid the 1970s' attention to SSC, Rosenbaum and Tyler (1975:271) stated that "the newly prosperous LDCs [less developed countries] have been slow to recognize that they have a responsibility for nations outside their own regions". The authors' assertion was that 'wealthy' developing countries did not appear to feel a moral obligation to aid *all* developing countries. And except for the OPEC member's *financial* development assistance, South-South aid was "largely of a token nature" and "provided within a political subsystem", as "more powerful developing countries have begun to use economic assistance to establish and maintain client-patron relationships in the areas that they consider to be their spheres of influence" (Rosenbaum & Tyler, 1975:270).

Following the increased wealth from high oil prices, the provision of grants and loans to developing countries specifically by OPEC members was nothing short of impressive.[23] According to Stokke (2009:535), "the share of ODA from non-DAC donors peaked in 1975 at 40 percent of total ODA when OPEC countries were at the top as aid donors". However, the recipients of this ODA were very few. Between 1976 and 1978, approximately two-thirds of all of OPEC aid went to other Arab countries, with the other third being roughly distributed in half between Islamic countries and 'others' (ODI, 1980:1). OPEC donors were unapologetic about their limited choice of recipients. In 1973, the director general of petroleum at the Iranian Ministry of Finance stated, "Industrial countries have to take care of those who are developing. The fact that they have no resources – that is not our fault. We ourselves, in this area are developing countries and our help should be limited" ('Iraquis

Increasing', 1973). In a similar line, Kuwait's Minister of Oil and Finance was explicit about his country's interest in providing aid for Arab countries and Muslim countries in Northern Africa: "Nobody looked at the Arabs before, why does everybody expect us now to be the godfather?" (De Onis, 1974:1).[24]

Notwithstanding these early signs that SSC might not have always been as horizontal or altruistic as many claimed, this issue was not explored in-depth for quite some time. The 'default' position of most policy and academic analyses until the early 2000s – and even many current ones – is to take at face value the assertion that the practice of South-South *is* different and even 'morally' superior to North-South's approach to development assistance and technical cooperation. Writings on these lines tend to view the interplay between the principles and the practice of SSC/TCDC as rather unproblematic.

Published by the UNDP, Browne's (2002) analysis is exemplary of this approach. For this author, the contrast between South-South and 'traditional' donors is quite tangible, with the latter's interaction serving as a convenient tool for "rich countries [seeking] to extend post-colonial patronage through transfers of capital and skills into the gaps that appeared to hamper development progress" (Browne, 2002:7), where demand was manufactured, not self-generated. Rosseel et al. (2009) follow a similar approach: "SSC lacks the overtones of cultural, political, and economic hegemony that is sometimes associated with traditional North-South aid. SSC is altering the global balance of power" (Rosseel et al., 2009:19). Some authors have gone even beyond, labelling "the South as a *norms leader* in the international system" (Alden et al., 2010:4; emphasis added).

More recently though, there is an increasing number of authors that embrace the possibility – and the reality – of 'real life' deviations of SSC/TCDC actions from its principles. The increased volume and data availability of SSC/TCDC projects has led to more nuanced understandings of its empirical uses. For Ayllon Pino (2009:2), SSC is only different than traditional donor's ODA – not better or worse. A tendency for 'romanticizing' SSC would then overlook the possibility that the power balances it generates is not necessarily different to the ones characterizing the North-South cooperation (Lassey, 2010:8). Gurria's (2010) interpretation, abundant with verbs and adverbs highlighting uncertainties and indefinite frequencies, is worth reproducing:

> It *appears* that South-South technical cooperation respects country ownership, supported *often* by high-level political commitments to set up and implement SSC. SSC also *seems* to be *often* aligned with partner country policies. (...) It is *often* emphasized that SSC does not impose conditions – a key priority for partner countries. Further, it does *seem* that South-South technical cooperation is more efficient, *often* using cheaper and more adapted human resources and methods. Mutual benefit and 'horizontal partnerships' *appear* to be a key aspect of SSC, based on perceptions of shared development challenges and experiences.
>
> (Gurria, 2010:11; emphases added)

The question over horizontality in developing countries' interactions can be seen from different perspectives. First, even in a dyad where both parties are faithfully committed to a horizontal structure, the most common type of cooperation arrangement will have one party providing something for the other (e.g., knowledge, money). While the overall context might be of many agreements between the two partners working together and cooperating towards mutual development, *each* agreement by itself tends to be unidirectional: from the supplier to the receiver. In a dynamic where the overwhelming majority of SSC actions between two developing countries are characterized by this two-tiered structure of giver/taker, it will be easier for the former to take advantage of the latter. While it cannot be said that the country with the upper hand *will* do so, the 'power arrangement' will be in its favour.

Going back to the idea that there are social expectations attached to 'giving', one can argue that even if there is a horizontal vision and no strings are attached to the initiatives, "the recipient government is likely to be, or believe itself to be, under pressure to conform to the wishes of the donor, if it wants to qualify for further aid in the future" (Wolfers, 1965:104). If this is the case, there would always be *some* expectation from the donor to get something back from its good deeds, even if it goes unsaid. In addition, there are undeniable cleavages between countries. This has been an issue quite present in the case of SSC between 'wealthy' developing countries and their 'destitute' peers. It is a fact that individual developing countries do not have the same levels of economic or military power, legitimacy in certain area, or knowledge over certain themes. There is a myth that SSC is between 'equals' (Jules & Silva, 2008:58). This obscures the reality that Southern countries could be subjected to the "same criticized vertical dynamic of concern when talking about the North-South cooperation that is to say conditionality, expected opinion support or political pressure" (Lassey, 2010:8). Hence, great care is necessary when dealing with the concept of SSC, as the presumption of a "horizontal and equal interaction neglects the existence of economic and power asymmetries as well as the possibilities of dependencies between the countries of the South themselves" (De la Fontaine & Seifert, 2010:11).

Nevertheless, even if absolute *de facto* asymmetry between nations is a given, this does not necessarily nor automatically result in a vertical relationship. 'Richer' developing countries can be pro-active – or not – in attempting to minimize this unbalance and foster a structure to promote *relative symmetry.* In any case, some authors call attention to dangers of equating cooperation to horizontality, and more importantly the contentious question: horizontality according *to whom*? There is always the risk of a mismatched interpretation as to "what to one actor seems like affinity might look like authority to another" (Abdenur, 2002:65), and the underlying

> ambiguity around who exactly gets to determine whether a technical cooperation initiative has been authentically 'led' or 'driven' by the recipient government, and what incentives there might be for governments to

> claim that technical cooperation was 'Southern-led' when in fact it was heavily influenced by donors, possibly via informal mechanisms.
>
> (Scott, 2009:5)

There are also questions over the capabilities of TCDC that are worth taking into consideration, all of which could critically impact the development and implementation of projects. One frequent issue relates to the sustainability of the partnerships over time. For Andrade (2009:1), "apart from the ministries working on foreign policy, developing countries still lack the means to engage in effective cooperation". Most 'Southern' nations would only have limited institutional capacities, implying limitations for coordination with other development actors and for scaling up (Gurria, 2010:11). While committing verbally to SSC, few developing countries have made it a priority in terms of establishing clear policies and institutional mechanisms to coordinate, monitor, and fund sufficient large-scale or strategic cross-border initiatives (UN, 2009:7).

All developing countries themselves – even the 'emerging' ones – face huge challenges "in terms of a high prevalence of poverty, malnutrition, and unemployment, serious deficits in infrastructure and productive capacities and the impact of external shocks" (UN-LDC, 2011:7). This leads to more uncertainty as to the assurance of funds in mid/long-term scenarios. In addition, opportunity costs matter: in accepting technical cooperation from one country, the recipient may forgo an alternative agreement from another country. As emphasized by Ajayi and Jerome (2002:24), TCDC would tend to be "naively" considered as a free good or resource for the recipient country, when in fact there is always a potential downside of not embracing an option of a more 'stable' assistance from developed countries.

One frequent critique made regarding 'Northern' development consultants is their 'tendency' for arrogant behaviour towards the recipients (Amis et al., 2005:375). They have largely been seen as "incompetent and often judged to be too young, inexperienced, culturally insensitive and completely lacking in knowledge of the local context in which they have arrived" (Scott, 2009:7). Not going into the debate over how truthful these accounts are, in reality, there are also no *guarantees* that the public employees from developing countries in charge of providing the knowledge exchanges to other developing countries will be devoid of these negative characteristics and refrain from condescending behaviours. There is always the chance that power asymmetries will be embraced by individuals in their interactions, whether consciously or unconsciously. Other elements can hamper the ideal of a horizontal dialogue between 'Southern' actors' on-the-ground relationship, including the potential impact of historical grudges, cultural prejudices, language barriers, not to mention the problems that can arise if the individuals sent from developing countries are seen by the locals as taking their jobs (Ekoko & Benn, 2002:146; Singh, 2002:64–65).

***

The concepts of 'South-South Cooperation' and 'technical cooperation among developing countries' are entrenched with several specific principled and normative beliefs. However, as is frequent with abstract concepts, interpretations vary as to what they (should) mean in practice. SSC and TCDC do in fact signal a particular framework and specific values. However, this does not mean that each developing country will translate these concepts into policy in the same manner. Nor does it mean that these translations are immutable as many countries' *own* interpretation of what SSC/TCDC means, foreign policy wise, has changed over time, or even varied depending on whom the country was partnering with.

As in the case of development assistance by 'traditional' donors, it is incorrect to state that *all* developing countries provide development assistance in the *same* manner or with the *same* intentions – notwithstanding similarities that emanate from adopting a SSC/TCDC framework. The South-South 'spirit' does not imply that developing countries will not tie their provision/exchange of knowledge to commercial gains. While most of them do not, some very important developing countries *do* attach ties to their technical cooperation agreements. The next chapter will deal with this heterogeneity in the foreign policy practices of emerging countries, including details over the practice of TCDC involving emerging countries. This will provide the empirical ground necessary to highlight Brazil's 'unique' approach of unconditional and untied technical cooperation within the context of SSC.

## Notes

1 No former colony whose independence occurred post-World War II is currently a member of DAC.

2 Least Developed Countries are those with not only a low income per capita but also with severe economic vulnerability and human resource weaknesses, such as problematic indicators related to population health and nutrition (ex: high adult illiteracy, high child mortality rates, and life expectancy).

3 Available information suggests that in response to the Indian Ocean tsunami of 2004, December 26, some 70 non-DAC donors responded with pledges of support (World Bank, 2008:12).

4 For the full project, see www.unep.org/south-south-cooperation/case/casedetails.aspx?csno=74.

5 UN principles, regulations, or guidelines that are not binding are typically referred to as 'soft' international law; for more on this concept see Abbott and Snidal (2000).

6 Under the DAC definition, a loan must have a grant element of at least 25% to be considered ODA.

7 According to SEGIB (2008:10), the first 'concrete' SSC initiatives can be traced back to 1954, when Thailand engaged in providing for small developing-oriented projects in the region.

8 Among many achievements, Prebisch occupied two very prominent positions regarding developing countries in the international stage: first director of the United Nations Economic Commission on Latin America and Caribbean (ECLAC/CEPAL), and first director-general of United Nations Conference on Trade and Development (UNCTAD).

9 Rosenbaum and Tyler (1975:248) noted at the time "within particular regions, some elites may remain psychologically attached to certain Northern nations", and cited Argentina as an example.

10 Created in 1974, the Office's mission is to promote, coordinate, and support South-South and triangular cooperation globally and within the United Nations system.

11 http://ssc.undp.org/content/ssc/about/what_is_ssc.html.

12 Merriam-Webster Dictionary.

13 The back-and-forth communication between the two parties, reproduced in the book's Appendix, is fascinating.

14 As already mentioned, after a 1959 Resolution from the General Assembly, the UN began to adopt the term technical *cooperation* instead of technical *assistance*, an initiative led by developing countries who felt that 'assistance' implied a rather patronizing and vertical relationship.

15 Resolution 2974 (XXVII) (1972, December 14), *Co-operation among developing countries in the United Nations technical co-operation programmes and increased efficiency of the capacity of the United Nations development system.*

16 Resolution 3251 (XXIX) (1974, December 09), *Technical co-operation among developing countries.*

17 Resolution 33/134 (1978, December 19), *United Nations Conference on Technical Co-operation among Developing Countries.*

18 The Organization of American States (OAS), for instance, created a 'Horizontal Cooperation' model to serve as "a facilitator and catalyst for [South-South] cooperation" (Berenson, 2002:7).

19 Resolution A/RES/49/96 (1994, December 19), *United Nations conference on South-South Cooperation.*

20 Also in 1995, the Non-Aligned Movement Centre for South-South Technical Co-operation (NAM-CSSTC) was established.

21 Including the UN General Assembly's 2003 resolution declaring December 19th the "United Nations Day for South-South Cooperation."

22 Resolution A/RES/64/1 (2009, December 19), *High-level United Nations Conference on South-South Cooperation.*

23 Aid from OPEC countries had begun before the 1973/1974 rise in oil prices. Kuwait, for instance, had begun its development programme in 1961, and several Arab countries (notably Saudi Arabia) had provided grants for regional allies since the 1960s.

24 Nonetheless, the global importance of Arab aid has now faded out, with only 4 out of 12 OPEC member-states still being a provider of 'aid' (Kragelund, 2008:565).

## Bibliography

Abbott, K., & Snidal, D. (2000). Hard and soft law in international governance. *International Organization*, *54*(3), 421–456.

Abdenur, A. (2002). Tilting the North-South axis: The legitimation of southern development knowledge and its implications for comparative education research. *Current Issues in Comparative Education*, *4*(2), 57–69.

Ajayi, S. I., & Jerome, A. (2002). Opportunity costs and effective markets. *Development Policy Journal*, *2*, 23–46.

Alden, C., Morphet, S., & Vieira, M. A. (2010). *The South in world politics*. New York, NY: Palgrave Macmillan.

Amador, E. A. (2001). El nuevo rostro de la cooperacion tecnica entre paises en derarrollo (CTP) y las nuevas tendencias internacionales. *Ciencias Sociales, 94*(IV), 169–188.

Amis, P., Green, L., & Hubbard, M. (2005). Measuring aid costs: What has been learnt and what still needs to be leant? *Public Administration and Development, 25*, 373–378.

Andrade, M. (2009, February). Is the South ready for South-South Cooperation?. *International Policy Centre for Inclusive Growth*, One Pager no. 77.

Ayllon Pino, B. (2009). *Cooperación Sur – Sur: Innovación y Transformación en la Cooperación Internacional.* Madrid, Spain: Fundación Carolina.

Balandier, G. (1956). Le "tiers monde": Sous-développement et développement. *Populacion, 11*(4), 737–741.

Bauer, P., & Yamay, B. (1982). Foreign aid: What is at stake? *National Affairs, 68*(Summer), 59–69.

Berenson, W. M. (2002, September 17–18) *The Process of Technical Cooperation within the Organization of American States: The Legal Blueprint,* Seminar on the New OAS Legal Agenda and the Caribbean Region. Nassau Beach Hotel and Resort. Nassau, Bahamas.

Betancourt, M. C. S., & Schulz, N. J. (2009). *South-South Cooperation in Latin America and the Caribbean: Ways ahead following Accra.* Madrid, Spain: FRIDE – Fundación para las Relaciones Internacionales y el Diálogo Exterior.

Bobiash, D. (1992). *South-South Aid – How developing countries help each other.* New York: St. Martin's Press.

Browne, S. (2002). Introduction, In S. Browne (Ed.), *Developing capacity through technical cooperation country experiences* (pp. 1–14). London: Earthscan.

Chandy, L., & Kharas, H. (2011). Why can't we all just get along? The practical limits to International Development Cooperation, *Journal of International Development, 23*, 739–751.

Davies, P. (2010). *A review of the roles and activities of new development partners.* CFP Working Paper Series No. 4.

De la Fontaine, D., & Seifert, J. (2010). The role of South-South Cooperation in present Brazilian Foreign Policy: Actors, interests and functions. *Stockholm Papers in Latin American Studies.*

De Onis, J. (1974, March 7). Kuwait to invest riches in Arab channels. *New York Times*, page 55.

Eckl, J., & Weber, R. (2007). North-South? Pitfalls of dividing the world by words. *Third World Quarterly, 28*(1), 3–23.

Ekoko, F., & Benn, D. (2002). South-South cooperation and capacity development. *UNDP Development Policy Journal, Special issue: Technical Cooperation, 2*, 119–129.

Gurria, A. (2010, October). Aid effectiveness – Why does it matter to partners in South-South Cooperation? *Development Outreach.*

Hayter, T. (1971). *Aid as imperialism.* London: Penguin Books.

Horowitz, D. (1966). *Economic disparity among nations.* Baltimore: Johns Hopkins Press.

Jules, T., & Silva, M. M. S. (2008). How different disciplines have approached South-South Cooperation and transfer. *Society for International Education Journal, 5*(1), 45–64.

Knorr, K. (1973). *Power and wealth: The political economy of international power.* New York: Basic Books.

Kragelund, P. (2008). The return of non-DAC donors to Africa: New prospects for African Development?. *Development Policy Review*, *26*(5), 555–584.

Lassey, P. (2010). South-South & triangular cooperation – With a focus on multilateral platforms acknowledging the aid effectiveness agenda, *mimeo*.

Lengyel, M., & Malacalza, B. (2011). What do we talk when we talk about South-South Cooperation? The construction of a concept from empirical basis. IPSA-ECPR Joint Conference "Whatever Happened to North-South?", Panel: South-South Cooperation: History, Concepts, Trends, São Paulo, 2011, February 16–19.

MacFarlane, N. (2006). The 'R' in BRICs: is Russia an emerging power?. *International Affairs*, *82*(1), 41–57.

ODI – Overseas Development Institute. (1980, August). *OPEC Aid*. Briefing Paper No. 4.

OPEC – Organization of the Petroleum Exporting Nations. (1968, June 25). Declaratory Statement of Petroleum Policy in Member Countries. Resolution XVI.90.

Patel, I. G. (1971). Aid relationships for the seventies. In B. Ward, L. D'Anjou, & J. D. Runnalls (Eds.), *The widening gap, development in the 1970s* (pp. 295–311). New York, NY: Columbia University Press.

Puente, C. A. I. (2010). *A cooperação técnica horizontal brasileira como instrumento de política externa: A evoliução da cooperação técnica com países em desenvolvimento – CTPD- no período 1995–2005*, Brasília: FUNAG.

Quilligan, J. B. (2002). *The Brandt Equation: 21st century blueprint for the new global economy*. Brandt 21 Forum.

Rosenbaum, H. J., & Tyler, W. G. (1975). South-South relations: The economic and political content of interactions among developing countries. *International Organization*, *29*(1), 243–274.

Rosseel, P., De Corte, E., Blommaert, J., & Verniers, E. (2009). *Approaches to North-South, South-South and North-South-South collaboration. A policy document*. Belgium: KULeuven.

Sachs, J. (2002). Science, technology & poverty: Five ways to Mobilize Development in low-income countries. *IAEA Bulletin*, *44*(1), 7–10.

Scott, Z. (2009). *Southern perspectives on Technical Cooperation – Analytical review and annotated bibliography*. Governance and Social Development Resource Centre (GSDRC).

SEGIB – Secretaria General Iberoamericana. (2008). *II Informe de la Cooperación Sur-Sur en Iberoamérica*.

Shimazu, N. (2011, October). 'Diplomacy as Theater': Recasting the Bandung Conference of 1955 as Cultural History. Asia Resarch Institute (ARI), Working Paper Series No. 164. National University of Singapore.

Singh, S. (2002). Technical cooperation and stakeholder ownership. *Development Policy Journal*, Special Issue on Technical Cooperation, vol. 2.

Six, C. (2009). The rise of postcolonial states as donors: A challenge to the development paradigm?, *Third World Quarterly*, *30*(6), 1103–1121.

Smith, K., Fordelone, T. Y., & Zimmermann, F. (2010, May). *Beyond the DAC the welcome role of other providers of development co-operation*. OECD – DCD Issues Brief.

Stokke, O. (2009). *The UN and development: From aid to cooperation*. Bloomington: Indiana University Press.

UN – United Nations. (1978, September 12). *Buenos Aires plan of action for promoting and implementing technical co-operation among developing countries*.

UN – United Nations. (1995, April 07). *Technical cooperation among developing countries*. UN Doc. TCDC/9/3.

UN – United Nations General Assembly. (2009, October 27). *Promotion of South-South Cooperation for development: A thirty-year perspective* – Report of the Secretary-General, A/64/504.

UNCTAD – United Nations Conference on Trade and Development. (2010). *Economic Development in Africa Report 2010: South-South Cooperation: Africa and the new forms of development partnership*. New York: United Nations.

UNDP – United Nations Development Programme. (2008, July 21). Draft fourth cooperation framework for South-South Cooperation (2009–2011), DP/CF/SSC/4/Rev.1.

UN-GA – United Nations General Assembly. (1974, May 01). Declaration on the Establishment of a New International Economic Order. A/RES/S-6/3201.

UN-GA – United Nations General Assembly. (2009). Nairobi outcome document of the High-level United Nations Conference on South-South Cooperation – Resolution adopted by the General Assembly, A/RES/64/222.

UN-LDC IV – United Nations Conference on Least Developed Countries. (2011, February 19), Background Paper "Harnessing the Positive Contribution of South – South Co – operation for Least Developed Countries' Development" New Delhi.

Vieira, M., Alden, C., & Morphet, S. (2010). *The South in world politics*. London: Palgrave Macmillan.

Widstrand, C. G., & Ctervenka, Z. (1971) *Scandinavian development agreements with African countries*. Uppsala: Nordiska Afrikainstitutet.

Wolfers, A. (1965). *Discord and collaboration – Essays on International relations*. Baltimore: John Hopkins Press.

World Bank. (2008). *Aid architecture – An overview of the main trends in official development flows*. Working Paper.

Zhou, E. (1955) *Texts of selected and final communique of the Asian-African conference, Bandung, April 18–24, 1955*. New York: Far East Reporter.

Zhou, Y. (2010, October 01). *The future of South-South development assistance and the role of the UN*. Remarks given at the OECD meeting of National Focal Points for Policy Coherence for Development.

# 5 International development and technical cooperation

## Emerging donors

This chapter focuses on emerging donors as a subcategory of Southern donors, representing the leading actors in South-South Cooperation (SSC). While probably all developing countries have engaged in South-South activities, some have played a pivotal role as drivers of multi-country programmes, hubs for knowledge and experience-sharing, and as sources of expertise, technology, and funding (UN, 2009:25). As each country prioritizes different mechanisms for providing development, the emphasis given to technical cooperation in each emerging donors' overall 'assistance' programme is not the same. While for some, it seems to be the preferred instrument, for others it appears as more auxiliary. At the same time, there are differences in how these donors position themselves regarding tying technical cooperation agreements to commercial gains: while some unapologetically tie agreements, others condemn the practice.

Emerging donors' decisions regarding the provision of development to other developing countries have great impact, including the collective power these countries have to affect the DAC-based 'development assistance' governance. Whether collective and individually, the dynamics created from which partners and regions are privileged by 'emerging donors', the mechanisms used to provide development, and the relationships they have with the recipients, all combine to embed a power component that extends beyond the actions in isolation.

This chapter focuses on four emerging donors: Brazil, India, China, and South Africa. Not only are they the most relevant emerging donors, they are also the most prominent countries among those 'emerging', representing the bulk of the BRICS countries (Russia is the only exception). The chapter is divided in two sections, with the first shedding light on emerging countries in general, seeking to understand the concept of 'emerging donor,' along with an analysis of the power dynamics involving SSC between emerging donors and developing countries in general. The second section briefly describes and compares China, India, and South Africa as emerging donors, with attention to their provision of technical cooperation. The Brazilian case as an emerging donor will be explored individually and with greater depth in the next chapter.

## Defining 'emerging donors'

Emerging donors, in a simplified explanation, can be defined as the most important 'new' players in the international development arena, which overlap with the most powerful 'new' actors in the current international system (i.e., emerging countries). The present research embraces the 'emerging donor' nomenclature while acknowledging that problematic occlusions or associations make it far from being ideal. Nonetheless, if its proxy status and porous boundaries are acknowledged, it can be useful as a parsimonious reference to countries that used to be under the radar as providers of development assistance and now are internationally recognized as important players (see Mawdsley, 2012a).

Three main issues make 'emerging donors' a contested concept. First, the word 'emerging' invokes the impression of something that was obscure, has come to light, and is now apparent. It can also refer to the idea of 'coming into existence'. This can mistakenly imply that these key developing countries have only engaged in development actions *recently*. It implicitly conceals the history of providing development that most of these key countries have had, which in many cases is as old as the ones of 'traditional' donors.[1] It also brings forth the question of *emerging for whom?* After all, they might be 'rising' only for 'Northern' countries (and literature) who only recently begun to acknowledge their actions. In addition, there is the risk of seeing this 'emergence' as implying an intermediary stage towards the goal of rising to the 'superior level' of becoming an ODA member. A second important concern is that some explicitly reject the *donor* designation. The Brazilian government is one who is adamant in its refusal being called a 'donor', positing that it is a *partner*. The word 'donor' would connote a top-bottom, vertically arranged structure of active-donor/passive-recipient, normatively in disagreement with what SSC is all about.

> [F]or many in the South the word 'donor' is burdened with associations of paternalism, hierarchy and neo-colonial interference. Some of the (re-)emerging actors prefer to call themselves 'development partners' in a conscious promotion of a discourse of horizontal relations of mutual benefit, non-interference and respect for sovereignty, rather than the vertical hierarchy invoked by the terms 'donor' and 'recipient'.
>
> (Mawdsley, 2012b:257)

The term 'donor' is also challenging for practical reasons: SSC explicitly embraces a much broader list of actions, including private and for-profit activities between developing countries, which have little to do with the idea of 'donor'. In addition, the term can be problematic from a perspective of domestic politics, as there can be little/no public support for a developing country being itself the giver of development aid (Konijn, 2013). Not that the people from these developing countries would be against other countries' development. The question policymakers can have to answer: why be a donor to the poor in other countries when there are many poor inside of the 'donor's' *own* country? Hence, the word *partner* can serve as a political purpose since it is less likely to raise questions than the term *donor*. This problem seems to be a concern mostly for democracies (like Brazil, South Africa, and India), as non-democratic 'donors' – such as China and Arab/OPEC 'donors' – don't appear to mind the label.

Third, even if the words themselves were not problematic, there would remain the issue of *who* should be called an 'emerging donor' or not. With no exact measure or specific threshold to determine whether a specific country is or is not one of the *key* developing countries to provide development 'assistance', each author or institution can come up with their own assessment. This lack of consistency poses an obvious methodological difficulty. Yet, even if there is not a clear set criterion of over which exact countries are or are not 'emerging donors', the triad China-Brazil-India are basically always referenced as examples, and increasingly South Africa as well. This bears a clear connection to the BRICS group, with Russia being the obvious exception. Russia might be an emerging country, but it is not an emerging donor. It has ties to the DAC and has never been labelled 'South' or developing. Also, compared to the Cold War period Russia has *declined* its provision of assistance, even becoming a recipient during the 1990s. Considering a more recent timeframe (since the early 2000s), the country has re-engaged as a donor more actively. Yet, it is far from giving as much attention to 'development assistance' in its foreign policy as the other four BRICS countries currently do (Chin & Malkin, 2012). Gray (2011:5) raised a pertinent on this issue: "Should the Russian government's efforts to join the global community of donors be understood as a defence mechanism against what Mauss called the 'wounding' experience of being treated as a perpetual recipient"?

Also, Brazil, China, India, and South Africa overlap in an important category connected to last chapter's analysis: they are 'pivotal countries', or 'prime movers'. The identification of a select number of developing countries as lead actors of technical cooperation was explicitly made in the 1995 United Nations High Level Committee for Technical Cooperation among Developing Countries (TCDC). There, the concept of 'pivotal countries' was introduced as those "positioned to play a 'lead' role in the promotion and application of TCDC, mainly by sharing their capacities and experience with other developing countries in their region or in other regions" (UNDP, 1995). The UNDP's Special Unit for TCDC listed 22 countries as 'pivotal', including Brazil, China, and India. In 2003, the term 'prime movers' was introduced as an alternative to 'pivotal countries' although the idea remained the same: the existence of strategic developing countries for the promotion of SSC/TCDC.

The domestic capacities of Brazil, China, India, and South Africa to provide development-oriented knowledge to other developing countries were specifically singled out by the United Nations' Report on 30 years for South-South Cooperation. The document stated, "Brazil, China, India and South Africa, the leading pivotal countries, exemplify how years of indigenous effort to build technical competence develop capacity to provide assistance, technology transfer, policy exchanges and funding" (UN-GA, 2009). All four of these emerging donors have embraced technical cooperation in their SSC initiatives and have framed its use within SSC principles. Nonetheless, two points are very relevant: (1) each one has given different *emphasis* to TCDC within their overall provision of development assistance; and (2) while their positions are similar in rejecting conditionalities, they are different regarding tying technical cooperation agreements.

## 'Emerging donors' and hierarchy

Borrowing from one of George Orwell's *Animal Farm* most famous lines, even if all developing countries are equal, some are more equal than others. There are indisputable differences among developing countries. Whether measured by economy, size, population, military strength, ability to influence others, or knowledge in particular areas, it is a fact that some countries have more power than others. This leads to a reflection over a "growing hierarchy of the South" (Korany, 1986:90), as an 'emergent' developing country might consciously use its 'donor' status to reassert power positions vis-à-vis less endowed developing countries. So, while the principle of mutual benefit is a central tenet of SSC, reality might show a different picture, as "middle-income donor countries often have markedly unequal relationships with the poorest countries in which the foreign policy thrust or strategic interests of the former" (BetterAid, 2010:3). As noted two decades ago, "the differences between a Southern donor and a recipient may be just as profound as the differences between a Northern donor and its developing-country aid recipient" (Bobiash, 1992:13). So, even if an 'emerging donor' does not reproduce an active-rich-donor/passive-poor-recipient structure, and both embrace a South-South logic, there is still room to explore the silent hierarchy that exists in a donor-recipient relationship. As said by a senior Brazilian diplomat interviewed, "One thing is the discourse, another is practice, and this is valid for North-South as well as South-South. And for more fragile countries, they tend to accept [anything], anything is welcome, so it is easier [to have it the donor's way]".

Each of the 'emerging donors' under investigation appears to be aware of the clear asymmetries that exist between them and most of their recipient 'partners'. All of them vocally and unquestionably position themselves as '*developing* countries' and 'Southern partners' in their 'development assistance' initiatives. One of the main goals of these semantic distinctions is to accentuate the differences between the approach of rising donors to promoting socio-economic development in the South and the rhetoric and practices of the Western/Northern donors (Chin & Quadir, 2012:494).

Another is to try to mitigate the uncomfortable overlap between (principled) horizontality and (real) asymmetry. In the case of each of the four BRICS 'donors' studied, all of them seem to believe that there is little to gain and much to lose from *highlighting* existing asymmetries. In fact, their rise as net donors have been accompanied by continuous efforts to reaffirm their 'Southern' and 'developing' identities, with Brazil and South Africa being particularly sensitive to being called *donors*, much preferring the term *partners* (Rowlands, 2008:7). Nevertheless, despite the effort to deflect connotations of hierarchy from the language on cooperation between developing countries, these collaborative ties still imply complex political processes. What to an 'emerging donor' might seem like South-South *affinity* can look like a (*quasi*) North-South *authority* structure to the recipient, as regional leaders such as Brazil, South Africa, and India may use their lending capacities to reassert their positions within their respective geopolitical arenas (Abdenur, 2002:65).

In the present context of development assistance, 'emerging donors' are much more likely than traditional ones to be sensitive to their reputation as promoters of horizontal cooperation. Recipients' perception and critiques of an authoritative relationship in development initiatives will probably cause more damage to 'emerging' than traditional providers. Hence, it can be said that 'emerging donors' face a narrower set of options than traditional ones. While their (relative) strength *provides* them the opportunity to take advantage of weaker 'Southern' partners, their limits for *exploring* this opportunity are smaller if they want to continue to frame their 'aid' as horizontal, and identify themselves as 'Southern partners'. The more a country's foreign policy identity is entangled with or hinges upon the idea of being a developing country, the more sensitive it will be to be called a hypocrite – as it has more to lose.

There is one final aspect of the interesting power dynamics concerning Brazil, China, and India as 'emerging donors' that would have been unimaginable until recently: the slow but growing prospect of these countries actually being *providers* of 'development assistance' to DAC donors. There is strong reason to believe that this 'South-North' structure will become more frequent, demanding a much deeper rethinking of what it means to be 'South', 'North', developed, and developing. Taking the reality of 2012 as reference, a negotiation involving China, India, or Brazil with Greece, Ireland, or Portugal could very well be re-interpreted by having the former be the 'Northern' countries and the latter as 'Southern' ones. There are already some examples that could signal this shifting landscape. In 2009, China was a provider of 'development assistance' projects to 12 Eastern European countries; Brazil has signed technical cooperation agreements with Spain and Portugal to transferred knowledge over human milk banks; and India's agreements with the Czech Republic and Hungary under the Indian Technical and Economic Cooperation (ITEC) Programme. Hence, there are grounds to concur with the assertion that "developing countries have become major providers of high technology goods and services to developed countries" (UN-GA, 2009:4; see McFarlane, 2006:1416).

## 'Emerging donors': key characteristics

As is the case with developing countries, the motives for 'emerging donors' to provide development assistance are mixed. A genuine interest in promoting development may be intertwined with the immediate political, commercial, and strategic goals of the 'donor', and the significance or weighting of various motives for specific aid projects may be difficult to ascertain (Bobiash, 1992:9). More importantly, the specific objectives and motives for *each donor* can vary greatly among recipient countries, aid projects, and over time.

There are great risks in treating the SSC/TCDC actions of 'emerging donors' as a homogeneous unit. As already seen, some methodological choices are certain to produce significant variation in the results, such as which countries are considered 'emerging donors' and what the data for 'development assistance' or SSC is actually measuring. Even if these issues are overcome, there is great variance among these donors' individual financial capabilities to provide SSC/TCDC (e.g., China vis-à-vis South Africa). This means that a simple sum of what these 'donors' aggregately spend on development assistance/SSC, or how many technical cooperation agreements are signed between developing countries, can easily obfuscate the numbers and characteristics related to each 'emerging donor's' actions and strategies.

In the case of technical cooperation among developing countries, while it is normatively conceived to be horizontal and to refrain from seeking to create or promote any dependence on foreign expertise, this has not always been the practice. In fact, China and India have frequently – and in many cases unapologetically – tied their technical cooperation agreements to the purchase of their national goods and services. These countries tend to mix and deliver different forms of assistance in so-called package deals which include other financial flows beyond aid (Davies, 2010:12–13). Moreover, when financial cooperation does become part of a South-South relationship, commercial considerations can be an integral component of it (Smith et al., 2010:6). So, though there may not be policy conditionalities, "mutual assistance means that the majority of aid from Southern countries, especially China, India, and Venezuela, is tied (...) to the use of donor-country contractors and companies, donor-country goods, or oil imports" (Walz & Ramachandran, 2011:17). Nevertheless, not all 'Southern donors' tie their provisions of development assistance. By and large, bilateral aid from OPEC nations is *untied*, with only a small number of oil contracts which contradict this general picture (Kragelund, 2008:567), although this can be explained simply by a lack of a range of goods and services to tie procurements to (Neumayer, 2004:295). As will be detailed in the next chapter, Brazil's stance is to refrain from attaching commercial ties onto its development assistance projects (even when it easily *could*), something that is quite visible in its technical cooperation programmes.

Notwithstanding these considerations of variations within 'emerging donor' behaviours, there are important commonalities between Brazil, China, India, and South Africa. Three issues stand out: (1) focus on regional partnerships and increasing presence in Africa; (2) absence of conditionalities, political or macroeconomic; and (3) technical cooperation based on indigenous research conducted mostly by public institutions. They will be addressed before moving to the specific analysis of each country's approaches to SSC in general and technical cooperation in particular.

### *Main partners ('recipients')*

One commonality among 'emerging donors' is their strong focus on regional 'recipients'. In fact, it is fair to say that when providing development assistance, the tendency of *all* developing donors is to primarily focus on their immediate region. This is the reality for Brazil in its strong record of partnership with South American countries, China and India with their closest Asian neighbours, and South Africa committed to nations in the southern portion of the African continent. Such is also the case of Turkey, which overwhelmingly favours partners in South and Central Asia, and Balkan and Eastern European countries (Turkey/MFA, undated), with strong links to Pakistan and Afghanistan. And Arab 'donors' have consistently focused on countries in the MENA (Middle East & North African) area, with some 'donors' giving special attention to recipients in close vicinity to Israel, namely, Egypt, Jordan, Lebanon, and Syria (Villanger, 2007:9–10; Kragelund, 2008:565).

This phenomenon can be explained through various theoretical lenses. In a Realist approach, this can be due to geopolitical interests and calculations, which could even include fostering recipients' *dependence* upon the donor. Political considerations would influence the geographical direction of development assistance flows of new development partners (as does the promotion of trade and investments), something that would not be unique to 'emerging donors' as it is also the case of many traditional donors (Davies, 2010:9). Providing assistance would be a way for each 'emerging donor' to strengthen and amplify their status as A (or *The*) Great Regional Power. In a Liberal perspective, this can be an expression of putting regional cooperation in practice by concretely improving relationships with neighbours, and a recognition that one's progress is intertwined with its closest partners (which in most cases are in the immediate region) so that all benefit from collective improvement.[2] A Constructivist approach can see this as being due to a process of identification with the neighbours, and an easiness of making and implementing agreements with countries with a shared similar language, culture, and problems, etc. It could also relate to some greater sense of 'responsibility' to help neighbours (or help them *before* 'strangers'), as well as greater expectations – and demands – *from* neighbours that it is the duty of the (relatively) wealthy among them to help them. This final point connects well to academic research in other areas, such as sociology and psychology, where one can find relevant arguments regarding this dynamic. For example, "the closer the relationship between the interacting persons, the stronger the expectations that help should be offered; less gratitude expressed when help is offered; and the more resentment felt when help is refused" (Bar-Tal et al., 1977:293).

There is one very important point in which Brazil, China, and India do separate themselves from other developing countries and even from other which could also be labelled 'emerging donors' (including South Africa). Since the early 2000s, these selected countries have consistently increased their provision of 'development assistance' to countries not only outside of their traditional immediate geographic proximity, thus extending the concept of their own geographic 'reach', to going outside of their regions altogether. Under President Lula, Brazil expanded from its regional presence to include Central American and Caribbean countries. India has increased its development 'provision' to Central Asia, Pacific islands, and all around Southeast Asia. China has reached out the most broadly of all, with growing presence not only throughout the *entire* Asian continent, but to otherwise 'non-traditional' areas such as the Caribbean and even moving towards Central and Eastern Europe. But since the early 2000s, the African continent has been the one place all three 'emerging donors' have most actively pushed to strengthen their ties with. Brazilian, Chinese, and Indian links with African nations are not new phenomena. They can easily be traced back to the decolonization processes of the 1950s and 1960s, international articulations regarding the Third World identity, and Cold War dynamics' of supporting certain 'sides' (including the non-aligned position). What is different is that more recently there has been a veritable explosion of engagements related to economy, diplomacy, trade, finance, as well as development. Compared to the past, projects are more ambitious; more money is invested; partnerships are more diversified; and interactions are more frequent, consistent, and structured. Hence, Brazil, China, and India's closer development ties with African nations have occurred within a much larger context, which could be framed as embodying the broad 'spirit' of SSC, and one where development is just *one of many* spheres to be promoted.

### *Conditionalities*

One of the core principles of SSC discourse is the rejection of conditionalities. Whether political or economy-oriented, developing countries have long protested them. Conditionalities are perceived as a (mis)use of 'development assistance' to (poorly) disguise what would in fact be intervention and disrespect to sovereignty. There is strong reason to believe that 'emerging donors' do in fact follow through on the rejection of conditionalities in their development commitments. The only exception noted in the literature is China's pressure upon its recipients to embrace a 'One China' policy – i.e., that they do not recognize Taiwan as a sovereign nation. This appears to have a particular relevance for understanding Chinese disbursement patterns in Central America and Caribbean. Nonetheless, there does not seem to be a direct tit-for-tat dynamic in place as China engages in SSC/TCDC initiatives with countries that continue to recognize Taiwan as a sovereign nation.

One possible reason for Brazil, China, India, and South Africa's rejection of conditionalities in their development assistance can be that they simply are not powerful enough to demand other countries to change domestic structures. Under this understanding, 'emerging donors' do not impose conditionalities because they *cannot*. But this explanation is problematic: it assumes that all countries that demand conditionalities such as good governance, commitments to human rights, or respect to the Rule of Law to provide 'development assistance' do so because they have the *power* to demand them (if they were 'weak donors' they would not call for conditionalities). Another power-based account is that a no conditionalities policy is actually driven by a desire to do business with countries that are considered 'rogue states'. Such seems to be Naim's (2007:95) opinion, who classifies the 'foreign aid' programmes of China, Venezuela, and Saudi Arabia as "toxic". However, more in-depth analyses have shown that this is not the case, with the largest beneficiaries of Southern assistance being the same as for OECD/DAC aid (UN-ECOSOC, 2008:36), with very few exceptions.[3]

Two non-excluding explanations seem to be much more reasonable. First, 'emerging donors' might not apply conditionalities due to a normative stance. They have all gone through negative experiences as aid recipients and the still very fresh memories of external impositions, whether from colonialism or related to the 'Washington Consensus', might have their policymakers embrace the idea that conditionalities are *wrong*. The second reasoning is that there is a historical attachment of the idea of conditionality as part of a 'Northern identity', as something that only '*they*' do when providing 'foreign aid'. Moreover, regardless of whether policymakers *believe* in the 'conditionalities-are-bad' normative framework, Brazil, China, India, and South Africa's policymakers do not want to have their countries perceived as hypocrites. If their foreign policies are based around a 'developing' identity, critical of actions, and attempts by 'rich' countries and international organizations such as the IMF, any potential gains from 'invading' another country's sovereignty would be very costly. Promoting conditionalities would mean running the risk of losing legitimacy to complain if someone else (like a DAC donor) demand these towards them.

Nonetheless, it is possible to argue that Brazil, India, and South Africa will be increasingly pressured to impose *political* conditionalities. These include good governance and respect to human rights, both connected to concerns that non-interference makes it "difficult for the civil society to be included especially in the country showing a democratic deficit" (Lassey, 2010:8). Thus, a serious lack of transparency in the terms and conditions of many SSC transactions precludes "any meaningful citizen participation in shaping policies and holding development partner governments accountable for their aid interventions" (BetterAid, 2010:4). Hence, for democratic emerging donors, their own constituents might perceive the increased domestic visibility of 'questionable' friendships as deeply problematic. This can lead politicians in the opposition to take advantage of when criticizing the government in office. One way out of this conundrum can be to *formally* maintain the vows to no-conditionalities and non-intervention while having the domestic 'development bureaucracy' drag their feet regarding any negotiation or execution of a previous agreement with an undesired partner.

### *Public knowledge*

As already stated, the bulk of knowledge shared through technical cooperation agreements by 'Southern donors' has its origins in state-sponsored development-related research. Most of the innovations in development that are shared with other developing countries – whether related to health, energy, technology, agriculture, poverty mitigation, reduction of inequality, etc. – have their origin in the country's *own* needs. It is still very common for development-related knowledge to still be fully under the state's grip and the know-how being shared to be under the control of a Ministry/Secretary, a government institute, a state-owned enterprise or a publicly funded research body. Also, unlike in the case of most developed countries, 'emerging donors' in general have no significant histories of public-private partnerships in producing knowledge (whether 'social' or technological). The bottom line is that when it comes to technical cooperation agreements from 'emerging donors', the knowledge they share is mostly *state-owned.*

Two corollaries follow this arrangement. First, the knowledge transfer is almost always done by people who work directly with the subject, i.e., public employees. Writing about India, but describing a situation that fits the reality of other 'emerging donors', "in areas such as social development, reproductive health, education, and taxation, *the only experts available* in India *are those employed in the public sector*" (Agrawal, 2007:10; emphasis added). This reinforces the State's presence and fosters clear and strong links between the projects undertaken and the 'donor' State's (foreign policy) interests. The second corollary is that under this sort of arrangement, the private sector, in general, plays a small role in creating knowledge to foster development. The historical quest for development shared by most 'emerging donors' – particularly China, Brazil, and India – was one that occurred when they had either none or very weak private sectors. The only strategies were to grow via the State or by relying on foreign partners. Considering the context of the Cold War and these three countries' embrace of a non-aligned position, along with the seriousness of the challenges these nations faced to develop, it is unsurprising that the private sector was never a meaningful player. The challenge of proving even basic levels of food, healthcare, water, energy, and housing for hundreds of millions of people was conceived as a *public* mission. The legacy is that even as these countries have opened their economies to the private sector in the past two decades, even as these enterprises have thrived and flourished in many areas, most of what is conceived as essential parts for the State's development has remained in public hands. Compounding to all of this is the public sector, which has rights over the knowledge it obtains (and wishes to share).

## 'Emerging donor': China

China is now the world's largest economy, measured in GDP (PPP).[4] Nonetheless, its government firmly categorizes the country as a *developing* nation, usually highlighting the enormous number of Chinese living on less than $2 a day. It also claims to conceive and provide 'development assistance' under the tenets of SSC, consciously presenting itself as a Southern partner (see Eckl & Weber, 2007). There is great difficulty in finding exact figures regarding how much is provided by China under the rubric of foreign aid, much less details as to *how* and *where* the amounts were spent, as "aid figures are treated as state secrets" (*The Economist*, 2011a). If one uses a broader definition of foreign aid,[5] China is probably one of the top three largest bilateral donors (Chin, 2012; Brautigam, 2013; Kitano & Harada, 2016).

China's official forms of foreign aid are the following: "complete projects, goods and materials, technical cooperation, human resource development cooperation, medical teams sent abroad, emergency humanitarian aid, volunteer programmes in foreign countries, and debt relief" (China, 2011). Brautigam (2013) explains that this number would cover all the short-term training courses, the youth volunteer programme, military aid, some turnkey projects funded by grants, and zero-interest loans (like stadiums, hospitals, schools, agrotechnical demonstration centres, government buildings) but does not include the concessional loans. Regardless of the exact number, it suffices to know that this country is the strongest '*emerging*' donor in terms of financial capacity, and increasingly one of the strongest of all donors of development assistance (including DAC members) in this rubric. Due to its importance, China's case will be investigated in more detail than India and South Africa's.

Just as many other 'Southern' donors, China has a long history as a provider of development assistance. The country's first incursions in this landscape began already in the early 1950s: it gave material support to North Korea and Vietnam (1950), participated in the Bandung Conference (1955), and began to provide aid to African countries (1956). The political dynamics of the Cold War ended up having important direct and indirect influences upon China's aid strategies. Its partnerships, for instance, sought to promote the recognition of Beijing (and not Taipei) as being '*the*' voice for

China, as well as strengthening the non-aligned movement. Still, for many decades, its foreign policy ambitions had to coexist with the reality of a country that struggled with domestic economic constraints. The government was able to provide some financial aid to most partners, but the situation did not allow the government the luxury of providing voluminous grants and loans to all desired partners in a systematic manner. The establishment of diplomatic ties with China/Beijing was normally accompanied by an offer of assistance: usually, a zero-interest credit, made available for a specific number of years, and which could be drawn on to finance projects agreed on by both governments (Brautigam, 2008:8–9). Technical cooperation however, was readily available and doable, being a worthy mechanism for low-cost and continuous engagement; for example, according to official sources, from 1953 until 1979, China hosted many trainees from countries like North Korea, Vietnam, Albania, Cuba, and Egypt (China, 2011). As said by Cooper (1976:14), China's technical assistance programmes served as "a tool of its external relations".

Technical cooperation has never stopped being a part of China's approach to foreign aid. It continues to be a foreign policy mechanism used under the framework of South-South development engagements. However, as China's economy opened in the late 1970s and began the process of growing at impressive rates, the country embraced and expanded the use of *other* SSC mechanisms with much more impetus. In the 1990s, the government took a series of measures to reform its foreign aid structure, focusing on *diversifying* the sources and means of funding, all the while continuing to enlarge the scale of technical training (China, 2011). Nowadays, Chinese aid is generally given through projects, and has been used to finance the purchase of (*Chinese*) vehicles, equipment, and material goods. The two main instruments of aid used by China are "complete plant projects (turn-key projects that involve construction or repair of buildings, infrastructure or facilities of some kind) and *technical cooperation* projects that involve training and assistance" (Brautigam, 2008:15–16; emphasis added). Hence, despite the absolute increase in number of technical cooperation projects, its *relative* weight as a foreign policy tool in China's current overall approach to providing development assistance has become much smaller in the past two decades. Therefore, while technical cooperation still matters in China's development assistance, it does not matter as much as it once did.

As said, when it comes to China's foreign aid, it is very difficult to gauge exact figures and details. This challenge is even more dramatic when it comes to finding thorough information and analysis focusing solely on the country's technical cooperation programmes. Technical cooperation tends to be only briefly mentioned in the literature, usually when authors talk in broad strokes about the mix of mechanisms used. When there is some further detailing, it is usually concerning funding mechanisms (grants, loans, lines of credit, etc.). As these are incredibly significant in volume, this is somewhat understandable. The combination of little information to work with, and technical cooperation's (relative) minor significance within China's full aid provision framework have led to a situation where it is almost impossible to analyse in depth China's technical cooperation. Still, this does not mean that relevant assessments cannot be made. Despite the deficiencies, the literature available does allow for a more thorough analysis of China's position to *tying* the provision of technical cooperation to commercial gains. The consensus is that China does in fact tie its foreign aid in general, including technical cooperation agreements. In fact, there are accounts dating from the 1960s that tied agreements were an intrinsic part of the *modus operandi* for Chinese aid: "Almost all of China's aid has been in the form of Chinese product or credits to purchase Chinese goods, rather than in foreign currency" (Ching-Chu, 1964:18).

From a broader perspective, China (like most countries) does not have a single motivation to provide development assistance in general, and tying technical cooperation projects can serve more than a single need. For Brautigam (2009:15), one of the most recognized researchers in Chinese foreign aid, "like the US, China gives aid for three reasons: strategic diplomacy, commercial benefit, and as a reflection of society's ideologies and values". Rowlands (2008:6) explains that as the country's industrial sector began to expand, and as the Cold War subsided, *commercial* motivations gained strength as the government sought to secure access to natural resources. At the same time, as the country's global role expanded, so did the reach and magnitude of its assistance. Former World Bank country director for China, Yukon Huang, highlights that the country has been using its formidable financial assets to further its own interests, such as expanding its exports and promoting the internationalization of the Chinese currency (Voice of America, 2011). Brautigam (2012) points out that tying export credits to your own country's exports is still the norm, and asks "why else would countries have a government instrument to intervene in trade"?

China's development assistance extends throughout all continents, with visible attention given to African nations. Sino-African assistance has taken "several shapes, and forms, from health and education projects to the construction of official buildings, stadiums and roads" (UN, 2010:44). Aid and FDI "are coordinated so closely that it is not clear what components of interaction with African countries can be classified as aid or FDI" (UN, 2010:51). For example, the $5 billion China-Africa Development Fund can be used as a case of tied policy related to financial investments. Here, the agreement was structured in a way that the money was to be used to invest exclusively in Chinese enterprises and their projects in the African continent, with investments concentrated in companies and projects related to natural resources, as well as infrastructure, agriculture, manufacturing, and industrial parks set up by Chinese companies in Africa.

China's decision to tie its foreign aid – and technical cooperation projects – seems to be most easily explained by (1) commercial interest and (2) a normative reasoning that reinforces this path. To begin, the overall picture of

Chinese foreign aid points to a picture of an unclear – perhaps even *non-existent* – boundary between aid and commercial interests (Brautigam, 2009; De Haan & Warmerdam, 2011). Chinese tied foreign aid generally implies in assistance being provided on condition that the projected work is undertaken by Chinese companies, the bulk of fund transfers are from the Chinese government and banks to those Chinese companies, and quite commonly, with Chinese labourers being sent to work on the projects. This means that Chinese aid usually "involves a complete package of measures, combining technical solutions with financing backed by state-owned banks, together with Chinese labour to implement them" (Wang & Ozanne, 2010:13).

This situation certainly bears a close connection to China's institutional arrangement relative to the coordination and provision of aid. The link between Chinese aid and trade is not new or accidental, but a legacy of its history of planned economy: since 1952, the provision of materials and international flows of all materials related to foreign aid were controlled by the Ministry of *Foreign Trade* (Cheng et al., 2012:5; emphasis added). Currently, the central department managing development assistance is in the Ministry of Commerce (Rowlands, 2008:10). More specifically, it is organized by the Department of Foreign Aid in the Ministry of Commerce (MOFCOM), which cooperates with the Ministry of Foreign Affairs (Brautigam, 2009, 2010, 2011a). As put by Cheng et al. (2012:6), "No wonder that commerce is inevitably one of key features of China's international aid policy. For good or bad, the market elements are part of [the] gene of China's foreign aid policy". The standard practice seems to lead to an Economic and *Technical Cooperation Agreement that is essentially a line of credit* and then ask the government to suggest projects that could be funded under the credit (Brautigam, 2008:21; emphasis added). Chinese aid projects financed through grants and zero-interest loan projects source almost all their procurement from a list of approved Chinese firms (Brautigam, 2011b:2). While *state-owned* enterprises are not part of the State's aid policy formulation process, they are believed to play an important – and growing – role in recent years, driven by interests to secure raw materials and expand markets.

Compounding to this institutional framework is the underlying issue that seeking commercial gains in the provision of foreign aid is seen as quite natural and unproblematic. This position is almost diametrically opposed to the one adopted by both the Brazilian and South African governments, and certainly much more vocal and visible than the one embraced by the Indian government. Therefore, while the Chinese government embraces the SSC principle of non-conditionality, the idea of tying of the foreign aid given to the purchase of Chinese goods and services does not appear to be seen as problematic or as a contradiction to the spirit of SSC.

The idea of *mutual benefit* is a key element in understanding the normative logic behind tying Chinese foreign aid in the context of SSC. In fact, it has been said that the notion of untied aid is *absent* in China (De Haan & Warmerdam, 2011:10). To understand the roots of this position, a good place to start is by looking closely at the 1964 Chinese speech called 'Eight Principles for Economic Aid and Technical Assistance to Other Countries'.[6] To this day, this declaration is promoted as representing the basic principles for China's foreign aid. Among other things, it states that the Chinese government "always bases itself on the principle of equality and *mutual benefit* in providing aid to other countries" (emphasis added), and that it "strictly respects the sovereignty of recipient countries, and never attaches any conditions or asks for any privileges". Under this light, tying is not 'exploitative' – quite the contrary. It can be (unapologetically) embraced as part of a win–win relationship. The Chinese government has publicly argued *in favour* of tying its foreign aid by claiming it minimizes the opportunities for corruption, since it would help lower the risk of financial mismanagement and misappropriation of funds (Wang & Ozanne, 2010; Mwase & Yang, 2012). According to Chin (2012), this positive view of China's approach is not just rhetoric, but is a part of a more entrenched ideational framework. In the case of Chinese aid to African nations,

> the official view of the Chinese government—and the conventional understanding among Chinese scholars—is that China gives aid to Africa in ways that are selfless, demand driven, without conditionality and based on mutual respect and understanding, effectively integrates aid, trade and investment and gives priority to fast and efficient delivery of promised projects.
>
> (Chin, 2012:588)

Nonetheless, there might be a limit to how acceptable recipients are to Chinese claims of *mutual* benefits. In recent years, the reports of African nations pushing back on the terms and conditions of Chinese aid have increased significantly. The word "colonial" is being tossed around, and the Chinese have come more frequently to be viewed with mixed feelings—especially in smaller countries, where China's weight is felt more (*The Economist*, 2011a). Leaders from some African recipients have started to verbalize publicly that the current economic arrangements are not sustainable over the long term, and have put in question the environmental and social standards in China's aid projects, the quality of imported Chinese goods, the use of Chinese workers and suppliers, and the lack of transparency in the whole process (Chin, 2012:587). Even some cash-starved African nations are pushing back and suggesting that the days of unbridled influence by the African continent's mega-investor may be waning, for as grateful as they are for Chinese-built roads and ministry buildings, many are choosing to no longer be passive partners (Nossiter, 2013).

### *'Emerging donor': India*

One of the most fascinating aspects about India's position as an emerging donor is that not too long ago, it was the world's largest aid recipient (in total volume) for almost four decades.[7] It is estimated that between the early 1950s and early 1990s it received somewhere around $55 billion of foreign aid.[8] Nevertheless, times have changed, and the country appears to have transitioned to a net donor of development assistance. Nonetheless, it sits in a more fragile situation than the other emerging donors in one important point: over two-thirds of its population are still very poor. In 2010, there were more than 800 million people (!) in the country still living on less than $2/day, meaning there are more people living in poverty *inside* of India than in Sub-Saharan Africa (approximately 600 million).[9] This led Fuchs & Vadlamannati (2013) to call India 'the *needy* donor'.

While traditionally India's development assistance programme has at best been a marginal component in the overall foreign policy framework (Chaturvedi, 2012), like other emerging countries it is now actively "using aid to win friends and influence people abroad" (*The Economist*, 2011b). This transformation can be understood as driven by a combination of factors, including India's self-conscious role as an emerging power, its competition with China for political influence and energy resources, and the rapid growth of its economy, including both its non-profit and private sectors (Agrawal, 2010:43). India has come to see its receipt of assistance as antithetical to its vision, as an emerging, self-reliant nation, with global ambitions and influence, and sees its role as a donor as an important facet of its regional hegemony and as representative of its growing global political and commercial ambitions (Rowlands, 2008:6). Becoming an emerging donor would also reflect the government's interest in developing the country's soft power credentials, something that had long been neglected as a tool of statecraft (Lee, 2010; Purushothaman, 2010).

The federal government's 2003–2004 budget speech is considered a milestone in India's road to becoming an emerging donor. The then finance minister, Jaswant Singh, announced that a stage had come in the country's development where it should (1) review its dependence on external donors, (2) extend support to the national efforts of other developing countries, and (3) re-examine the line of credit route of international assistance to other countries. While grateful for aid it had received, India would now prefer to provide relief to certain bilateral partners, and the country *would no longer accept tied aid.* Although the actual policy changes were softer in the beginning than the speech seemed to imply, the government made clear its intention to play an important role in the world of international development cooperation (Fuchs, 2013:111). At the same time, the Minister Singh also announced a proposal to create the India Development Initiative (to be established in the Ministry of Finance) as a way to promote the country "as both a production centre and an investment destination [and] leverage and promote [India's] strategic economic interests abroad" (India, 2003:§117).

In 2007, there was another attempt to establish a specific body for governing its outgoing development assistance, which failed because of a lack of agreement between the Ministries of Foreign Affairs and Finance on the location of the proposed agency (Konijn, 2013). Only in 2012 would India have such a structure, the Development Partnership Administration. Placed under the control of the Ministry of External Affairs, this can be read as a tacit acknowledgment by the Indian government "that development cooperation cannot be divorced from the broader foreign policy strategy and national interests" (Sharan et al., 2013:5). However, as all other emerging donors and most developing countries, India is by no means a novice to the provision of some sort of development assistance. Its actions began a few years after gaining independence with the Colombo Plan, the Bandung Conference, and the context of a nascent South-South Cooperation and Non-Aligned Movement. Unsurprisingly, the norm of unconditional interference evolved to be a tenet of Indian foreign policy (Jobelius, 2007:6).

Technical cooperation was the main mode of engagement as 'assistance', something unsurprising, given the country's cash-strapped reality. This was part of a conscious effort to build solidarity with other Afro-Asian nations and promote economic cooperation among post-colonial states (Sharan et al., 2013:3), with much of concrete actions going to neighbouring countries. The bulk of India's overseas assistance still goes to Bhutan and Nepal, and it is estimated that Bhutan alone represented almost 30% of all Indian overseas aid between the 1990s and mid-2000s (Agrawal, 2007:6). The idea of SSC through technical cooperation was given as major boost with the Indian Technical and Economic Cooperation (ITEC). Its chief architect was the country's first Prime Minister, Jawaharlal Nehru, who ardently pushed for 'modern temples of science', and established the framework and the priority for India to become a technologically self-sufficient country (Agrawal, 2007:9–10). Established in 1964, ITEC was conceived under the idea that

> it was necessary [for India] to establish relations of mutual concern and inter-dependence based not only on commonly held ideals and aspirations, but also on solid economic foundations. *Technical and economic cooperation was considered to be one of the essential functions of an integrated and imaginative foreign policy.*[10]

Although ITEC began small in monetary terms, it is estimated that over $2 billion were provided in technical assistance to developing countries through the ITEC programme in its first 40 years (Chaturvedi, 2012:570). Among its over 40,000 alumni are many senior public officials, bureaucrats, and politicians from other developed countries – such as Afghan President Hamid Karzai – who received their educational training in India. There is no clear answer to if this programme has generated positive rewards over time. The government's position is that they have a friendly disposition toward India, under a conceptualization that ITEC's technical cooperation is a very visible and successful part of Indian diplomacy, a view shared by Mullen and Ganguly (2012) and Sharan et al. (2013). On the other hand, it might just be that "ITEC programs have not resulted in long-term political value for India" (Agrawal, 2007:9). In any case, ITEC remains India's main reference for technical cooperation to this day. Although the following assertion could not be confirmed or updated from other sources, the same author reports that "currently almost 50 percent of all ITEC program slots [were] related to information technology [and] much of the training in this area is *subcontracted to private companies*" (Agrawal, 2007:9).

Agrawal (2010:44) argues, "the single-most defining characteristic of India's overseas aid program is that it attempts to share India's own experience in poverty alleviation and development", with notable expertise in information technology, auditing, pharmacology, public administration, and textiles research (Mathai, 2013). Nevertheless, there is reason to believe that technical cooperation's *relative* weight as a foreign policy mechanism is smaller nowadays. Since the mid-2000s, the Indian government has been actively engaged, and with greater impetus than even, in many other facets of SSC such as financial investments, trade promotion, credit lines, debt cancelations, humanitarian assistance, etc. India is now able to provide direct cash transfers and subsidized loans (Mullen & Ganguly, 2012), and there is a significant volume of money available for a variety of actions, along with incentives *from* and *towards* the government to expand its South-South actions through these other mechanisms. Therefore, while technical cooperation is still an integral part of India's 'development assistance' project, the government now has many other options for engagement.

India's project as an 'emerging donor' seems to involve several goals beside the altruistic and humanitarian ones, including geopolitical, diplomatic, and commercial interests as well. Its 'development assistance' is couched in a discourse of mutual benefit and economic cooperation (Konijn, 2013). India's choices seem to have been based primarily to ensure secure sources of energy for an expanding economy, opening markets for India's increasingly export-oriented industrial and service sectors. Also, bolstering geostrategic ties with key neighbours, with larger mercantilist goals underpinning the country's overall provision of 'development' (Mullen & Ganguly, 2012), with increasing interest and partnerships in Africa. Commercial interests play a very important role in India's development assistance programmes. In fact, "many foreign diplomats and donors consider a large part of what India spends on development assistance as *nothing more than an export subsidy scheme for surplus goods*" (Agrawal, 2007:8; emphasis added). It has "learned from China" that development assistance can provide seed money to enable the entry of private commercial interests (Mullen & Ganguly, 2012), a position that does not seem to be exactly secretive. A high-ranking member of the Ministry of External Affairs, Special Secretary Shri PS Raghavan, recently declared that measures were "being explored for combining development partnership with India's private sector investments as an effective way of expanding India's development footprint abroad" (Raghavan, 2013; see also Sharan et al., 2013).

India rejects conditionalities in its South-South 'development assistance' projects but it does not extend the sentiment to *tying* the projects it provides to the purchase of Indian equipment or services, such as automobiles and trucks, ground-water pumps, pharmaceuticals, public health infrastructure, or railway equipment. This is exemplified by India's relationship with African nations, where "historically, there has been little integration of trade, FDI and aid by India in Africa". Yet, in very recent years, "aid and FDI have been bundled together in a package, and the Indian State has also played a role as an investor in collaboration with one of its largest firms" (UN, 2010:59). In a 2013 speech given by the country's Foreign Secretary, Ranjan Mathaim, the position was that the country's "underlying philosophy remains that which underpins South-South Cooperation", where "we [India] do not attach conditionalities, we do not prescribe policies and we do not challenge national sovereignty" – but no mention made to tying agreements (Mathai, 2013). Since India refuses to accept tied aid, this implies that the government consciously applies different standards in its roles as donor and recipient of development aid (Fuchs & Vadlamannati, 2013:126).

### *'Emerging donor': South Africa*

South Africa's 'development assistance' programme began in the context of apartheid and Cold War related struggles in the African continent. In the late 1960s, the 'Economic Cooperation Promotion Loan Fund' was set up to direct funds to developing countries, especially African ones, as well as to its so-called 'Homelands' in an attempt to 'legitimize' their (fictional) independent existence. Assistance was provided to countries with three main goals. First, gathering diplomatic support from the recipients in the UN and international negotiations, as the world increasingly isolated the racist regime. Second, as a mechanism to support its anti-Communist campaign in the continent. Finally, to facilitate trade relations with some countries, as international sanctions grew against apartheid.

With the shift towards political and racial democracy, its conception of development assistance has emphasized regional integration, post-conflict reconstruction, and humanitarian assistance. All the while, it has remained focused on the African continent, with few initiatives – mostly humanitarian aid – outside of the region (see Sidiropoulos, 2011). This is in many ways a consequence of a broader goal to promote the country's *African* identity and the vision of an 'African Renaissance'. In 2000, the government created the African Renaissance Fund (ARF), envisioned not as an instrument to provide aid but rather to establish partnerships, demonstrate solidarity, and support the economic empowerment of Africa by funding activities of co-operation, democracy and good governance, conflict resolution, social and economic development, humanitarian and disaster relief, technical co-operation, and capacity development (Besharati, 2013:19).

Although the absence of systematically collected aid data value leads to varied estimates (Davies, 2010:30), it is safe to say that South Africa became a net development 'donor' in the early 2000s. While its development projects are smaller in scope, scale, and ambition than those of Brazil, China, and India, its total aid contributions were the largest of the BRICS countries in per capita gross domestic product (GDP) terms in the early 2010s (Chin, 2012:585). While Chin (2012), Vickers (2012), and Besharati (2013) posit that South Africa was spending more than 0.7% of their GDP in development assistance, O'Riordan (2013:3) vehemently challenged this. For this author,

> South Africa is miles away from meeting that target. The 2011/2012 budget records revenue of R734bn on a GDP of R3tn. The R500 million or so South Africa allocates to development cooperation would need to increase forty-fold to R21bn simply to reach 0.7% of GDP (lower than GDP).

In April 2013, the government created the South African Development Partnership Agency (SADPA), to structure and coordinate the country's development assistance activities. The South African government has been clear in its desire to be referred to as a development *partner* and not as a *donor.* This has not been haphazard: there is an awareness of the undissolved discomfort and suspicion from countries in the region over South Africa's 'true' intentions, and the references to the country as 'imperialist' or 'regional hegemon' (Taylor, 2011:1235–1239) and its contested continental leadership in Africa (Vickers, 2012:536). The term *partner* also reflects sensitivity to the continent's perception that South Africa may be replicating the role of a dominant economy in colonial relations (Braude et al., 2008:6). South Africa often faces tension between its foreign policy and its constitutional democratic and human rights values, as critiques point out acts of leniency towards despots, warlords, and corrupt leaders on the continent under the 'Southern banner' and the 'African brotherhood' frameworks (Besharati, 2013:23). Concerns over semantics might reflect the government's sensitivity to (perceived) regional power dynamics. This might also help explain its approach to provide technical cooperation without commercial ties. Even with "hints that commercial interests have gradually crept into South Africa's development assistance agenda" (Rowlands, 2008:6), these interests still appear to be minor.

Technical cooperation agreements play a significant role in South Africa's development strategy. The country has been strongly engaged in institution building, capacity-building, and human-resource development of African public servants across the continent, through training offered by its Public Administration Leadership and Management Academy (PALAMA), the Independent Electoral Commission, the South African army and police services, and other departments, along with its universities which charge students from neighbouring countries the same or similar fees as local students (Besharati, 2013:28).

South Africa has a small budget for development provision in general, but it is in a unique position of credibility when it offers to cooperate *with*

Africa and *for* Africa, and to claim a better understanding of the problems that affect the continent's nations. Just as many other donors, elements of egotism and altruism coexist in South Africa's assistance, since "support for regional growth is both an act of solidarity and a way to enhance economic opportunities" (South Africa, 2010:25). With less cash available, "Pretoria's preference has been for technical cooperation to strengthen governance and build institutional capacity in Africa, indirectly extending the country's soft power and democratic norms and values across the continent" (Vickers, 2012:552–3). A similar assessment was made by Besharati (2013), stating even more firmly that "without a doubt, development co-operation has been used in the past and present by Pretoria as a tool for soft diplomacy to promote foreign policy objectives", which include the promotion of the MDGs, SSC, the African agenda, and regional integration (Besharati, 2013:24).

## Concluding remarks

The main goal of this chapter was to provide some more detail to the characteristics of the so-called 'emerging donors'. These countries are unique since their provision of development assistance simultaneously have similarities and differences to 'traditional' OECD/DAC donors and to other 'developing' countries that abide to SSC. They overlap with 'traditional' donors in their ability to provide assistance systematically (as opposed to occasionally), to a broad range of recipients, and through an increasing number of mechanisms. At the same time, they retain their normative footing in the SSC paradigm, explicitly rejecting conditionalities, and self-identifying as 'developing countries'. Moreover, while they are better able to provide development assistance with more frequency, through more paths, and with larger volume than their other 'Southern' peers, in general they still do not have the same financial power as most DAC donors.

This chapter focused on a few number of 'emerging' donors: Brazil, China, India, and South Africa. While other countries can fall under this classification, these four nations are particularly relevant in other dimensions of current international affairs – being also labelled emerging countries and four of the five BRICS nations. Thus, their development actions are more likely to have greater regional and/or global repercussions than other emerging donors. As shown, there are considerable challenges in attempting to analyse 'emerging donors' as a group. The term itself is difficult to be defined, and with fuzzy boundaries over which countries fall in or out. The possible overlaps of the category 'emerging donors' with other ill-defined country classifications (particularly 'emerging countries' and 'middle powers') reinforces the complexity involved in researching 'non-traditional' donors and 'somewhat-powerful' countries. If behaviours are understood through categories – "emerging donors do this...", "middle powers act like this...", "emerging countries prefer that..." – then definitional issues must be observed with care. As anticipated in Chapter 2, just because a country can

*Table 5.1* Emerging donors' characteristics, selected countries

| | *China* | *India* | *S. Africa* |
|---|---|---|---|
| History of provision (1) initial, (2) expansion | 1 Early 1950s<br>2 since late 1990s | 1 Early 1950s<br>2 since mid–2000s | 1 Late 1960s<br>2 since early 2000s |
| Labels: (1) 'Donor'; (2) 'Development Assistance provider' | 1 Both apparently comfortable being called 'donors'<br>2 Both apparently comfortable with giving 'development assistance' | | 1 Rejects label; prefers 'partner'<br>2 Uncomfortable |
| Main recipients | Global; strong attention to Asian and African nations (esp. resource rich) | Asian neighbours; East Africa (Indian diaspora); growing w/ resource–rich African countries | Southern African nations (esp. neighbours) |
| Main SSC instruments | Great importance to trade, FDI, grants, loans, military aid, debt cancellation; Tech. Coop.: important but relatively small in big picture | Increased attention to FDI, trade, lines of credit; Tech. Coop still important but decreased relative importance | Technical cooperation: main instrument |
| Conditionalities – notes | Sometimes used for 'One China' policy; strong outside criticism for 'supporting' undemocratic leaders | So far unconditionality is not a controversial topic | Growing regional pressure to balance non-interference with human rights' protection in relationship with non–democratic nations |
| Ties | Both: immediate commercial gains are clear; tying frequent, used unapologetically; framed as acceptable SSC stance (i.e., 'mutual assistance')<br>Ch: common to send own labour to work on projects | Ind.: important private sector involvement | Untied; ties not appropriate in SSC: reproduces N–S dynamic |
| Gains from Tech. Coop | 1st: Commercial gains<br>2nd: Diplomatic gains | 1st: Commercial gains<br>2nd: Diplomatic gains | 1st: Diplomatic gains<br>2nd: Commercial gains |

be categorized as a 'middle power' does *not*: (1) directly imply it will be an emerging donor; (2) determine the country's level of engagement to provide technical cooperation; and (3) indicate a donor's interest to giving aid with or without commercial ties.

This chapter also showed that even after debates regarding definitions and categories are dealt with, and certain boundaries are chosen, the need to refine the analysis does not end. Echoing the assessment that "developing countries are hardly a homogeneous group" (Ekeko & Benn, 2002:128), emerging donors are also not a homogeneous group. Thus, even if there is agreement that Brazil, China, India, and South Africa 'fit' in the emerging donor's category, their behaviour cannot be expected to be identical. Since this book is interested in *variation* of countries' foreign policies – i.e., why do some countries tie technical cooperation agreements and others do not? – it was necessary to provide at least a brief comparison among some emerging donors. Table 5.1 provides a summary of findings of China, India, and South Africa's development assistance programmes. It serves two main purposes: (1) highlight overlaps and divergences between these emerging donors, and (2) allow an easier comparison to Brazil's case – the subject of the next chapter.

## Notes

1 Woods (2008) somewhat bypasses this problem by understanding 'emerging donors' as a shortcut to contrast OECD/DAC's *'established'* donors.
2 A former European Commissioner for External Relations and European Neighbourhood policy clearly exemplified this understanding in a speech aptly entitled "The European Neighbourhood Policy: *Helping ourselves through helping our neighbours*" (Ferrero-Waldner, 2005; emphasis added).
3 In this report, only Burma/Myanmar was labelled as an exception.
4 Source: World Bank (online statistical database).
5 This would include grants and no-interest development loans as well as the lines of concessional financing that are issued under the rubric of 'international economic cooperation'.
6 The speech was given by Premier Zhou Enlai, in Accra (Ghana), on 1964, January 15.
7 Bijoy (2010:65) does highlight that "when translated into per capita terms [the country] appears much less reliant on aid".
8 While this number is mentioned by various authors (Bijoy, 2010; *The Economist*, 2011b; Chin, 2012; Mullen & Ganguly, 2012), there is no mention to its original source.
9 Source: World Bank's online database.
10 Source: ITEC's webpage (http://itec.mea.gov.in/).

## Bibliography

Abdenur, A. (2002). Tilting the North-South axis: The legitimation of Southern Development Knowledge and its implications for Comparative Education Research. *Current Issues in Comparative Education*, *4*(2), 57–69.

Agrawal, S. (2007). *Emerging Donors in International Development Assistance: The India Case. One of five reports on the role played by emerging economies in funding international development*. Ottawa, Canada: IDRC.

Agrawal, S. (2010). Emerging aid donors: India. Network for Policy Research Review and Advice on Education and Training (NORRAG), Special Edition: *A Brave New World of 'Emerging', 'Non-DAC' Donors and their Differences from Traditional Donors*, *44*, 43–45.

Bar-Tal, D., Bar-Zohar, Y., Greenberg, M. S., & Hermon, M. (1977). Reciprocity behavior in the relationship between donor and recipient and between harm-doer and victim. *Sociometry*, *40*(3), 293–298.

Besharati, N. A. (2013, August). *South African Development Partnership Agency (SADPA): Strategic aid or development packages for Africa?*. South African International Development Agency (SAIIA), Economic Diplomacy Programme, Research Report 12.

BetterAid. (2010). *Policy paper on South-South development cooperation*. www.betteraid.org/images/Documents/policy_paper_on_south_south_development_cooperation_eng.pdf

Bijoy, C. R. (2010). India: Transiting to a global donor. *The reality of aid, special report on South-South Cooperation*, 65–76. www.europe-solidaire.org/IMG/pdf/India_-_from_Debtor_to_Donor_-_Case_Study_C-R-Bijoy_1_.pdf

Bobiash, D. (1992). *South-South aid – How developing countries help each other*. New York: St. Martin's Press.

Braude, W., Thandrayan, P., & Sidiropoulos, E. (2008). *Emerging donors in international development assistance: The South Africa case*. Ottawa, Canada: IDRC.

Brautigam, D. (2008). *China's African aid: Transatlantic challenges*. Brussels: German Marshall Fund of the United States.

Brautigam, D. (2009). *The Dragon's gift: The real story of China in Africa*. New York: Oxford University Press.

Brautigam, D. (2010). China, Africa and the International Aid Architecture. *African Development Bank*, Working Paper Series, No. 107.

Brautigam, D. (2011a). Chinese development aid in Africa: What, where, why, and how much? In J. Golley & L. Song (Eds.), *Rising China: Global Challenges and Opportunities* (pp. 203–223). Canberra: Australia National University Press.

Brautigam, D. (2011b). U.S. and Chinese efforts in Africa in global health and foreign aid: objectives, impact and potential conflicts of interest. In X. Boyton (Ed.), *China's emerging global health and foreign aid engagement in Africa* (pp. 1–12). Washington, DC: Center for Strategic & International Studies (CSIS).

Brautigam, D. (2012, January 22). *China's foreign aid: The economist still doesn't get it*. www.chinaafricarealstory.com/2012/01/chinas-foreign-aid-economist-still.html.

Brautigam, D. (2013, October 14). *Chinese aid: How much?*. www.chinaafricarealstory.com/2013/10/chinese-aid-how-much.html.

Chaturvedi, S. (2012, September 05). Aid from India, coming to a country near you. *The Hindu*.

Cheng, S., Fang, T., & Lien, H. T. (2012). China's International Aid Policy and its implications for global governance. *Research Center for Chinese Politics and Business*, Working Paper 29.

Chin, G. (2012). China as a 'net donor': Tracking dollars and sense. *Cambridge Review of International Affairs*, *25*(4), 579–603.

Chin, G., & Malkin, A. (2012, March 08). *Russia as a re-emerging donor: Catching up in Africa*. Waterloo, ON: CIGI.

Chin, G., & Quadir, F. (2012). Introduction: Rising states, rising donors and the global aid regime. *Cambridge Review of International Affairs*, *25*(4), 493–506.

China, The People's Republic of. (2011). *China's foreign aid*. http://english.gov.cn/official/2011-04/21/content_1849913.htm

Ching-Chu, A. (1964, August 21). China's economic and technical aid to other countries. *Peking Review*, *7*(34), 14–18.

Cooper, J. F. (1976). *China's foreign aid: An instrument of Peking's foreign policy*. Lexinton: Lexington Books.

Davies, P. (2010). *A review of the roles and activities of new development partners*. CFP Working Paper Series No. 4. Washington, DC: World Bank.

De Haan, A., & Warmerdam, W. (2011). *New donors and old practices: Does the rise of China challenge aid effectiveness?. Rethintking development in an age of scarcity and uncertainty – new values, voices and alliances for increased resilience*. University of York, 2011, September 19–22.

Eckl, J., & Weber, R. (2007). North-South? Pitfalls of dividing the world by words. *Third World Quarterly*, *28*(1), 3–23.

*Economist, The*. (2011a, April 20). The Chinese in Africa: Trying to pull together, Africans are asking whether China is making their lunch or eating it.

*Economist, The*. (2011b, August 13). Official Development Assistance, Aid 2.0.

Ekoko, F., & Benn, D. (2002). "South-South Cooperation and Capacity Development". *UNDP Development Policy Journal, Special issue: Technical Cooperation*, *2*, 119–129.

Ferrero-Waldner, B. (2005, October 31). *The European Neighbourhood Policy: Helping ourselves through helping our neighbours*. Conference of Foreign Affairs Committee Chairmen of EU member and candidate states (London). Speech 05–658.

Fuchs, S. D. (2013). China, India and Brazil in Africa: Effects on Development Policy. *KAS International Reports*, *1/2*.

Fuchs, A., & Vadlamannati, K. C. (2013). The needy donor: An empirical analysis of India's aid motives. *World Development*, *44*(April), 110–128.

Gray, P. A. (2011). Looking 'The Gift' in the mouth: Russia as donor. *Anthropology Today*, *27*(2), 5–8.

Gray, K., & Murphy, C. N. (2013). Introduction: Rising powers and the future of global governance. *Third World Quarterly*, *34*(2), 183–193.

India, Government of. (2003, March). Budget Speech 2003–2004.

Jobelius, M. (2007). New Powers for Global Change? Challenges for the International Development Cooperation. *FES Briefing Papers*.

Kitano, N., & Harada, Y. (2016). Estimating China's foreign aid 2001–2013. *Journal of International Development*, *28*(7), 1050–1074.

Konijn, O. (2013, March 04). India: aid donor or development partner? www.thebrokeronline.eu/Blogs/Emerged-Powers/India-aid-donor-or-development-partner

Korany, B. (1986). Hierarchy within the South: In search of theory. In R. Gashar (Ed.), *Third world affairs yearbook* (pp. 85–100). London: Third World Foundation for Social and Economic Studies.

Kragelund, P. (2008). The return of non-DAC donors to Africa: New Prospects for African development?. *Development Policy Review*, *26*(5), 555–584.

Lassey, P. (2010). South-South & Triangular Cooperation – With a focus on Multilateral platforms acknowledging the Aid Effectiveness agenda, *mimeo*.

Lee, J. (2010, June 04). *Unrealised potential: India's 'Soft Power' ambition in Asia. The Centre for Independent Studies (CIS)* – Foreign Policy Analysis, No. 4.

Mathai, R. (2013, April 15). Keynote address by Foreign Secretary at Conference of Southern Providers-South-South Cooperation: Issues and Emerging Challenges. www.mea.gov.in/Speeches-Statements.htm?dtl/21549/Keynote+address+by+Foreign+Secretary+at+Conference+of+Southern+Providers+SouthSouth+Cooperation++Issues+and+Emerging+Challenges

Mawdsley, E. (2012a). *From recipients to donors: Emerging powers and the changing development landscape.* London: ZED books.

Mawdsley, E. (2012b).The changing geographies of foreign aid and development co-operation: contributions from gift theory. *Transactions of the Institute of British Geographers, 37*(2), 256–272.

McFarlane, C. (2006). Crossing borders: Development, learning and the North – South divide, *Third World Quarterly, 27*(8), 1413–1437.

Mullen, R., & Ganguly, S. (2012, May 08). The rise of India's soft power. *Foreign Policy.*

Mwase, N., & Yang, Y. (2012, June 19). When resources come from 'Partners' instead of 'Donors'. *IMF*, Survey Magazine: Policy.

Naim, M. (2007). Rogue aid. *Foreign Policy, 159* (March–April), 95–96.

Neumayer, E. (2004). Arab-related bilateral and multilateral sources of development finance: Issues, trends, and the way forward. *The World Economy, 27*(2), 281–300.

Nossiter, A. (2013, September 17). China Finds Resistance to Oil Deals in Africa. *New York Times.*

O'Riordan, A. (2013, September). South Africa seems woefully unprepared to be an effective donor. *South African Foreign Policy Institute* (SAFPI), Policy Brief No. 47.

Purushothaman, U. (2010). Shifting perceptions of power: Soft power and India's foreign policy. *Journal of Peace Studies, 17*(2&3), 1–16.

Raghavan, P. S. (2013, July 18). Talk by Shri PS Raghavan, SS (DP) on Development Partnership Administration (DPA). Round Table Event. Institute for Defence Studies and Analyses.

Republic of South Africa. (2010). *The new growth path: The framework.* Pretoria: Economic Development Department.

Rosseel, P., De Corte, E., Blommaert, J., & Verniers, E. (2009). *Approaches to North-South, South-South and North-South-South collaboration.* A Policy Document, KULeuven.

Rowlands, D. (2008). *Emerging donors in international development assistance: A synthesis report.* International Development Research Center (IDRC) – Canada.

Sharan, V., Campbell, I., & Rubin, D. (2013). *India's development cooperation: Charting new approaches in a changing world.* Observer Research Foundation (ORF), Special Report #2 (July).

Sidiropoulos, E. (2011). *Perspectives from the BRICs: Lessons for South Africa.* Report on a seminar held by the South African Institute of International Affairs, Pretoria, 2011, March 1.

Smith, K., Fordelone, T. Y., & Zimmermann, F. (2010, May). *Beyond the DAC the welcome role of other providers of development co-operation.* OECD – DCD Issues Brief.

Taylor, I. (2011). 'South African "Imperialism" in a region lacking regionalism: A critique'. *Third World Quarterly, 32*(7), 1233–1253.

UN – United Nations. (1995, April 07). *Technical cooperation among developing countries.* TCDC/9/3.

UN – United Nations. (2010). *Africa's cooperation with new and emerging development partners: Options for Africa's development.* Office of the Special Adviser on Africa. New York.

UN – United Nations General Assembly. (2009). *Promotion of South-South cooperation for development: A thirty-year perspective* – Report of the Secretary-General, A/64/504, 2009, October 27.

UNDP. (1995) New directions for technical cooperation among developing countries. http://dag.un.org/handle/11176/198679.

UN-ECOSOC – United Nations Economic and Social Council. (2008). *Background study for the development cooperation forum: Trends in South-South and triangular development cooperation.*

UN-GA – United Nations General Assembly. (2009, October 27). *Promotion of South-South cooperation for development: A thirty-year perspective* – Report of the Secretary-General, A/64/504.

United Nations Millennium Project (2005). *Investing in development: A practical plan to achieve the millennium development goals.* New York: UN.

Vickers, B. (2012). Towards a new aid paradigm: South Africa as African development partner. *Cambridge Review of International Affairs, 25*(4), 535–556.

Villanger, E. (2007). Arab foreign did: Disbursement patterns, aid policies and motives, *Forum for Development Studies, 34*(2), 223–56.

*Voice of America* (2011, January 25). *Global development aid from China on the rise.*

Walz, J., & Ramachandran, V. (2011, November). Brave New World: A literature review of emerging donors and the changing nature of foreign assistance. *Center for Global Development*, Working Paper 273.

Wang, X., & Ozanne, A. (2010). *Two approaches to aid in Africa: China and the west.* Paper Prepared for the Conference "Ten Years Of 'War Against Poverty': What Have We Learned Since 2000 And What Should We Do 2010–2020?", hosted by the Brooks World Poverty Institute, The University of Manchester, 2010, September 8–10.

Woods, N. (2008). Whose aid? Whose influence? China, emerging donors and the silent revolution in development assistance. *International Affairs, 84*(6), 1205–1221.

# 6 Brazil as an emerging donor of technical cooperation

As is the case of other 'emerging donors', Brazil's rise as a provider of development assistance has gained increased academic, media, and political attention. This country is not alone in promoting the use of technical cooperation in its provision of development assistance – all donors tend to use this mechanism as well. However, it stands out as a country whose foreign policy has been explicit about using technical cooperation as the basis for its development assistance programme, as opposed to concessional aid mechanisms such as grants or loans.

The most significant contrast Brazil's provision of development assistance vis-à-vis most 'traditional' and 'emerging' donors is its choice to provide technical cooperation through unconditional and untied agreements. The assertion that Brazil's policy is *not* to attach conditionalities or ties to its technical cooperation agreements rests upon a solid empirical base. It comes from an evaluation of the relevant literature and policy documents, and dozens of interviews conducted in Brazil with diplomats, federal civil servants working with technical cooperation, and leading academics in the field. Of course, it's possible that exceptions to this untied character exist and were not reported. Still, even if a couple of cases were to be found, they would not automatically disprove the arguments posited. What matters more for this book is the *general direction* of how conditions and ties are interpreted as serving the country's 'national interest'.

There is awareness of the great likelihood of informal *quid pro quo* arrangements between the individuals involved in the negotiations. In fact, quite a few diplomats and academics alluded to how these do exist. However, when asked for more on the subject, all interviewees explained that when this occurred, the expectation of reciprocity was *implied* between the parties as a normal – i.e., customary – reflection of the 'rules of the game' in diplomatic negotiations. Even more important, the direct expectations sought by Brazil were at first of a diplomatic nature, such as counting on support and votes in international organizations and multilateral negotiations. Commercial interests are present in many (although not all) cases, and were generally expected to *indirectly* derive from the improved relationships, as opposed to coming directly from the technical cooperation agreements themselves.

This chapter's main goals are to understand the broad contours of Brazil's provision of technical cooperation and the gains sought from choosing to provide technical cooperation with no-strings-attached. The timeframe focuses on President Lula's (2003–2010) tenure, with brief discussions over Dilma Rousseff's (2011–2016) tenure, along with contextual references going back to the mid-20th century. To evaluate these issues, this chapter is divided in two main sections. The first section presents Brazil's path in becoming a 'donor' from its very early steps to the post-2000s and current contours. The second analyses the three factors informing the foreign policy decision to provide technical cooperation with no conditionalities or commercial ties: (1) the role of ideas and principles; (2) domestic institutional framework, notably the Constitution, the presidency, and Itamaraty; and (3) a desire to set/improve Brazil's position in the international system.

## Brazil: from recipient to provider

Three important points can be derived from a historical analysis of Brazil's provision of development assistance. First, it reaffirms that so-called 'emerging' donors are not *new* donors. As shown in Chapters 4 and 5, most developing countries have, at least at some point, provided some form of what could be called development assistance. This is certainly the case for Brazil's own experience as a provider, which can be traced back to the 1970s. Second, technical cooperation has always been the main mechanism of Brazil's development assistance provision. This can be greatly explained by weak financial capabilities limiting the options available, as well as significant outside demand for Brazil's knowledge in certain areas. Third, the country initially adopted an unconditional but tied approach to its provision of technical cooperation, which changed throughout the 1990s, and since the 2000s, unconditional and untied has been the norm.

Before moving forward, a couple of definitional notes should be reinforced: the Brazilian government (1) rejects being labelled a 'donor' and (2) is adamant that it does not provide 'development assistance', but is engaged in development *cooperation*. Both terms 'donor' and 'development assistance' are said to be understood as reinforcing a hierarchical structure between the parties involved: while the donor is the active/dominant party, the recipient is passive/dominated. 'Assistance' is also framed in a negative light, as embedding a paternalistic connotation and a vertical relationship, as opposed to a cooperation among equal partners (Rowlands, 2008:7). For the head of the Brazilian Cooperation Agency (2012–2015), Ambassador Fernando José Marroni de Abreu, the Government's position was that Brazil was a *partner*, since "even if the contribution for the other partner is modest, there is always something to learn" (interview). In his view, Brazil should not be defined as an 'emerging donor', but as an "emerging (or developing) country which develops cooperation activities with other countries, preferably in the South-South domain" (interview). A similar account was reported by Inoue and Vaz (2013:527) in their interviews with Brazilian authorities emphasizing the country is not an 'emerging donor' or 'new donor', with the interviewees "[believing] that aid is related to a vertical relationship and that Brazil instead favours a 'horizontal approach'". Notwithstanding these issues, for the sake of consistency of terms, 'emerging donor' and 'development assistance' will be used to address the Brazilian case.

### *Historical context and evolution*

In 1950, Brazil's federal government created the National Commission for Technical Assistance (*Comissão Nacional de Assistência Técnica* – CNAT), whose goal was to deal with development assistance *received* by Brazil.[1] About two decades later, in 1969, CNAT was replaced by two bodies. One was the Sub-Secretary of Economic and Technical International Cooperation (*Subsecretaria de Cooperação Econômica e Técnica Internacional* – SUBIN), controlled by the Ministry of Planning, responsible for policy*making* in this area and insuring integration with the government's broad domestic goals. The second one was the Division of Technical Cooperation (*Divisão de Cooperação Técnica* – DCOPT), part of the Ministry of Foreign Affairs and in charge of the "foreign policy of technical cooperation" (Valler Filho, 2007:67). At that point, still no mention was made to Brazil as a provider of cooperation – only as a recipient.

The history of Brazil as a provider of development assistance begins to take shape between 1969 and 1978. This period can be characterized as Brazil's first attempts to create a system to coordinate technical cooperation and the first agreements with other developing countries (Inoue & Vaz, 2013:509). Brazil's economy grew at great strides between 1968 and 1973, with low inflation and an average of 11% GDP growth per year – a welcoming time for Brazil to begin providing development assistance within its approach to SSC. During this time, there was a growing conviction that Brazil should take advantage of the experience acquired from receiving technical cooperation and transform it in an instrument of domestic development and as a foreign policy tool (Puente, 2010:103). Its foreign policy became increasingly guided by the quest to open markets, expand its political presence beyond its geographic region, and internationally reflect Brazil's status of an 'emerging power' (to use current jargon). There was a clear governmental goal to strengthen political, economic, and cultural links between Brazil and other Southern countries, not only in Latin America but also in Africa.[2]

Brazilian technical cooperation in this early phase would serve to demonstrate Brazil's technological capacities, without the need of great financial commitment. But more importantly, it would be used to maximize opportunities to increase exports and the entry hard currency (Valler Filho, 2007:75). General Geisel (1974–1979) was designated as president when Brazil's economy began to collapse, with the Oil Crisis serving as a key trigger. The country's foreign debt grew at a staggering pace due to ever-rising interest rates and an enormous dependency on foreign oil. General Geisel's direction to the country's international engagements was rooted in one word: *pragmatism*. In a time when "international trade was taken as an instrument of international assertiveness" (Spektor, 2004:200), Geisel's Minister of Foreign Affairs, Azeredo da Silveira, was clear in what Brazil should seek in its foreign policy engagements: economic development. Hence, Cold War ideologies and Third World principles were overridden to improve the country's weakening economic condition. Thus, Brazil's provision of development assistance should serve as a mechanism to generate commercial gains for Brazilian companies, in a guaranteed and short-termed setting. In the President's own words to his Ministers, "we will propel our diplomatic actions, always alert to the discovery of new opportunities, to serve – particularly – our foreign trade interests" (*apud* Leite, 2011:127).

However, on the practical side, the commercial (and diplomatic) impact of tied agreements was minimal – if any. Most technical cooperation agreements involved the training of technical staff from the recipient countries, which took place in Brazilian public institutions (Conde, 1990:72, *apud* Puente, 2010:104). The struggle to find civil servants willing to go for missions abroad, and the lack of proper institutional structure or mechanisms to organize and coordinate actions with signed agreements made their execution difficult (Cervo, 1994:61; Leite, 2011:150). By the end of the 1970s, resources for cooperation dwindled, and technical cooperation became a marginal instrument within a shrinking provision of development assistance of an economically struggling country. Still, despite dire macroeconomic conditions and significant domestic political turmoil, Brazil still managed to provide some technical cooperation in the 1980s. Much of this came from external *demands* of knowledge from renowned Brazilian public institutions like EMBRAPA, SEBRAE, SENAI, and FIOCRUZ (see Valler Filho, 2007). Cervo's (1994) numbers are impressive: out of 694 requests for Brazil to provide technical cooperation between the 1960s and 1980s, only two were proposed in the 1960s, and 26 in the 1970s – all others emerged during the 1980s. Cervo (1994:49) credits this enormous demand to a positive image Brazil had as a developing country, which has spread in the late 1970s, especially in the aftermath of the 1978 Buenos Aires Conference.

For most of the 1980s, the prospect of Brazil as a 'donor' continued to be more of an intention than a real possibility. Very few requests became projects, and even fewer were executed. The change towards democracy (1984/1985) allowed new room for rethinking the idea. In 1986, the First National Development Plan for the New Republic (*I Plano Nacional de Desenvolvimento da Nova República*) was published. Its chapter on Foreign Relations (Chapter IX) includes a specific mention to technical cooperation: it was to be incentivized especially in areas where "the contribution of bilateral and multilateral cooperation has a special meaning for the consolidation and opening of regional and sub-regional opportunities", with emphasis on Latin American and African partners due to "geographic, historic, and cultural affinities". Between 1986 and 1987, three agreements were signed between the UNDP and the Brazilian government to provide a solid structure for Brazil's provision of technical cooperation with developing countries (TCDC).[3]

In 1987, the Brazilian Cooperation Agency (*Agência Brasileira de Cooperação* – ABC) was created, replacing both SUBIN and DCOPT. The new Agency was fully nested within the Ministry of Foreign Affairs, and its competence incorporated both development assistance received *and* provided (see Puente, 2010). The general assessment is that up until that point, whatever technical cooperation had been provided by Brazil, it had served 'non-diplomatic' goals, like strengthening economic links (FUNCEX, 1985:20; *apud* Cervo, 1994:43). In this sense, there are interesting parallels between Brazil's approach to providing development assistance (and technical cooperation) in the 1970s and 1980s and China's current policy: agreements without conditionalities, yet with ties meant to secure commercial gains for few big national companies.

With the creation of ABC, solely under the Ministry of Foreign Affairs (aka Itamaraty), Brazil's technical cooperation agreements were explicitly intended to serve *foreign policy* goals. Yet, the agreements' tied character did not change immediately following this new institutional arrangement. According to Bobiash (1992:10), a document from the Brazilian Economic and Technical Cooperation Secretariat from the late-1980s/early-1990s stated "Brazilian technical assistance has become an important instrument 'for the commercial promotion of export of goods and services to other developing countries'". One interviewee with ample experience in the cooperation provided in this period described it in the following way:

> What is practiced today [2012] is not necessarily what was done 30 years ago. When ABC was created, late 80s, early 90, we did cooperation with a commercial interest. ... But this was in the early days of the agency, when it derived from the Dept. of Trade Promotion; maybe they sought to give an economic vision to technical cooperation, or an economic vision of the role of technical cooperation. I think we settled into a new model, and nowadays this is our discourse – our discourse and our *practice* also.

According Inoue and Vaz (2013:507), during the 1990s, Brazil was not fully engaged in technical cooperation among developing countries. Of course, they are not claiming it did not occur. They explain that the period preceding the presidency of Lula da Silva did not see a 'big leap' in Brazil's external development assistance – only incremental growth (Inoue & Vaz, 2013:517; see also Puente, 2010:240). Thus, the 1990s can be said to be a decade of (re) building Brazil's institutional framework for providing technical cooperation. A growing rationalization of ABC's role in coordinating received technical cooperation and more regularized procedures for providing technical cooperation created the foundations for growth in Brazilian development assistance after the mid-2000s (Puente, 2010:240). These efforts were crucial. Cervo (1994) revealed very interesting numbers on how disorganized that system was in the early years of ABC. The compiled number of demands for Brazilian cooperation registered until 1989 were close to 700, but the lack of documentation was so dire that over 600 cases analysed lacked any information regarding results; in almost 500 cases there was not even a confirmation of whether the project had been approved.

It is not surprising that the 'Brazil-as-donor' project was, once again, left in the side-lines during the 1990s. Along with managerial issues, Brazil's reality was not inviting of deep and meaningful South-South engagement. The first half of the decade witnessed significant political and economic turmoil, although both would be slowly stabilized during Cardoso's presidency (1995–2002). The relatively low importance given to the broad context of South-South in Cardoso's foreign policy contributed to a timid profile in this realm. During his tenure, South America and Portuguese speaking countries were the only real 'Southern' priority. International cooperation was part of the discourse, but there was little spill over in concrete actions (Puente, 2010:223–224). Regardless of difficulties, in 1997, the UNDP labelled Brazil one of the developing countries playing a 'pivotal role' in SSC (UN-GA, 2009:9). By the end of the 1990s, there was growing request for technical cooperation from Brazil in its national AIDS/HIV policies and other pharmaceutical and health programmes connected to FIOCRUZ (Valler Filho, 2007; Barbosa, 2011a). Thus, while *some* actions were taking in *some* areas, Brazil's broad international profile as a development assistance provider was not yet one of influential global impact. This would change notably by the next decade.

### *Brazilian development assistance since the 2000s*

Brazil would truly become a relevant 'donor' of development assistance in the 2000s, under President Lula (2003–2010). Notably in the second half of the 2000s, there would be a significant deal of attention given to the use of technical cooperation as a foreign policy tool. Changes in presidency can deeply affect a country's foreign policy. This was certainly the case for the shift from presidents Fernando Henrique Cardoso (1995–2002) to Lula. However, there are disagreements over how dramatic this change was. For some, it represented a deep shift, with the arrival of President Lula signalling "a *drastic change* in relation to the Cardoso period" (Bernal-Meza, 2010:206; emphasis added). For others, such as Ambassador Rubens Barbosa (2011b) – closely connected to former President Cardoso and his party (PSDB) – "the near totality of Itamaraty's main lines of action were maintained". For the latter author, some foreign policy actions which had originated in previous administrations were presented by President Lula's administration as advances, achievements, or novelties, based upon the ideological 'veneer' they were given. Nonetheless, most analysts interpret the comparison between Cardoso and Lula as revealing elements of both continuity *and* rupture (Almeida, 2004; Burges, 2008; Lessa et al., 2009; Cason & Power, 2009; Power, 2010; Inoue & Vaz, 2013). Brazil's foreign policy under the Cardoso and Lula tenures show an enormous deal of stability in many themes. Examples include the continuous attention to South America, active engagement with the World Trade Organization, and great direct presidential involvement in foreign policymaking. Still, each presidency had their own unique characteristics, with varying priorities, approaches, and 'preferred' strategies for attaining what they perceived to be 'the national interest'. Compared to his predecessor, President Lula's foreign policy showed a much greater degree of attention to the issue of SSC, Brazil's 'developing country' identity, and growing attention to alliances with other emerging countries.

The 'emergence' of Brazil as a provider of development assistance in the 2000s did not occur in a vacuum. It would take place within a broader context of social, political, and economic changes, as well as shifts in both domestic and foreign policy priorities. The country would begin the 2000s with a (relatively) stable economy and political structure. Having reached yearly inflation peaks of almost 3,000% in 1990 and over 2,000% in 1994, after 1996 inflation would finally settle to manageable single digits.[4] Its GDP (PPP) crossed the $1 billion mark in 1995, Brazil's economy would grow by close to half a billion dollars by 2004, practically reach $2 billion in 2009, and finish 2013 almost at $2.5 billion.[5] This positive scenario in economic and – especially – *human* development would have two reinforcing consequences for Brazil's provision of technical cooperation. First, the Brazilian government would be able 'offer' a bigger variety of knowledge to other countries, and do so with evidence of its real-life 'effectiveness'. The intrinsically public nature of policies (i.e., 'owned' by the State) were based upon the experience accumulated by national governmental institutions regarding formulating, planning, executing, and following-up public policies seen as 'innovative' in the international stage (IPEA, 2013:25). This feature allowed the government to offer a greater variety of policies and techniques to other countries in the foreign policy context. Second, it concurrently generated/increased *demand* for 'made in Brazil' successful experiences, and countries with similar problems became very interested in knowing more about Brazil's 'solutions'. If 'for every African problem there is a Brazilian solution', desirability of such knowledge is evident.[6] These two reinforcing factors are fundamental in explaining the significant expansion in the number of technical cooperation agreements signed between Brazil and other countries since the mid-2000s.

The 2000s also witnessed Brazilian foreign policy move in the direction of a stronger and more diversified global – and 'Southern' – presence. This was reflected in the country's push for greater visibility in international negotiations, its vocal desire for more power in global governance structures, and the increased pro-active interaction with countries and issues outside of its traditional 'comfort' zones. Much of Brazil's actions towards these foreign policy goals have been done through multilateral arrangements, with the most common partners in these endeavours during Lula's tenure being other 'emerging' countries – such as China, India, and South Africa. The main point of convergence between Brazil and its partners, as pushed by that administration, was the claim that power is not adequately distributed in the current international system, a position frequently accompanied by a strong discourse highlighting the under-representation of developing countries. This was the case for Brazil and for these other emerging countries' bid for more voice in: global financial matters, particularly regarding G-8 and International Monetary Fund (IMF); international trade, and issues of agriculture in the World Trade Organization (WTO); international climate change negotiations, notably through the BASIC arrangement (Brazil, South Africa, India and China); Brazil's collective attempt (along with India, Germany, and Japan) to reform the United Nations Security Council, etc.

SSC would be an essential element of President Lula's foreign policy. He turned the relations with other Southern countries into "*the* policy priority" (Inoue & Vaz, 2013:514). There was considerable dedication to fostering Brazil's bilateral relations with developing countries outside of South America. During his eight years in power, an average of 10 new diplomatic posts were created *each year*. In 2002, Brazil had 150 overseas posts. By 2010, that number had reached 230, with the creation of: 52 embassies, six missions to International Organizations, 22 consulates, and one diplomatic office (in Palestine). More than 70% of these new posts were in 'Southern' countries (Amorim, 2010:226), leading Brazil to have more embassies in Africa than the UK.

As Brazil's global stature increased, there was a concomitant expansion in its development assistance programmes to other regions. Technical cooperation would be thoroughly embedded in this internationalization process for two key reasons. First, it served as a concrete gesture of approximation from the Brazilian government. Second, it was an easy fit for a president wanting to engage directly in foreign policymaking. In comparison to other mechanisms of bilateral cooperation (such as grants, loans, and trade concessions), technical cooperation could be provided in high volumes at a relatively low cost. Compared to other options, these agreements usually present much less legislative, political, or bureaucratic hurdles. The possibility of being able and willing to provide 'legitimate' knowledge to (usually already) eager recipients – all the while with no ties or conditionalities – was explored in presidential visits and operationalized with the help of the growing web of physical representations of Brazil abroad. Technical cooperation could easily serve as a go-to tool for Brazil's foreign policy interests, especially since about three-fourths of all 83 countries President Lula visited during his tenure were developing countries.[7]

The overall importance of technical cooperation as a foreign policy tool, particularly in the context of SSC, was clearly acknowledged by the administration. President Lula's Minister of External Relations, Celso Amorim, in his first speech immediately signalled that "policies of cultural, technical, scientific, and technological cooperation will be essential elements in the foreign policy of the Lula (*sic*) administration". By the last year of President Lula's first term, in 2006, Amorim would be even more direct: "[technical] cooperation is an instrument for Brazilian foreign policy (...) [with] extreme relevance for bringing Brazil closer to other countries, especially those in the developing world" (Amorim, 2006:16). The overall use of technical cooperation as a foreign policy tool could also be found in the administration's final assessment of Brazil's foreign policy under this presidency:

> Technical cooperation developed by Brazil was broadened according to the guidelines of the policy to strengthen the South-South dialogue, as a foreign policy instrument of Luiz Inácio Lula da Silva's government. This cooperation seeks to strengthen Brazil's bilateral relations with the rest of the world, elevating Brazil's profile in the world stage. As a result of recent economic growth, the country has been taking one a more protagonist role in international discussions and spearheading the movement for integrating and strengthening developing countries. In this sense, technical cooperation has been one of the most important elements in Brazilian foreign policy.
>
> (MRE, 2010; topic 7.1.1)

As in the transition from Presidents Cardoso to Lula, Dilma Rousseff's rise to the presidency (2011–2016) would also entail elements of continuity and rupture in Brazil's foreign policy. Coming from the same political party and having been her predecessor's Minister of Mines and Energy, the expectation was of more 'natural' similarities in foreign policies between Lula/Rousseff than for Cardoso/Lula. President Rousseff's foreign policy maintained the attention to SSC (particularly with the BRICS nations), Brazil's 'developing' identity, and preference for power-seeking through multilateral arrangements with developing countries. However, while there was continuity in many aspects, President Rousseff's foreign policy also had its own unique elements, and she moved away from her predecessor's choices in some noticeable respects. First, attention to international issues was visibly reduced. A symbolic example is reflected in direct presidential involvement in international missions. In her first two years in power she travelled less than her predecessor did in his *first* year alone, and even less than President Cardoso did in his two first years. Compared to her predecessor, "the *absence* of rhetoric is what is most apparent" in Rousseff's foreign policy speeches (Hochstetler, 2013; emphasis added).

To say that President Rousseff was more focused on domestic than international issues is uncontroversial. A common understanding by Brazilian analysts is that President Rousseff was much less avid to be under the international spotlight than President Lula was, as well as more 'pragmatic' (as opposed to 'symbolic') in her policy choices. Then again, leaving aside personality traits, since 2011, Brazil's economy and domestic political scenario has been going through difficulties which President Lula did not have to deal with. The country still boasts an impressive GDP, but its growth rate decreased significantly after 2013. Political turmoil – including Rousseff's controversial impeachment in 2016 – and economic recession forced the presidency to 'look inward' with a lot more impetus. In President Rousseff's presidency, technical cooperation remained a key component of Brazil's overall development assistance, and agreements remained unconditional and untied, although there was a clear decrease in the number of new agreements signed. One important takeaway is that just because a president has the *possibility* of exploring the use of technical cooperation with greater ease than other foreign policy mechanisms does not mean they *will*.

## Drivers of Brazil's use of technical cooperation as a foreign policy tool

Providing unconditional and untied technical cooperation has been a cornerstone of Brazil's 'development assistance' programme. While both diplomatic and commercial gains are actively sought, the former has been prioritized over the latter. Essentialist explanations for Brazil's no-strings-attached approach – such as 'Brazilians care about poverty *because they are Brazilian*' or 'Brazilians have better values *because they are Brazilian*' – are inadequate. These 'answers' create an illusion of an innate and immutable character to the Brazilian identity, denying its constructed character and the divergent interpretations of what this has meant over time. This section covers three factors which inform Brazil's decision to leave its development assistance unconditional and untied: (1) ideational, (2) institutional, and (3) positional factors.

### *Ideational forces*

One way to understand Brazil's decision to provide unconditional and untied technical cooperation is by looking at prominent ideas and principles informing foreign policymaking. While this interpretation is quite strong for explaining unconditionality, the same cannot be said for explaining Brazil's untied cooperation. The country's diplomatic tradition has been informed by essentially the same core values for decades and unconditionality has remained untouched and essentially unquestioned. And yet, in the 1970s and 1980s, Brazil provided technical cooperation *with* ties, only moving to an explicit and all-around *untied* stance in the 2000s – all the time under the same overarching diplomatic principles. So, while the idea of unconditionality is deeply entrenched in Brazil's foreign policy, providing untied aid is not.

Brazil's embrace of unconditionality is not recent. It has its visible roots in the early 1960s, years before this country's initial provisions of development assistance and *decades* before its 'emergence' as a donor. In the history of Brazil's foreign policy, major shifts in values have been rare and short-lived (Amorim, 2010:214). Among the most important and constant features are: a strong diplomatic tradition, centred upon the Ministry of Foreign Affairs (*Itamaraty*) and its patron Baron of Rio Branco; non-aggressive solutions to conflicts (e.g., consensus building, legal proceedings, mediation); staunch support for multilateralism; and high value given to international law and international organizations. For Professor Miriam Saraiva, "the tradition of a non-imposing nature is a part of Brazilian foreign policy's profile" (interview). It is clear, there has been a consistent attempt "to dissociate itself from the paternalism, conditionality and political interference in domestic affairs which has often been linked to the image of the traditional donor countries" (Inoue & Vaz, 2013:510).

In the case of conditionalities attached to development assistance, there was never a rupture in the principled belief that they were *undesired*. Rather, this negative connotation has been reinforced through time, as the country has experienced its own subjection to unwanted external conditionalities by more powerful parties (developed countries and international organizations). Conditionalities demanded of Brazil to receive foreign aid were not welcomed nor seen as benevolent actions by concerned donors who had Brazil's best interest at heart. Even worse were the conditionalities 'requested' – for many, they were nothing short of *imposed* – by the IMF and the World Bank, especially in the 1980s and 1990s. Because the legal understanding was that Congressional approval was not required for each loan made with the IMF (only sanctioning from the Executive government), the country's acceptance of the conditionalities was perceived as belonging to an undemocratic structure.

A common perception shared by interviewees was that 'traditional' donors' approach was selfish and patronizing; and international organizations led by developed countries were usurping the sovereignty of all developing countries, in a process commonly described (especially in Latin America) as 'economic imperialism'. While there were voices in Brazil believing there was a need to implement economic changes in the country, criticism still existed. At the crux of the matter lied the perception that the conditionalities did not take into consideration (nor respect) the country's *own* pace or priorities, and had little to no public debate concerning important decisions that were being made. Hence, the continued historical and political understanding regarding conditionalities in Brazil has always been a negative one: a top-bottom, paternalistic, undemocratic, and ultimately undesired inclusion to development assistance received.

Paradigm shifts between providing tied and untied assistance which occurred in Brazil were intimately related to the foreign policy vision held by each President. For example, the explicitly tied approach was chosen by President Geisel's 'pragmatic' diplomacy, while President Lula's was in great part responsible for the Brazil's untied cooperation. Hints of changes to the unconditional and untied paradigms were briefly mentioned by President Rousseff, but there was no move forward. Fieldwork interviews revealed a significant level of *convergence* between values praised by diplomats and civil servants involved in technical cooperation, regardless of the latter's' academic background, institutional affiliation or time in service in the government. To use Goldstein and Keohane's (1993) language, it appears that the worldviews and principled beliefs (distinguishing right from wrong) of diplomats and civil servants dealing with technical cooperation were very similar. During a technical cooperation workshop with some 30 federal civil servants in Brasília – all directly engaged in the operational side of agreements – the words 'sharing', 'cooperation', 'partnership', and 'exchange' were constantly repeated as positive values Brazilian foreign policy should abide to. Horizontality, for instance, was seen not only as something the State should promote, but as a *principle* that individuals sought to embrace. 'Aid' and 'assistance' were generally addressed with a negative interpretation, as denoting a condescending attitude. All expressed that in their dealings with SSC the projects should always begin from an eye-to-eye approach, regardless of which other country was involved. There was an overwhelming normative rejection to the idea of imposing conditions unrelated to the project for economic or political gain; commercial ties were also portrayed in a negative light, although not as vehemently.

Interviews also revealed a strong emphasis from government officials – both diplomats and non-diplomats – to highlight Brazilian unconditional cooperation. The understanding that adopting conditionalities would be *wrong* was shared by practically all diplomats and public civil servants interviewed. Fieldwork revealed that public servants with experience on negotiations to *receive* assistance from DAC donors were particularly critical of conditionalities, and were the most vocal ones to abide to this negative image (both during the workshop and in individual interviews). Professor Cristina Inoue (interview) confirmed the impression that "many diplomats do believe in cooperation, solidarity, and horizontality" as a valid foreign policy approach. Again, this position should not be automatically equated to altruism. As stated by one high level diplomat,

> This practice of non-conditionality, of searching for the autonomy with the country with which Brazil is cooperating, this search for answering to external demands from other countries... it corresponds to a genuine perception that this is Brazil's interest too.... The more my partner is developed, satisfied with that which I can give him, and by itself reach higher development levels, more Brazil benefits from the bilateral point of view.

President Lula's rise to power would once again reinforce the condemnation to conditionalities. During his tenure, Brazil became a powerhouse on its own and transitioned from essentially a recipient to mostly a provider of development assistance. The project of transforming Brazil into an emerging donor, consistently providing significant volume of development assistance programmes, only became a reality in the mid-2000s – prior to this, Brazil's economy was still in the process of becoming stabilized. The material reality of *not having funds* to implement or sustain a significant number of projects undoubtedly played an enormous role. But once the situation improved, President Lula was able to reverse this situation. The normative position of framing conditionalities in a negative light would be cemented in Brazil's role as an emerging donor.

Civil servants with direct experience in agreements to *receive* cooperation from developed countries highlighted how much they disliked when countries sought to impose a model or conditionalities upon an agreement with Brazil. They acknowledged the current situation for Brazil (as a recipient) as being much better than before the early 2000s. Nonetheless, many of those working with traditional donors reported that the top-bottom model still existed. According to a non-diplomat with several years of experience at Brazil's Cooperation Agency, "[DAC donors in general] they come with a posture of imposition, and have their specific interests very well defined" (interview). Brazilians had to fight for the country's own interests vis-à-vis DAC donors in an "exercise of counterbalance" (interview). The broad assessment made by civil servants working with technical cooperation was that the Brazilian model of international cooperation was not only different but more 'just/fair'. These findings mirror those made by Cristina Inoue and Alcides Vaz:

> This current sensitivity of the Brazilian government and its insistence on framing its assistance as 'cooperation' and 'partnership' are motivated by Brazil's own past experiences as an aid receiver and preconditioned by a longer-held belief and conscious desire to confront the traditional assumption that international relations is a zero-sum game of realpolitik and unending power contestation.
>
> (Inoue & Vaz, 2013:527)

Given the long history of upholding unconditionality, it is not a surprise that Brazil would provide unconditional development assistance. However, tradition should not be mistaken for destiny. The idea of unconditionality was born and evolved in Brazil under a context where (1) it was a recipient, and (2) its capacity to provide assistance was so limited that it probably would not be able to demand conditionalities from others even if it wanted to. The shift towards being not only a donor but a *relevant* one had the potential to change the interpretation of unconditionality. President Lula did not do this, with his Minister of External Affairs arguing that with countries which have a history of human rights violation, "dialogue and cooperation are more effective than condemnation and sanctions" (Amorim, 2009:74). Many foreign policy analysts in late 2010 anticipated a major change in Brazil's provision of development assistance after President Rousseff was sworn in 2011 January. However, this shift did not take place. In practice, President Rousseff ended up adopting her predecessor's position on the implementation of human-rights-based political conditionalities, and continued with the fully *un*conditional approach. For example, in 2012, she visited Cuba and was questioned by Brazilian journalists about the Brazil's extensive cooperation with a country considered by many to violate many human rights. Her response was "people who live in glass houses shouldn't throw stones", to what many interpreted as Brazil, with its own problems with human rights, was not in a condition to pass judgment on anyone else.

Unconditionality has thus been a systematic characteristic in Brazil's provision of development assistance (including technical cooperation). This is evidently due mostly to the country's history as a recipient of foreign aid and its embrace of 'Southern' values. As all other countries providing assistance under the SSC banner, unconditionality is a pivotal value. But as previously discussed, the idea and concepts of SSC are prone to varied interpretations in many fronts – with the normative value of providing tied assistance being one. While China and India embrace SSC and unconditionality, both countries are known to tie assistance they provide to other developing countries. Hence, the variables 'abiding to SSC values' and 'defending non-intervention' yield a low explanatory value for understanding *if* or *why* an emerging donor country will tie its technical cooperation agreements or not.

The Brazilian case demonstrates this conceptual ambiguity in a remarkable way. The country has a record of providing both tied and untied technical cooperation – even though consistently following the SSC framework. While the country's military and democratic leaders before President Lula maintained Brazil's embrace of the broad conception of SSC, the Southern/'Third World' *identity* was never wholeheartedly adopted, symbolized by Brazil's decision to only have an observer status to the Non-Aligned Movement. In other words, Brazilian foreign policy was not a case of SSC ideas 'all the way down'. President Geisel's (1974–1979) 'pragmatic' diplomacy exemplified this point. In the 1970s, Brazil was actively participating in North/South, First/Third World debates, with its foreign policy closely trailing the main theses defended in these *fora*. However, when it came to foreign policy actions, the country's leadership was more interested in immediate and concrete gains than long-term possible benefits. In a later memoir, President Geisel stated:

> We went to the meetings and conferences, were in favour of their [Third World] demands, since we were also a subdeveloping [sic] country (...) but we did not make any commitments. They had our sympathy, but we did not engage. [We had] a policy of solidarity with the Third Word and economic preference for the North. (...) But even in this Third World solidarity, Brazil never fully committed to it.
>
> (*apud* D'Araujo & Castro, 1997:337–338)

The economic crisis under which the country was in during the 1970s also contributed to framing tied assistance as normatively 'good', under the reasoning that the country could not afford to miss commercial opportunities to mitigate its dire financial needs. At the same time, this choice could still be presented as abiding to the SSC paradigm: tying Brazil's provision of development assistance was simply an expression of 'mutual gains'. Foreign policy was expected to open new markets and opportunities for economic cooperation with developing countries. This legacy of the Import-Substitution Industrialization model (*developmentismo*) initially remained after the economic crisis and official abandonment of the economic mode, in a case of what Soares de Lima and Hirst (2006:24) called "paradigmatic resilience".

The shift in conceptualizing development from an economic to a social perspective would greatly impact how technical cooperation would be framed, allowing a much easier path from a tied to an untied structure. Under President Lula, Brazilian foreign policy adopted an explicitly negative interpretation of tying cooperation. Regardless of whether this positioning echoes 'true' moral values or not, since the early 2000s, both the discourse and practice Brazilian technical cooperation agreements have been intertwined: tying condemned in discourse and absent from practice. For one diplomat interviewed, "our [Brazil's] external discourse has never been more closely connected to our internal practices than now". A non-diplomat at ABC shared their experience during Director Marco Farani's tenure (2009–2012) in the following way:

> When there was an open call for purchasing machinery, or a car, and it needed to determine the specifications, the guideline was to find a way to have the most rational option – best quality, specificity, cost-efficiency... – and buy it. The office never received a specification demanding that Brazilian products were to be purchased – *never*. It was always about efficiency. I believe that there weren't any changes with new ABC administration: it's still 'buy what is cheaper and deliver whatever is best for the partner's needs'. It is not selling aid. (...) I can really say there is no direct commercial gain. I guarantee that this strategy does not exist, many reasons: most of the people involved with TC at ABC do in fact believe in what they are doing, that they are doing a solidary cooperation.

The normative value of untied assistance has thus been reinforced by a discourse which highlights the overlap between SSC values – e.g., 'demand-driven', 'solidarity' – and Brazil's foreign policy *actions*. The option for untied cooperation can also be conceptualized as an extension of a 'diplomacy of development', i.e., the immediate goal of Brazil's technical cooperation is to assist in the recipient's development. According to Corrêa, Brazil is a country "openly committed to the idea of development as an instrument of reduction of asymmetry among nations"; for him, Brazil does not remain only in the *discourse* of solidarity in the international area, but "seeks to *practice* this solidarity, mobilizing what we have in terms of the country's conditions" (interview; see Corrêa, 2010). However, unlike the well-established unconditionality principle, it would be a stretch to claim that untied cooperation already has the same grounded position. Rather, such assessment would be better made given time and continued reinforcement and practice. For now, it would be more appropriate to conceive untied cooperation as representing a principle-*based* 'expression' of the country's commitment to upholding the recognized principles of non-interference, solidarity, and horizontality. Hence, from an ideational perspective, the higher the value placed upon these principles, the higher the chances of untied cooperation being embraced.

### *Institutional forces*

Brazil's current Constitution (from 1988) appears to be a powerful force sustaining the country's unconditional stance as the *status quo*. At the same time, the document only provides a weak base for justifying or explaining the decision to provide untied technical cooperation agreements. The Brazilian Constitution explicitly embraces 'non-interference' as a principle to be followed in the country's international relations. This stance automatically makes any attempt to introduce political or economic conditionalities extremely cumbersome – and thus, highly unlikely. Nonetheless, if the principle of non-interference is framed as clashing with other Constitutional principles – such as respect and protection of human rights – there is a possibility that some conditionalities might be perceived as ethically and legally justifiable.

The present Constitution was the first in the country's history to explicitly incorporate guiding principles to Brazil's international relations. Unsurprisingly, many of these principles had been part of the country's traditional discourse for decades when the Constitution was being crafted. Its Preamble provides an insight into which values were – and still are – deemed an integral part of the country's legal and political *ethos*. The opening sentence for the Constitution affirms that the State's purpose is to ensure "the exercise of social and individual rights, liberty, security, well-being, *development*, equality and justice as supreme values [...] and [the State is] committed, in the internal and international orders, to the peaceful settlement of disputes" (emphasis added). The Constitution's Article 4 is specifically devoted to Brazil's foreign policy, enumerating 10 principles which should govern the country's international relations:

I national independence;
II prevalence of human rights;
III self-determination of the peoples;
IV non-intervention;

V equality among the States;
VI defence of peace;
VII peaceful settlement of conflicts;
VIII repudiation of terrorism and racism;
IX cooperation among peoples for the progress of mankind; and
X granting of political asylum.

Sole Paragraph [*Parágrafo único*]: The Federative Republic of Brazil shall seek the economic, political, social and cultural integration of the peoples of Latin America, viewing the formation of a Latin-American community of nations.

Many of these values and principles have an undeniable resonance with those embedded in SSC. Hence, concepts like 'non-interference', 'horizontality', and 'development' are more than part of Brazil's stated principles as a 'development donor' or part of a foreign policy discourse. They are Constitutional directives, which (at least in theory) are expected to be embedded in every single international action or commitment undertaken by the country. Under this light, it could be argued that attaching conditionalities to development assistance projects is *unconstitutional,* i.e., an interference in another country's right to self-determination. Nonetheless, there is still room for a slightly different interpretation of unconditionality under the law. President Rousseff, for example, in the beginning of her first term, initially discussed an idea (which did not advance) to include human rights considerations in the provision of development assistance. Because Article 4's principles are not placed in a hierarchical order, one could argue that 'prevalence of human rights' could be given primacy over 'non-intervention'. Notwithstanding the legal possibility of giving primacy to human rights over non-interference, this has not been the approach chosen so far. Brazil's diplomatic tradition is to abstain from – if not *condemn* – direct interference in other countries' politics. In the exceptional cases it has supported interference, these have involved multinational actions and transitions towards democracy, not military attacks or direct involvement in deposing 'problematic' leaders. Hence, while the Constitution does not fully impede an eventual adoption of conditionalities, it certainly discourages actions in this direction.

In contrast to conditionalities, it is much harder to make the case that the provision of untied cooperation is constitutionally justified. Connections can certainly be made with the Constitution's principles, but it requires some creativity: untied agreements could be constitutionally protected if interpreted as an *expression* of commitment towards one of the legally established principles. Two potential choices of interpretation emerge, both fragile. First, tied agreements could be violating the principles of "self-determination of the peoples" and "non-intervention". Under this logic, commercial attachments *interfere* in the other recipient's sovereign right to purchase from whomever it would find adequate. Another option, demanding what appears to be an even wider legal and conceptual stretch, would be to frame untied agreements under the banner of "cooperation among peoples for the progress of mankind". In this case, if the ultimate purpose of Brazil's 'foreign aid' – particularly if related to development issues – is not to accrue commercial gains but promote 'the progress of mankind'. Nonetheless, this framing is done *ipsi literis* in the Ministry of Foreign Affair's website page for 'Technical Cooperation': "Brazil's South-South technical cooperation (...) is founded upon the Constitutional principle of cooperation among peoples for the progress of mankind" (MRE, undated). The main problem here is that this constitutional principle is the most poorly defined of all; in its most simple assessment, Brazil should not cooperate for *destructive* purposes (Nascimento, 1997:219). Ultimately, while untied cooperation could be inspired by constitutional principle, the link is clearly very tenuous – and thus easy to be dismissed.

In terms of government players, the Executive Power is – *de jure* and *de facto* – the single most important force in determining the direction of the country's foreign policy. The Legislative Power has been traditionally uninvolved in discussing these matters and mostly limited to fulfilling the Constitutional requirement of authorizing the ratification of international treaties, which is usually done with little controversy. Inside the Executive Power, the Presidency holds a key position in foreign policymaking, immediately followed by the Ministry of Foreign Affairs. These have been the undisputed main players in setting the direction of Brazil's international cooperation projects.

In Brazil, President Cardoso (1995–2002) was the first to truly engage in 'presidential diplomacy' (see Danese, 1999). This concept signals a transition from foreign policymaking being essentially a bureaucratic process to an *individual* and *personified* one – with the President at the centre stage. Most presidents before Cardoso focused on domestic policy, mostly serving as the 'physical' manifestation of the nation in international meetings and engaging in courtesy and protocol visits with other foreign dignitaries. While they had the power to command the country's diplomacy, most were not very enthusiastic about exerting this power to its fullest potential. President Cardoso introduced this new structure in Brazilian foreign policymaking, wholeheartedly embracing the role of Diplomat-in-Chief through direct and active engagement. Unlike previous presidents, he was "*personally* involved in international conferences and multilateral and bilateral negotiations, to a degree and intensity unparalleled by any of his predecessors", actions normally exerted by the Minister of External Relations or diplomats (Lampreia & Cruz, 2005:109; emphasis added). Presidential Diplomacy reached yet another level with President Lula, who took this active involvement to (so far) its highest degree of intensity. One of the greatest characteristics of his diplomatic activism was the degree of personification he gave to Brazil's foreign policy. More than 'just' being the President of Brazil he became known as somewhat of an international celebrity – being called by US President Barack Obama "the most popular politician on Earth" in 2009.

Presidential Diplomacy has had a direct impact upon the domestic architecture of Brazil as an 'emerging donor'. To start, the surge in Brazil's provision of development assistance after 2005 was not a 'natural' process. It came about as a clear direction from President Lula, who became personally involved in this mission, actively encouraging developing countries to take advantage of Brazil's no-strings-attached technical cooperation agreements. According to a high-level political advisor interviewed (with over two decades of active work in various institutions of the Federal government), the President *"pushed Itamaraty"* to expand this agenda. Many diplomats and academics interviewed pointed out President Lula's personal commitment to increase Brazil's soft power and South-South interaction. In this context, diplomatic gains were highly valued and sought after. At the same time, technical cooperation agreements were "a pretty thing to sell", as an interviewer said. Compared to other options such as grants and loans, technical cooperation agreements were easy to promote, since many countries already manifested their interest in Brazilian knowledge. They were relatively cheap, thus possible to be provided in a significant scale, and legally simple. They also fitted well with the President's pro-development agenda and were something he could *personally* promote. President Lula's personal charisma and life-story – from Brazil's poorest region and an extremely impoverished family to the Presidency – probably helped to increase the legitimacy of this broader project. In his own words, "there is no other [world] leader who has starved" (*apud Folha de São Paulo*, 2004). President Rousseff, on the other hand, took a much more low-key international profile than her predecessor, while maintaining President Lula's broad foreign policy direction – including the overall guidelines for providing 'developing assistance' and a discourse in tune with SSC (see Oliveira & Onuki, 2010).

Ultimately, presidential diplomacy has brought important shifts in the institutional structure of Brazil's foreign policymaking process and directly and indirectly affected its provision of international development cooperation. Under such arrangement, foreign policy is more subject to the whims of presidents. This leads to a greater chance of decisions being made in a hurry and under the pressures of electoral calendars, unlike the long-term horizon of diplomats (Cason & Power, 2009:135). This concern was expressed explicitly by a high-ranking diplomat: "This is why diplomacy is state politics, concerned with continuity. We look at consequences beyond the immediate moment for the country's long-term image".

Aside from the Presidency, *Itamaraty* has been the bedrock institution of Brazil's foreign policymaking. Since the early 20th century, the Ministry has consolidated a significant degree of autonomy in foreign policymaking vis-à-vis any other federal bureaucracies. According to one interviewee, until the mid-2000s "the Ministry did not even report to the President's Chief of Staff" – only directly to the President. With the expansion of the international agenda, there has been an increase in the dispersion of policymaking attributions, although this 'outside' policymaking remains checked by *Itamaraty*. The consensus of Brazil's international relations elite is that the Ministry of Foreign Affairs has historically given little attention to the opinions and proposals of groups interested in contributing to foreign policymaking, even if these come from other federal ministries. The Ministry's hierarchical structure – with diplomats being referred to as '[military] officers in suits and ties' – was respected by the country's military rulers, explaining in great part the high degree of autonomy it maintained even during the two decades of dictatorship (see Cheibub, 1985; Soares de Lima, 2000). Combining a powerful resistance to bureaucratic threats to its mission and strong *esprit de corps*, its agenda-setting power has remained strong despite the rise of presidential diplomacy.

The Brazilian Cooperation Agency, formally responsible for the country's policies over development assistance (both provided and received), is fully nested within the Ministry. ABC's directors have always been diplomats appointed directly by the Minister of Foreign Affairs. This results in its mission, principles, and interests mirroring that of the Ministry's, and very limited autonomy as an agency. Direct interference of the Ministry of Trade in the Agency's development assistance policies from all account seems to be extremely weak. In fact, it appears safe to say that whenever there has been direct influence of the Ministry of Trade upon foreign policymaking in general, it has derived from a presidential decision to override the Ministry of Foreign Affairs. The big picture is one where regarding foreign policy, the Ministry of Trade and other ministries *sometimes* have *some* voice in *some* issues. The general rule is that diplomats are the ones who formulate Brazil's foreign policy, unless the President decides on a different direction. *Itamaraty* has never been particularly focused in promoting Brazil's foreign trade in *direct* terms, but rather as a *product* of improved bilateral relations and an optimal diplomatic environment. So, notwithstanding some hiccups and exceptions, the overall experience then has been one when having to choose between giving primacy to diplomatic or commercial interests, the former has 'won' over the latter.

The historical and contemporary discourse emanating from the Ministry of Foreign Affairs – to which the Brazilian Cooperation Agency is subordinate – is strongly supportive of the principle of non-interference, with unconditional development assistance being a fundamental corollary. The Ministry's official position is that Brazil's South-South technical cooperation is "founded upon the *constitutional principle* of cooperation among peoples for the progress of mankind [and is] *free of conditionalities*" (MRE, undated; emphasis added). At the same time, there does not appear to be governmental groups actively invested in trying to shift Brazil's rule of providing unconditional assistance. Archival research and fieldwork showed no clear direct involvement from the Ministry of Trade and Development in Brazil's provision of development assistance. This stands in clear contrast to the bureaucratic structure of most traditional and 'emerging' donors (such as China and India). However, this does not mean this Ministry can't influence foreign policy – it can 'bypass' the diplomatic channel and make their case directly to the Presidency.

As a rule, non-governmental actors tend to exert only a small influence in shaping Brazil's foreign policy. In the case of the country's provision of development assistance, this 'outside' influence is even fainter. There is no mainstream debate over the unconditional or untied character of the country's development assistance. This is situated within a broader context of little public awareness about Brazil's provision of this assistance itself. In recent years, ethical questions over agreements with countries with serious human rights violations have been occasionally raised in print media and in some academic circles but with limited repercussion. The group with the most obvious interest in questioning the untied character of Brazil's development assistance would be private companies. However, if this is their position, it is well hidden. Archival research (e.g., main print media outlets, material from industry associations) and fieldwork yielded no indication of organized movements to have the government introduce commercial ties. All interviews with diplomats and public servants, working directly with technical cooperation, pointed to the assessment of no direct pressure from private companies on technical cooperation projects. That said, this book *does not* claim the private sector is void of foreign policy interests or that it refrains from seeking to influence policy choice – this would be an erroneous assessment. Two mains point to be made are: (1) private companies do not appear to be explicitly focused on using technical cooperation agreements as their strategy for accruing commercial gains, and (2) they probably seek to influence policy directly towards the Presidency – 'bypassing' *Itamaraty* and ABC.

### *Positional forces*

A single technical cooperation agreement is very unlikely to help Brazil achieve any of these goals. However, a *collection* of agreements between Brazil and numerous donors, all under the same structure – unconditional and untied – has a much better chance of yielding diplomatic gains. These agreements are one of many tools used to support Brazil's strategy of an increased global presence. The desire to improve Brazil's *position* in the international system is the third element pushing Brazilian foreign policymakers towards unconditional and untied technical cooperation agreements. In this country's case, an 'improved position' has meant, among other things:

- greater power inside international organizations, such as in the United Nations Security Council, FAO, and WTO;
- being perceived as a legitimate voice for 'Southern'/developing nations when in negotiations with developed countries;
- being perceived as an honest broker and 'leader' of Latin America, while concomitantly presenting a non-threatening image towards the countries in the region;

- reaffirming its position as a cooperation partner thoroughly abiding to SSC values;
- differentiating itself from traditional donors (explicitly) and from some emerging donors, particularly China and India (implicitly); and
- being recognized as a necessary actor in international debates related to human development themes (e.g., poverty, hunger, education, maternal health), and others such as tropical agriculture, reducing deforestation, biofuels, etc.

There is an "absolute consensus" among Brazil's diplomats and elite that the country is destined to have a significant international role (Soares de Lima, 2005:10). An isolationist position in foreign affairs is practically a rare phenomenon in the country. According to De Souza's (2009) interviews among key actors in Brazil's academic, business, and diplomatic elite, only 1% believed the country should refrain from international problems. Still, building a global presence is something which requires more than just ideas – it requires concrete actions. The ability to provide valuable knowledge without demanding anything back from the recipient can support Brazil's engagement with a significant number of actors at a (relatively) low cost, at least compared to the provision of grants and loans. Simply put, this kind of no-strings-attached technical cooperation is "an instrument capable of giving support to the country's expansion of influence in an international scale" (Valler Filho, 2007:121). The expectation is not that unconditional and united technical cooperation agreements can, by themselves, transform Brazil into a global player. Rather, such agreements serve as an accessible and concrete way for promoting Brazil to a large number of countries (see Inoue & Vaz, 2013).

As part of this 'global project' pushed by President Lula, Brazilian diplomacy vastly increased its attention to developing countries outside of its 'traditional' areas, and increasingly sought to engage with as many developing countries as possible (see Lessa, 2010). Beyond improving bilateral relations, the provision of unconditional and untied technical cooperation was also used to achieve a prominent spot for Brazil within developing countries through two interconnected processes: positioning Brazil as (1) a Southern partner and (2) a development leader (see Dauvergne & Farias, 2012). Both were expected to be eventually translated into *concrete* diplomatic and commercial gains: endorsing Brazil's positions in international organizations through votes; (explicitly or implicitly) allowing Brazil to negotiate on behalf of a group of countries; not contesting Brazil's claim of leadership over certain themes (e.g., development, biofuels, HIV/AIDS); as well as improved commercial and trade opportunities for Brazilian companies.

Self-identification as a 'Southern' country has been present in the foreign policy of emerging donors for decades. In the Brazilian context, this has meant not just promoting SSC values but providing a supporting explanation for (1) going beyond a regional South-American focus and moving towards an engagement with developing countries in all continents, and (2) sometimes (but not necessarily) giving a higher degree of attention to the relationship with developing countries. Hence, it has been interpreted as signalling both a *position* in the international system (i.e., Brazil is a Southern country) as well as a *policy direction* (towards the global South). Notwithstanding periods of higher or lower prioritization in foreign policy, both understandings have been part of Brazilian foreign policy throughout the years. Unconditionality is a necessary element to sustain legitimacy for both cases. In the words of President Lula's Minister of External Relations, Celso Amorim:

> At the crossroads of all the main guidelines of Brazilian foreign policy is the effort to establish closer relations with other developing countries. South-South cooperation (...) helps expand Brazil's participation in world affairs. Cooperation among equals (...) reinforces our stature and strengthens our position in trade, finance and climate negotiations. Last, but not least, building coalitions with developing countries is also a way of engaging in the reform of global governance to make international institutions fairer and more democratic.
>
> (Amorim, 2010:231)

As discussed, unconditionality is at the heart of SSC, framed as an expression of respect for all countries' sovereignty and right to self-determination. Economic and political conditionalities are perceived as external impositions, even if justified by 'good' intentions. Unconditionality has become part of the 'Southern' *identity*. This implies (1) condemning and (2) refraining from demanding conditionalities in the interaction with peers. As with practically all developing countries, Brazil has historically been on the 'weak' side of relationships with powerful developed countries. Only very recently has this dynamic begun to change. From a historical perspective, even if 'Southern' countries such as Brazil wished to demand conditionalities from others, they probably would not be able to, as their capacity to provide aid (financial or other) was typically limited and with little leverage. Hence, the *condemnation towards* and *refrain from* conditionalities was quite easy. Providing unconditional and untied technical cooperation can – ideally – help to reduce doubts over Brazil's commitment to SSC and establish its *actions* as different from traditional donors and other powerful emerging donors. In sum, seeking a position as a 'Southern' donor implies unconditionality, but not necessarily unconditionality. Hence, Brazil's unconditional and untied approach should be seen as a way to (1) bring even more contrast to its actions than that of 'Northern' donors, and (2) highlight its deep commitment to SSC, even more so than China and India's.

Along with the 'Southern partner' image, President Lula's foreign policy was also infused with the idea of transforming Brazil into a development leader – increasing power based on the concept of development. Many of

Brazil's domestic development initiatives would end up having international repercussions, for two main reasons. First, by creating/increasing other countries' interests in Brazilian policy experiences. Second, due to President Lula and the Brazilian diplomacy's embrace of development as a key element of Brazil's foreign policy. This can be seen as a reinterpretation of the concept of 'development diplomacy': from a foreign policy seeking to improve Brazil's own development to one intended to improve *other countries'* development – with this latter approach falling within what has been sometimes referred to as Brazil's 'diplomacy of solidarity' (see Seitenfus, 2006; Barnabé, 2010). Cooperation was a political instrument and "as a policy of prestige, related to the desire to occupy a more central position in the international system" (Inoue & Vaz, 2013:515).

President Lula actively sought to transform Brazil's domestic social and economic successes into power on the international stage. Him and President Rousseff (albeit with less enthusiasm) promoted Brazil as a legitimate and innovative voice for development to build coalitions overseas, especially within the global South. Specially during President Lula's tenure, Brazilian foreign policy drew on concrete achievements to justify and legitimate leadership in international development, and not just rely on rhetoric or ideological commonalities. While the economic dimension of development remained high on the agenda, the social/human components of development – such as mitigating poverty and eradicating hunger – were incorporated and brought to the forefront. In this sense, it moved beyond the 'traditional' role of *calling* for development to being in a position of drawing from its own experience to *offer* development solutions.

Crafting Brazil's image of expertise in social/human development comfortably fit the concepts of 'middle power diplomacy' and 'niche diplomacy': focusing diplomatic actions upon selected topics, with the intention of leveraging gains from its reputation on effectively contributing to 'international public goods'. The strategy was more than simply sharing knowledge bilaterally: the goal was also to latch development to practically all international issues. Thus, if Brazil is perceived as a legitimate voice in matters of social/human development, and terrorism (for example) is framed as a lack of social/human development, then Brazil is a necessary voice in international terrorism debates. President Lula proposed this sort of logic in a 2004 speech at the World Bank on scaling-up poverty reduction:

> Hunger is actually the worst of all weapons of mass destruction, claiming millions of victims every year. Fighting hunger and poverty and promoting development are the truly sustainable way to achieve world peace...There will be no peace without development, and there will be neither peace nor development without social justice.

In a scenario where the international security agenda focuses on war and military interventions to violent conflicts, Brazil is indeed only a peripheral player. However, if the debate changes to securing peace and preventing conflicts – such as by addressing the 'root causes' of insecurity in the world – Brazil can position itself as a more powerful actor (or at least try to). President Lula's attention to the security-development nexus occurred within a very receptive international context which witnessed the "convergence of the global development and security agendas at the beginning of the new millennium" (Thomas, 2001:159). In the unhesitant words of the UN Secretary General Kofi Annan, "development and security are inextricably linked" (UN, 2004:viii), and "without security there is no development, and without development there is no security" (UN, 2005:6).

President Lula's overarching project was to have social and economic elements relative to both the domestic and the international spheres "unified under a single developmental agenda" (Almeida, 2003:10). In his speech given at the United Nation's General Assembly 2003 opening session, he stated "peace, security, development and social justice are indivisible" and "the true path to peace is to fight hunger and extreme poverty without truce". His successor also reiterated this approach: two days after taking oath, President Rousseff seized the opportunity of the UN Secretary General's call congratulating her on the new post to propose that the Security Council have a debate on security and social development, suggesting the creation of a United Nations University in Brazil on the same theme. By the following month – as Brazil took over the presidency of the Security Council – an open debate was announced on the subject of "Maintenance of international peace and security: the interdependence between security and development", with Brazil's approach to international security being: "sustainable peace requires a comprehensive approach to security – which involved consideration of the root causes of violence, as well as of the social and economic situation of the ground" (UN-SC, 2011). The narrative allows for a strong connection (at least in discourse) to Brazil's bid to become a permanent member of the UN Security Council and gain power from being a development 'leader'.

Brazil's quest for regional stability (and leadership) has also been sought *through* development. Here, the main motivation derives from an understanding that Brazil's internal security problems can be mitigated by the development of its neighbours, a logic made explicit in the 2005 National Defence Policy document: "a country's security is affected by the degree of instability of the region it is inserted". Hence, development-oriented actions which assist neighbouring countries is expected to reduce trans-border criminal activities which threaten Brazil, such as illicit trade (e.g., drugs, weapons, logging, mining), human trafficking, and illegal immigration. As simply put by a diplomat interviewed, Brazil's "national interest is connected with the development of our neighbours". If the lack of development (economic and social) can foster an unstable environment inside States by contributing to illicit activities, violence and conflict, then promoting development is an effective way to ultimately prevent conflicts – in which case Brazil gains power *through* others' development.

Finally, fostering Brazil's international prominence through development initiatives can be interpreted as another example of the country's leaning towards soft power actions and strategies – a point made by several academics and diplomats interviewed. Brazilian diplomatic history reveals a complex relationship with the positioning of Brazil as a leader. On the one hand, its behaviour can be interpreted as one wish *seeks* leadership positions. At the same time, there is a conscious refrain from the idea of *proclaiming* leadership. Assuming a leadership position involves expectations, like money or military protection. For a mid-level diplomat interviewed, it was best for Brazil to sell itself as a protagonist instead of a leader: "if people are counting on you, you must be reliable, and we [Brazil] aren't really. If you don't have financial stability you can be a victim of your own ambition". According to a senior diplomat, Brazil's

> neighbours in general are convinced that we are imperialists – this [vision] does exist. Brazil has a great dynamism: size, population... It doesn't interest us to have a hard relationship with them, but asymmetry is a reality and you can't ignore it.

A mid-level diplomat proposed a curious metaphor in this context:

> Brazil effectively is a soft-power based country. To start with, it doesn't have lots of hard power, and where it does, it deals poorly with this. Brazil has power projections that are clear, and we will have to develop mechanisms to deal with situations where we effectively have power. What do we do when we have power? We get embarrassed. Think of Gulliver in Lilliput: Brazil is like a Gulliver who asked to be tied down, [saying] "Tie me! I don't know what kind of damage I could do'!"

Ultimately, unconditional and untied technical cooperation agreements were not expected to carry the burden of achieving Brazil's diplomatic desire of leading through 'non-leadership'. But a strong case can be made that these agreements allowed a unique opportunity for 'humble-bragging', on the lines of "Brazil has never *claimed* to be a leader in development – we have so many problems of our own – but we are grateful that other countries see us as such".

## Brazil: possible gains from technical cooperation

This section looks for empirical indications of concrete gains Brazil has had from its provision of no-strings-attached technical cooperation: in other words, *has it worked?* Before moving forward, two important points must be made. First, this research has assumed there is no way to *prove* a direct and fully independent link between Brazil's provision of technical cooperation and diplomatic or commercial gains. There are numerous elements present in a bilateral relationship which work concurrently, with varying degrees of importance, to create a favourable predisposition for the recipient country to support Brazilian interests (Barbosa, 2011a:106).

Second, while an uncontested proof of causal link might be unattainable, it is nonetheless possible to find strong *indications* that such a link exists in some cases where data is available. So, instead of obtaining an unequivocal binary yes-or-no result to the question 'has Brazil gained from providing no-strings technical cooperation to a country or in regarding a specific theme', answers were sought within a range of (1) 'very likely' to 'very unlikely'. Barbosa (2011a:106) complements his thought by adding that while it might not be always possible to account for direct results from Brazil's provision of technical cooperation, it would however "be naïve to deny its role as a valid foreign policy instrument".

Based on the data obtained during research, technical cooperation has either been neutral or positive in promoting both diplomatic and commercial gains for Brazil. There are important signals that Brazil's decision to use its unique expertise as a foreign policy tool has very likely contributed to diplomatic gains in some areas. This is particularly the case for certain themes – like agriculture and health – where empirical data allows for more grounded analysis. But before these neutral/positive impacts are discussed, it is worth stating that evidence gathered points to an overall absence of *negative* feedback from recipients of Brazil's provision of knowledge. The only exception are generic critiques made towards all donors (including 'emerging' donors) that do not demand conditionalities in their cooperation actions with recipient countries which have poor human rights records. In comparison to other donors, Brazil is in a reasonably better situation. Most of its 'assistance' can be framed as a provision of 'global goods': knowledge directed towards human development. And as commercial gains are not directly connected to these initiatives, it can distance itself from these critiques with greater ease.

This is not to imply that critiques have not been made towards Brazil's 'international cooperation' in general. Loans for infrastructure projects and debt pardons are two examples of actions not officially classified as part of the country's 'development cooperation' portfolio. Yet, if they were to be analysed under the umbrella of Brazil's 'foreign aid' actions – notwithstanding the government's position on this classification – a different picture would emerge, as the past years have been especially ripe with serious controversies over government loans given to Brazilian companies operating abroad. This serves as reminder that (1) 'emerging' donors are bound to have their international actions increasing scrutinized by domestic constituents and international analysts, and (2) individual definitions of what is (and is not) 'development assistance' varies for each 'emerging' donor, prompting a great degree of care and attentiveness to cross-country comparisons.

### *Diplomatic gains*

Under President Lula, providing unconditional and untied technical cooperation was understood as an instrument used to promote increased density in political – as well as economic and commercial – relations with the recipient country (ABC, undated:1). While the provision of technical cooperation has clearly publicized and recognized political purposes (Puente, 2010:117), *purpose* does not ensure *results*. As such, there are no guarantees whether a country's initiative will entail the desired response from the other party. Nonetheless, the empirical data collected allows some reflections to be made based on how technical cooperation might have helped to translate legitimacy into *power* in the international stage.

The links between the recipients of Brazil's technical cooperation and the election of a Brazilian to the directorship of FAO illustrates the possibility of concrete diplomatic gains. Tropical agriculture has been one of Brazil's most well-known areas of expertise. It is likely that Brazil's decision to share its knowledge in this theme positively influenced the positions of recipients (and even third parties) in supporting Brazil's international interests in this area. There is too much evidence available to claim mere coincidence (Barbosa, 2011a:123). In 2011, FAO's 191 member-countries elected a new director. It would be a meaningful election for many reasons, and expected to start a new era for the organization (see Oxfam, 2011). A source from FAO is said to have stated that Brazil was "not going to miss the chance to take advantage of this" (*apud* Flemming, 2011). Six candidates made up the initial list, eventually narrowed down to two: Brazil's José Graziano da Silva and Spain's Miguel Cuyaubé.

The Brazilian candidate's qualifications were deeply tied to Brazil's focus on human development, SSC, and technical cooperation. In 2003, Graziano da Silva had been chosen by President Lula to be the Special Minister of Food Security and the Fight against Hunger, and was responsible for implementing the Zero Hunger programme ('*Fome Zero*'). In 2006, he became head of FAO's Regional Office for Latin America and the Caribbean, a position he held until the 2011 election. During the campaign period (2010–2011), SSC was clearly present in his discourse, with this being one of the five pillars in his platform. He travelled several times to African nations (with and without President Lula) to expose his programme, aware of the African electoral college's great deciding power (Costa, 2011). In the end, Graziano da Silva beat the Spanish candidate by 92 to 88 votes. His victory appears to have been strongly benefited by Brazil's standing with the countries with whom Brazil had technical cooperation agreements in agriculture. The election is said to have showed a split between developed and developing countries' interests, something Graziano da Silva was very aware of (Tran, 2011). For the new director, the alliance between developing countries "reflected the recognition of the Brazilian model's success in combating hunger, [and] a bet on South-South Cooperation" (*apud* Siqueira & Aggege, 2011).

The election for FAO director is based on secret voting. However, it is very common for countries to publicly declare which candidates they will support. During fieldwork, a very interesting piece of data was shared by an interviewee: an assessment of which countries had vouched to supported Brazil's candidate.[8] The list of countries was based not only on who were (at the time) recipients of Brazilian technical cooperation, but also specifically those which had received cooperation in *agriculture*. The numbers included both countries which had publicly and *privately* declared their support for Graziano da Silva, as well as those supporting other candidates, or whose position was unclear. The numbers revealed (1) a strong relationship between recipients of Brazilian technical cooperation (in general) and their support for Graziano da Silva, and (2) a very strong relation between recipients of Brazilian technical cooperation in agriculture and their support for the Brazilian candidate.

Out of the 78 countries listed, 59 stated their support for Graziano da Silva (78.7% in total); 14 (18.7%) declared support for other candidates, and two were unclear cases (2.7%). Regionally, 28 out of 29 countries in Latin America and the Caribbean supported Graziano da Silva, and 3/4 of African nations supported Brazil (27 out of 36). The only 'defeat' among developing regions was in the hodgepodge of 10 Asian, East European, and Middle Eastern nations receiving some sort of Brazilian technical cooperation: only four out of 10 declared their vote to be pro-Brazil. Given the fact that there were five other candidates initially – including from Indonesia, Iran, and Iraq – it is unsurprising that other elements (such as regional influence) could have had more weight in these 'distant' countries with which Brazil has a positive but *thin* relationship. Considering only the recipients of Brazilian technical cooperation in agriculture and their positions, the numbers were even more revealing. The number of countries in this cut narrowed the list from 75 to 45 countries: 18 in Latin America and the Caribbean, 25 in Africa, and two in Asia. In this group, only one did not support Brazil's candidate. Of the 30 remaining countries to which Brazil had provided technical cooperation but *not* in agriculture, half supported Graziano da Silva (10 of which were Latin American and Caribbean nations); in Africa, three supported Brazil, one was unclear, and seven supported others (four of these were countries in North Africa); elsewhere, two supported Brazil, one was unclear, and five supported other candidates.

Graziano da Silva's rise to the top position at FAO has since then reflected many important elements of Brazil's foreign policy, including the South-South focus and an incentive for the use of technical cooperation – all of which can be read as increased legitimacy for Brazil and power to push the FAO's direction in its favour. There was also a rise in partnerships between FAO and Brazil, including: an agreement between FAO and EMBRAPA so "to strengthen the transfer of experiences and technologies from Brazil's top agricultural research agency to developing countries within FAO's South-South Cooperation" (FAO, 2013); a trilateral agreement between

FAO, Brazil, and Angola to boost this Angola's agricultural and veterinary research (see FAO, 2014); and Brazil's $2 million contribution to new local food purchase programmes with FAO and the World Food Programme (WFP) to benefit farmers and vulnerable populations in five African countries (FAO, 2012). FAO's 'new' projection and its director might not have benefited Brazil in a tangible manner, but there is little room for denial over the potential for solidifying Brazil's legitimacy as a leader and 'indispensable' actor in international debates regarding food, agriculture, human development, etc. – a desirable situation particularly for 'middle powers'. In the end, this case shows that technical cooperation agreements do have the potential to foster non-trivial diplomatic gains.

Again, it can't be stated with certitude that the countries which voted pro-Brazil did so *because* they were recipients of Brazilian technical cooperation on agriculture – correlation does not imply causation. Nor can it be said that those who did not support Graziano da Silva would have voted differently if they had received Brazilian technical cooperation in agriculture. Also, because the votes are ultimately secret, a public statement of support might not correspond to the actual vote. Still, the numbers do allow for a strong case to be made that these agreements (at the minimum) helped Brazil to tilt the odds in its favour, as recipients become more likely to support Brazil's interest.

### *Commercial gains*

The official position from the Brazilian government is that technical cooperation "does not impose conditionalities to its recipients, and does not seek profit for Brazil" (MRE, 2010: topic 7.1.1). As with many governmental statements, this one should be taken with a grain of salt. Technical cooperation agreements might not be sought as a source of *direct* profit, but it would be naive to think that this consideration is absent from the minds of foreign policymakers. Even if the government *genuinely* was not motivated to act because of these gains, the logic of 'gift giving' and reciprocity posit that commercial gains could very well be a consequence of the donor's actions. Simply put: unconditional and untied technical cooperation can (potentially) foster commercial gains.

The data gathered points to technical cooperation being neutral/positive in generating commercial gains for Brazilian companies. However, causal links between the provision of untied technical cooperation and direct commercial gains are very hard to assert – if at all possible. A concomitant increase in the volume of trade relations and the number of technical cooperation agreements signed between Brazil and country 'X' does not imply causation – a logical fallacy known as *cum hoc, ergo propter hoc* ('with this, therefore because of this'). It was almost a consensus among diplomats, civil servants, and academics interviewed that while there are clear overlaps between the cooperation and the trade agendas, one does not determine the other. A good example relates to South America. This is the region with which Brazil has the greatest number of technical cooperation agreements but the commercial relationship between Brazil and countries such as Argentina, Bolivia, and Venezuela, involves a myriad of variables, of which technical cooperation is only one. This tool is part of a bigger *set* of tools used to bring the countries closer in all aspects – including commercial relations. In the case of Brazil and South American recipients, commercial gains are much better explained by bilateral and multilateral trade agreements, such as MERCOSUL.

Still, a valid case can be made for how no-strings-attached technical cooperation agreements help create a welcoming environment and profit opportunities for Brazilian companies. These agreements serve as an indirect support towards a "strategy of *internationalization of domestic companies*" (Bernal-Meza, 2010:205; emphasis added). They are a tool, fostering diplomatic gains as a *means* to accrue commercial gains. A cooperation project can facilitate subsequent sales of goods and services connected to the knowledge shared – albeit independently from the initial project itself. This interpretation fits well with the analysis posited by Brazilian experts in the area. For former ABC director Ambassador Elim Saturnino Ferreira Dutra, [technical] cooperation "is a *powerful mechanism of pre-investment*. It does not presuppose immediate gains, in which case it would cease to be cooperation, but it can also be the seed for future gains" (*apud* Puente, 2010:329; emphasis added). The physical presence of Brazilian representatives abroad helps to open and strengthen communication channels, and this can lead the way to "new fronts [which are] independent from technical cooperation, [such as] political, economic, financial, and commercial relations between Brazil and partner countries" (IPEA, 2013:25–26). Even if Brazil detaches its provision of technical cooperation from commercial ties,

> it is natural that (...) after the end of a project, the recipient country will reach out to Brazilian companies as partners, as these will be more accustomed to the technologies transferred or because they produce the machines and resources necessary for production.
>
> (Barbosa, 2011a:86)

Technical cooperation serves not as the direct source but rather as a *facilitator* of commercial gains for both Brazilian private and public enterprises.

It is worth reaffirming that nothing from the field research demonstrated that private interests had a particular preference for the use (or not) of technical cooperation as a mechanism for increasing Brazil's bilateral relations or international image. From the interviews conducted and archival data obtained, no cases were found showing *direct* gains from technical cooperation for Brazilian companies. Still, there was much private and public interest (i.e., government owned companies) to improve Brazil's relations abroad and to ease and increase trade and investments. This is demonstrated in the many businesspeople that were frequently part of Brazil's delegations abroad, accompanying President Lula to developing countries. While they undoubtedly had commercial interests, all indications are that their focus was on the macro-scale relations, not on the use or benefits from technical cooperation *per se*. From interviews with academic scholars and diplomats, the overall sense was that in Brazil, companies were lobbying for the Brazilian government to be present and act as a facilitator in certain places, and the question of means – i.e., *how* should the government be supportive – was not their focus. There was also no indication of private companies' *direct* involvement in the planning or execution of technical cooperation agreements to generate short-term profits. Of course, this is different from saying there has been *no* involvement whatsoever. But the data did point to a scenario where it can be stated, with a great degree of confidence, that private involvement – if it did occur – was not the norm. All civil servants interviewed, operating directly with planning and execution of such agreements (from various federal institutions), were unanimous in asserting they had never personally experienced direct participation of private companies or pressure from their superiors to cater to private interests. An interviewee with over 10 years of experience at ABC, when asked if the private sector ever directly pressured for a particular technical cooperation agreement answered "No, no, absolutely no. Zero. The private sector, I'd say, *never approached us*".

There have been however a few cases of big Brazilian multinationals (e.g., Petrobrás, Camargo Corrêa) becoming involved in technical cooperation projects executed by the government. The involvement of these companies run the risk of being reduced to a simplistic narrative of 'direct private involvement in Brazil's technical cooperation equals direct profit seeking', which would be a shallow – and erroneous – analysis. While these companies' actions are ultimately driven by profit-seeking behaviour, it would be too much of a stretch to claim that their involvements with technical cooperation projects were motivated by wanting to accrue *direct* profits from the projects themselves. Drawing from some interviewees, it was easier to speculate the other way around: it was the Brazilian government, probably at high levels of power, who might have *instigated* company directors to help with implementing the projects due to the government's limited financial capability. Commercial interests are undeniably present in the country's foreign policy, and there is a conscious push to attain them. But in the Brazilian case, technical cooperation agreements appear to serve as a tool to *improve the odds* of profit, not as a direct source for them.

Thus, it is possible to state that unconditional and untied technical cooperation has generated neutral/positive gains for the country – both in the diplomatic and commercial fronts. Direct causal links in this case are hard to guarantee. There are many intervening variables and intangible elements which don't allow for a straightforward assessment. Nonetheless, a qualitative evaluation of proxy indicators provided was able to establish connections that can't be attributed to coincidence alone.

## Concluding remarks

Technical cooperation is a useful tool for promoting Brazil's foreign policy goals, one which the country has amassed a considerable degree of tradition and reputation (Barbosa, 2011a:87). The analysis revealed an undeniable element of self-interest in Brazil's actions. The Brazilian government certainly hopes to attain diplomatic and commercial gains from giving technical cooperation, mostly through an indirect process.

Two elements have contributed to differentiate Brazil from 'traditional' and other emerging donors. First, the content of the knowledge shared. Most of what was provided related to policies and experiences related to human development and the provision of 'global public goods', such as mitigating poverty and hunger; and affordable techniques and technologies suitable for developing countries (especially in the tropical zone). Second, unlike what is still the norm for most DAC donors and some 'emerging donors', such as China and India, Brazil's provision is unconditional and untied. Still, Brazil's case illustrates the difficulties of comparing DAC and non-DAC countries' provision of development assistance. This is of great impact for those interested in emerging donor's numbers, as each country uses their own unique definition. Another problem related to these donors – and clearly for Brazil – is the frequent lack of transparency, availability, and/or reliability of numbers to allow proper quantitative analyses. Qualitative assessments are also affected by these problems, but to a lesser degree, as different sets of data are more easily available (e.g., interviews, policy reports, speeches, and official documents).

This chapter showed that Brazil's first incursions as a 'donor' began decades ago. As already alluded to in previous chapters, this is something common to other Southern countries like China and India. In this matter, the word *emerging* should not be interpreted as a synonym for *novel*. What is in fact new is the degree of importance of providing 'international cooperation' – used here as a proxy for Brazil's development assistance – in the country's foreign policy since the mid-2000s. The country began to give *more* through various mechanisms, incorporating more themes and making more financial commitments. It also expanded the list of recipients from neighbouring countries to an increasingly global reach. President Lula was very involved in personally promoting this Brazilian 're-branding' as an emerging *power*, with visible attention to South-South partnerships and a concurrent 'developing country' self-identification.

President Rousseff had much less personal involvement in foreign policy than her predecessor. Not only did she appear to have less interest in being in the international 'limelight', her presidency had to deal with (and prioritize) pressing domestic issues. Nonetheless, the unconditional and untied characteristics of Brazil's technical cooperation remained untouched. The 'special' attention to the full Latin America and Caribbean region and African nations, as well as the high provision of knowledge in agricultural and health-related themes, was also largely unaffected by the change in presidency.

The recent history of Brazil as an 'emerging donor' reveals the importance of presidential diplomacy. The structure of language used in framing technical cooperation, the direction of partnerships, and volume of initiatives, have had an undeniable connection to the vision held by the Presidency. These characteristics – as well as proposed changes – were not a consequence of popular or Congressional demand, nor did they appear to have originated from outside of Executive control. Unlike what takes place in most traditional donors' politics, there is no indication that this topic is on the attention radar of the public, media, or private companies. Hence, the decision-making process is overwhelmingly situated not only in the governmental arena, but in mostly two places: the Presidency and the Ministry of Foreign Affairs.

The status quo since President Lula's tenure is one of unconditional and untied technical cooperation. President Rousseff gave faint signals of change, but nothing occurred. The Constitution 'anchors' the unconditional position while being somewhat neutral towards tied/untied; and the Ministry of Foreign Affairs has not revealed interested in keeping the unconditional and untied characters. Yet, such arrangement should not be taken as a static structure, as any presidential election could open a 'policy window' (Kingdon, 1984). There is the possibility of currently silent or vaguely interested actors in conditionalities or ties deciding to come forward with their interests and push for change, especially if a 'norm entrepreneur' emerges (Finnemore & Sikkink, 1998).

Finally, the desire to achieve certain 'positions' in the international system has influenced Brazilian foreign policymakers to opt for providing unconditional and untied technical cooperation agreements: they serve as a *relatively* simple and inexpensive way to help place the country as a global actor; unconditionality reinforces its status as a Southern donor, whilst unconditionality *and* the absence of commercial ties differentiates it from 'traditional' DAC donors and other emerging donors such as China and India. Also, sharing knowledge serves to increase the country's power and status as a 'leader' by investing in a diplomatic niche: Brazil's legitimacy to speak on human/social development (or at least *framed* as being related). The expectation is that strong relationships and a good image can be translated, at some point, into concrete diplomatic and commercial gains.

## Notes

1 The sole hint of Brazil as an aid provider during the 1950s and 1960s was the concession of academic scholarships for foreigners wanting to study in Brazil.
2 This was especially the case with newly independent Lusophone nations, which increasingly requested assistance from Brazil (Leite, 2011:149).
3 UNDP documents: BRA/86/001, BRA/87/041 and BRA/87/032.
4 Source: World Bank's online statistical database.
5 Source: IMF's online World Economic Outlook database.

6 The phrase is attributed to Prof Calestous Juma, and was quickly incorporated in Brazilian discourse. It is worth mentioning his initial full thought, which dilutes the weight of Brazil's 'uniqueness': "China is not the only new player in Africa. For almost every African problem there is a Brazilian solution. *The same can be said about India.*" (available at www.economist.com/debate/days/view/469). He would repeat the Brazil-portion of the phrase many times after that (yet omitting the India).

7 Derived from numbers available in *Brazil* (2011).

8 The source requested anonymity, as well as to not reveal which countries had *privately* supported Brazil. Therefore, countries herein mentioned were those whose support was made public.

## Bibliography

ABC – Agência Brasileira de Cooperação. (undated). *Orientação Básica para a Apresentação de Projetos de Cooperação Técnica entre Países em Desenvolvimento – CTPD.* www.abc.gov.br/Content/ABC/docs/PORTFORM-2002.doc

Almeida, P. R. (2003). A Política Internacional do Partido dos Trabalhadores: da Fundação à Diplomacia do Governo Lula. *Revista de Sociologia Política, 20*(junho), 87–102.

Almeida, P. R. (2004). Uma política externa engajada: A diplomacia do governo Lula. *Revista Brasileira de Política Internacional, 47*(1), 162–184.

Amorim, C. (2006, June). A cooperação como instrumento da política externa brasileira. *Boletim ViaABC, June*, 16.

Amorim, C. (2009). O Brasil e os Direitos Humanos: em busca de uma agenda positiva. *Política Externa, 18*(2), 67–75.

Amorim, C. (2010). Brazilian Foreign Policy under President Lula (2003–2010): An overview. *Revista Brasileira de Política Internacional, 53*(special edition), 214–240.

Barbosa, P. H. (2011a). *O Brasil e a EMBRAPA: o viés instrumental da cooperação técnica horizontal.* Brasília: Instituto Rio Branco.

Barbosa, R. A. (2011b). Política externa de dois governos. Presented at Fundação Getulio Vargas' *8º Fórum de Economia da Fundação Getulio Vargas.* São Paulo, 2011, September 27.

Barnabé, I. R. (2010). O Itamaraty e a Diplomacia Presidencial nos governos FHC e Lula. *Revista de Estudos Internacionais, 1*(2), 29–45.

Bernal-Meza, R. (2010). International thought in the Lula Era, *Revista Brasileira de Política Internacional, 53*(special edition), 193–213.

Bobiash, D. (1992). *South–South aid – How developing countries help each other.* New York, NY: St. Martin's Press.

Brazil. (2011). *Relatório de visitas internacionais do Presidente Luiz Inácio Lula da Silva e de visitas ao Brasil de Chefes de Estado e de Chefes de Governo entre janeiro de 2003 e dezembro de 2010.* Brasília: Ministério das Relações Exteriores.

Burges, S. (2008). Consensual hegemony: Theorizing Brazilian Foreign Policy after the cold war, *International Relations, 22*(1), 65–84.

Cason, J. W., & Power, T. J. (2009). Presidentialization, pluralization, and the rollback of itamaraty: Explaining change in Brazilian Foreign Policy making in the Cardoso–Lula era, *International Political Science Review, 30*(2), 117–140.

Cervo, A. L. (1994). Socializando o desenvolvimento – uma história da cooperação técnica internacional do Brasil, *Revista Brasileira de Política Internacional, 37*(1), 37–63.

Cheibub, Z. (1985). Diplomacia e construção institucional: o Itamaraty em uma perspectiva histórica. *Dados*, *28*(1), 113–131.

Conde, C. (1990). *Cooperação Técnica Internacional: uma opção de intermediação nas relações internacionais.* M.A. thesis. University of Brasília.

Corrêa, M. L. (2010). *Prática Comentada da Cooperação Internacional – Entre a hegemonia e a busca da autonomia.* Brasília: Edição do Autor.

Costa, A.C. (2011, June 25). Um petista a caminho da FAO. *Veja.* http://veja.abril.com.br/noticia/economia/um-petista-a-caminho-da-fao

D'Araujo, M. C., & Castro, C., Eds. (1997). *Ernesto Geisel.* Rio de Janeiro: Fundação Getúlio Vargas.

Danese, S. F. (1999). *Diplomacia presidencial: História e crítica.* São Paulo: Topbooks.

Dauvergne, P., & Farias, D. B. L. (2012). The rise of Brazil as a global development power. *Third World Quarterly*, *33*(5), 903–917.

De Souza, A. (2009). *A Agenda Internacional do Brasil: A política externa brasileira de FHC a Lula.* Rio de Janeiro: Elsevier/CEBRI.

FAO – Food and Agriculture Organization. (2012, February 21). Brazil to fund food purchasing in five African countries. www.fao.org/news/story/en/item/123551/icode/

FAO – Food and Agriculture Organization. (2013, August 28). FAO-EMBRAPA partnership gets under way. www.fao.org/about/who-we-are/director-gen/faodg-news-archive/detail/en/c/195690/

FAO – Food and Agriculture Organization. (2014, January 24). Angola, Brazil and FAO sign South-South Cooperation agreement. www.fao.org/news/story/en/item/212887/icode/

Finnemore, M., & Sikkink, K. (1998). International norm dynamics and political change. *International Organization*, *52*(4), 887–917.

Flemming, T. (2011, July 10). Elections done right: The FAO. http://globalmemo.org/2011/07/10/fao-election-the-real-thing/

*Folha de São Paulo.* (2004, May 27). "Sou o único líder que passou fome".

FUNCEX – Fundação Centro de Estudos do Comercio Exterior. (1985). *Estudo do Sistema interministerial de cooperação tecnica.* Rio de Janeiro: FUNCEX.

Goldstein, J., & Keohane, R. (1993). Ideas and foreign policy. In Goldstein, J., & Keohane, R. O. (Eds.), *Ideas and foreign policy: Beliefs, institutions, and political change.* Ithaca, NY: Cornell University Press.

Hochstetler, K. (2013, December 11). The Changing Face of Brazil as an International Donor – From Lula to Dilma Rousseff. *CIGI.* www.cigionline.org.

Inoue, C. Y. A., & Vaz, A. C. (2013). Brazil as 'Southern donor': Beyond hierarchy and national interests in development cooperation? *Cambridge Review of International Affairs*, *25*(4), 507–534.

IPEA – Instituto de Pesquisa Econômica Aplicada. (2013). *Cooperação brasileira para o desenvolvimento internacional: 2010.* Brasília: Instituto de Pesquisa Econômica Aplicada, Agência Brasileira de Cooperação.

Kingdon, J. W. (1984). *Agendas, alternatives, and public policies.* Ann Arbor: University of Michigan Press.

Lampreia, L. F., & Cruz, Jr, A. S. (2005). Brazil: coping with structural constraints. In M. A. East & J. Robertson (Eds.). *Diplomacy and developing nations: Post–cold war foreign policy-making structures and processes* (pp. 97–113). New York: Routledge.

Leite, P. S. (2011). O Brasil e a Cooperação Sul–Sul em três momentos de política externa: os governos Jânio Quadros/João Goulart, Ernesto Geisel e Luiz Inácio Lula da Silva. Brasília: FUNAG.

Lessa, A. C. (2010). Brazil's strategic partnerships: An assessment of the Lula era (2003–2010), *Revista Brasileira de Política Internacional, 53*(special edition), 115–131.

Lessa, A. C., Couto, L. F., & Farias, R. S. (2009). Política externa planejada: os planos plurianuais e a ação internacional do Brasil, de Cardoso a Lula (1995–2008), *Revista Brasileira de Política Internacional, 52*(1), 89–109.

MRE – Ministério das Relações Exteriores. (2010). *Balanço de Política Externa 2003/2010*, 3.2.11: Temas Multilaterais Energias Renováveis. www.itamaraty.gov.br/temas/balanco-de-politica-externa-2003-2010/3.2.11-temas-multilaterais-energias-renovaveis.

MRE – Ministério das Relações Exteriores. (undated). Cooperação Técnica. www.itamaraty.gov.br/temas/cooperacao-tecnica.

Nascimento, T. M. C. (1997). *Comentários à Constituição Federal: Princípios fundamentais.* Porto Alegre: Livraria do Advogado.

Oliveira. A. J., & Onuki, J. (2010). Eleições, partidos políticos e política externa no Brasil. *Revista Política Hoje, 19*(1), 144–185.

Oxfam International. (2011, June 24). Election of new Director General must signal new era for FAO. www.oxfam.org/en/grow/pressroom/pressrelease/2011-06-24/election-new-director-general-must-signal-new-era-fao#sthash.Em8vOnkm.dpuf

Power, T. J. (2010). Brazilian democracy as a late bloomer: Reevaluating the regime in the Cardoso-Lula era. *Latin American Research Review, 45*(4), 218–247.

Puente, C. A. I. (2010). *A cooperação técnica horizontal brasileira como instrumento de política externa: A evolição da cooperação técnica com países em desenvolvimento* – CTPD– no período 1995–2005, Brasília: FUNAG.

Rowlands, D. (2008). *Emerging donors in international development assistance: A synthesis report.* International Development Research Center (IDRC) – Canada, http://publicwebsite.idrc.ca/EN/Documents/12447280141Synthesys_Report.pdf

Seitenfus, R. (2006). Elementos para uma diplomacia solidária: a crise haitiana e os desafios da ordem internacional contemporânea. *Carta Internacional, 1*(1), 5–12.

Siqueira, A., & Aggege, S. (2011, July 01). A revolução "duplamente verde" de José Graziano, *Carta Capital.* www.cartacapital.com.br/politica/a-revolucao-duplamente-verde-de-jose-graziano

Soares de Lima, M. R. (2000). Instituições democráticas e política exterior. *Contexto Internacional, 22*(2), 265–304.

Soares de Lima, M. R. (2005). A política externa brasileira e os desafios da cooperação Sul–Sul, *Revista Brasileira de Política Internacional, 48*(1), 24–59.

Soares de Lima, M. R., & Hirst, M. (2006). Brazil as an intermediate state and regional power: Action, choice and responsibilities, *International Affairs, 82*(I), 21–40.

Spektor, M. (2004). Origens e direção do Pragmatismo Ecumênico e Responsável (1974–1979). *Revista Brasileira de Política Internacional, 47*(2), 191–222.

Thomas, C. (2001). Global governance, development and humans security: exploring the links. *Third World Quarterly, 22*(2), 159–175.

Tran, M. (2011, June 07). FAO's new leader lays out his plans. *The Guardian.* www.theguardian.com/global-development/2011/jun/27/fao-director-jose-graziano-da-silva

UN – United Nations. (2004, December 02). *A more secure world: Our shared responsibility report of the high-level panel on threats*, Challenges and Change. UN Doc.A/59/565.

UN – United Nations. (2005, March 21). *In larger freedom: Towards development, security and human rights for all* – Report of the Secretary-General, UN Doc. A/59/200.

UN-GA – United Nations General Assembly. (2009, October 27). *Promotion of South–South Cooperation for development: A thirty-year perspective* – Report of the Secretary-General, A/64/504.

UN-SC – United Nations Security Council. (2011, February 02). Letter dated 2 February 2011 from the Permanent Representative of Brazil to the United Nations addressed to the Secretary-General. Doc. S/2011/50.

Valler Filho, W. (2007). *O Brasil e a crise haitiana: a cooperação técnica como instrumento de solidariedade e de ação diplomática*. Brasília: FUNAG.

# 7 Technical cooperation as a foreign policy tool

## Some lessons

This book explored the connections between foreign policy and the provision of development assistance. It focused on a specific mechanism of development assistance: technical cooperation, i.e., essentially the transfer of knowledge from one State to another. But instead of reflecting only upon the broad question of why would a country provide technical cooperation, the research aimed at an even more intriguing question: why would a country give knowledge to another country without demanding anything in return?

The starting point for answering the question of why countries provide technical cooperation was to assume States' foreign policies are driven by self-interest: they want to ultimately gain something from the initiative. The analysis assumed all donors would like to accrue commercial and diplomatic gains from their provision of technical cooperation. However, a donor's decision over whether to place conditionalities and ties (or not) has consequences that affect the odds for attaining commercial and/or diplomatic gains. Each choice of arrangement – with/without conditions, with/without ties – increases the odds to accrue one type of gain while simultaneously lowering the chances of obtaining the other. Donors might seek both gains but ultimately, they can only prioritize one, prompting reflections on what drives donors to choose to emphasize one over the other. Giving knowledge without conditionalities or ties is expected to increase the donor's odds to obtain diplomatic gains, while being a weak path for securing commercial gains. But answering why a country would choose this specific structure cannot be simply 'self-interest', since it would lead to a tautology: a country prioritizes diplomatic gains because it prioritizes diplomatic gains.

### IR theories on development assistance and the Brazilian case

The Realist approach brings strong explanatory power to Brazil's reasoning over specific choices in providing development assistance. Practically all interviewees interpreted Brazil's no-strings-attached technical cooperation agreements as instruments of soft power, given under the expectation of generating positive externalities. There is little doubt over Brazil's self-interest in providing development assistance. As bluntly stated by one senior diplomat, Brazil's technical cooperation "served to influence people and achieve goals". Giving no-strings-attached technical cooperation serves Brazil's self-interests in various ways: better relationships with recipients; expectation for more support in International Organizations; improved legitimacy and authority to speak in behalf of developing countries in certain areas, etc.

Nonetheless, the Realist approach fails to explain one key element. Assuming every country's 'national interest' involves seeking *both* commercial *and* diplomatic gains, what explains a country's choice to prioritize one over the other? In other words: why would Brazil *prioritize* diplomatic gains (through unconditional and untied agreements) if securing commercial gains is also in its interest? At the same time, why have other countries prioritized commercial gains (by conditioning and tying their agreements) if they also want diplomatic gains? To say that a country wants one thing more 'because it wants one thing more' is not an explanation. The Realist reasoning is also weak in explaining why Brazil did not take advantage of the opportunity to condition or tie its help when it *could*. Still, despite these flaws the general point that Realism makes in highlighting 'national interest' and the quest to gain 'power' as motivators for providing development assistance provide a theoretical framework for understanding the broad contours of Brazil's embrace of no-strings-attached technical cooperation.

At the same time, Brazil's decision to seek a 'non-predatory' approach to its development assistance can be partially explained through a Structuralist/Dependency theory lens: the country's foreign policy – especially under President Lula – embraced the perception of a world divided between the *powerful* and the *powerless*, actively pushing for a multipolar system and more representation for the voice of the marginalized. Brazil's South-South engagements were strongly articulated around horizontality and respect for the recipient's sovereignty. Most of its technical cooperation actions focus on human development, particularly sharing ingenious solutions for mitigating poverty and its nefarious consequences (hunger, diseases, lack of education, maternal deaths, etc.). Structuralist/Dependency Theory is also instrumental for tracing the origins of the South-South discourse. The worldviews and principled beliefs under this banner continue to be shared by most emerging donors in how they tend to frame their provisions of development assistance. Hence, this approach will be useful mainly for understanding the ideas and concepts that feed Brazil's foreign policy in general, and particularly development assistance.

However, closer scrutiny reveals important weaknesses. First, it is increasingly difficult to see a country like Brazil – or China and India, for that matter – as being part of the international system's 'periphery'. The level of power these countries have now and are projected to have in the next decades seriously defies their position as 'victims of the capitalist system'. Quite the contrary: they are *active* (capitalist) *players*. Even if their undeniable 'developing country' problems are considered – high levels of absolute poverty, income inequality, corruption, etc. – they are still "monster countries" (Kennan, 1993). Claiming to be the 'first' among equals, or *primus inter pares*, does not guarantee horizontal South-South relationships, particularly in cases of significant power asymmetry between the 'rich developing donor' and the recipient nation.

Still, embracing the Southern and developing *identities* matters. Brazil, China, and India are very vocal in identifying themselves under these two interconnected categories. These three countries all speak of a world that continues to be divided between North/developed and South/developing countries ('us-versus-them'), and do not impose conditionalities onto its development assistance projects. Nonetheless, when it comes to attaching commercial *ties* to their initiatives, China and India differ from Brazil significantly: while they place ties, Brazil does not. Simply put: categories are increasingly inadequate (who is in the 'core'/'periphery' nowadays, and where to emerging donors fit in this division?); main causal link is weak (i.e., is capitalism still the key driver?); and variation among emerging donors cannot be properly explained. Just because a country says it identifies itself as 'South' does not necessarily lead to a no-string-strings attached approach – just as a country *not* identifying as 'South' does not automatically imply conditionalities or ties. There is no direct causal link between a 'Southern identity' and commercial attachments made to development assistance projects.

The Idealist/Liberal framework could help explain one aspect of Brazil's provision of 'global public goods' with no conditions or ties. If the knowledge Brazil has is valuable for reducing poverty and mitigating human suffering, then sharing it through technical cooperation with no-strings-attached seems very reasonable from a moral/ethical perspective. After all, unlike private goods which hold no/little expectation of being freely shared among competitors, global public goods do not have exclusive owners, are seldom zero-sum in consumption, and can rarely be denied those who decide not to contribute to the supply of the goods themselves (Albin, 2003:367).

But while this line of reasoning can be used to explain Brazil's actions towards transferring its knowledge towards family agriculture, combating AIDS, deforestation, or hunger, it does not serve as a good framework to understand why the country chooses to transfer knowledge over such a clearly *commercial* issue. Another point this logic does not grasp properly is that almost all donors (including Brazil, China, and India) don't seem to provide development assistance based primarily on the recipients' *need* for development, but upon more strategic calculations. A close look at Brazil's bilateral partnerships, for example, reveal that factors such as geographic proximity, historical ties, and economic engagement matter (Bermeo, 2010:1). If the goal was to primarily assist in human development, the prioritized partnerships would be with Least Developed Countries (LDCs) – which is not the case.

The issue now becomes how to make sense of these partial explanations. The argument that a donor such as Brazil seeks self-interested gains ('power') in its international development actions is based upon a Realist analysis of why countries are donors. In (apparent) contrast, its choice of sharing knowledge without conditionalities or ties is very close to Idealists' point: countries can (and do) help people in other countries by *giving* (no-strings-attached), and cooperate towards win-win results. Adding to these accounts, Structuralists' conception of a world divided between developed/developing countries – and its impact on how development assistance is given – is very much part of Brazil's diplomatic discourse and practice. Nonetheless, each one of these approaches has issues in their explanatory power which can't be ignored.

Realism, Structuralism, and Idealism/Liberalism all introduce valid elements that (partially) explain Brazil's choices in international development. A fruitful way to connect the strengths and weaknesses from each of these theories is to bring in a constructivist 'lens'. As stated, Realism provides a strong explanatory power as to what guides countries' choices in how to provide development assistance: they are (usually) motivated by self-gain. The focus on the State, its calculations over national interest, and a recognition that (potential) donors are materially constrained places the analysis under a Realist framework. This research abides by the assertions that foreign aid is "first and foremost a technique of statecraft" (Baldwin, 1966:3), which "may productively be viewed as a microcosm of nation-states' broader efforts in foreign affairs" (Hook, 1995:34). Nonetheless, this still leaves open the question of what prompts countries to have *different* self-interests. As said by Wendt, "[Th]e distribution of power matters, but *how* it matters, the *meaning* it has for the actors, depends on what game they are playing" (Wendt, 1999:107).

To understand Brazil's choices, Structuralism and Idealism/Liberalism can be incorporated to the analysis (even if with less weight), since many of their *concepts* feed Brazil's identity and discourse regarding development assistance. But the main thrust of explanation for *all* countries' choices over how to provide development assistance and technical cooperation (with/without conditionalities or ties) occurs when Realism – particularly Classical and Neoclassical Realism[1] – is combined with constructivism. A Realist-Constructivist framework also allows important elements of both the Structuralist and Idealist/Liberal explanations to be taken in. The result is a theoretically sound account, not a forced or implausible patchwork of IR theories. The Structuralist vision of the world – divided in core/periphery, North/South, and developed/developing – can be incorporated under the *ideas* that inform Brazil's foreign policy, the vision of where it sits in the world, and what it perceives to gain from embracing this world vision in its discourse.

The choice of approaching this through a 'developing country' *identity* matters for its strategy of gaining power in the international system. This fits well with Schirm's (2012) evidence that emerging powers' leadership crucially depends on followership, as the inclusion of interest and/or ideas dominant *in the other country* (in this case, the recipient) into "an emerging power's leadership project is a necessary condition for this other country to accept the policy positions, shift in power and/or status desired by the emerging power and to follow its lead" (Schirm, 2012:213). This approach helps better grasp Brazil's foreign policy, one which "highlights how a State with limited military and economic power capabilities might attempt to leverage its idea-generating capacity to construct a vision of the regional system and quietly obtain the active acquiescence of other regional states to a hegemonic project" (Burges, 2008:65).

In thinking about why countries provide development assistance (such as technical cooperation), the research has shown that a dichotomy positing selfish *vs.* altruistic goals – often seen in the literature – is misleading. While it is true that development assistance has been frequently provided as a 'benevolent' disguise for dark intentions and with very little (if any) concern over detriments which the recipient might incur, this win-lose situation should not be taken as the rule. Donors can very well be motivated by a win-win structure, where the donor does not gain *from* the recipient but *with* or *through* the recipient. Thus, a donor can actively seek power based upon the recipient's development or 'success' to improve the bilateral relationship or the donor's image with other countries.

From a perspective of IR theory, the research provides yet another empirical validation to the theoretical argument that Realist theory (particularly Classical and Neoclassical Realism) is compatible with a constructivist approach. States are motivated by self-interest in their provision of development assistance, but each one has a specific understanding of what this *is* and *how* it should be pursed in practice. Social constructions such as values, institutions, and reputations are key elements in shaping decision-making processes regarding foreign policy, and the choices made regarding foreign policy resources, strategies, and tools. So, even if Waltz was correct in saying that "pride knows no nationality" (Waltz, 1993:66), countries can have very different interpretations of what they are (or wish to be) *proud of.*

Other IR theories should not be overlooked in their ability to explain at least some aspects of giving with no-strings-attached. The Idealist/Liberal framework highlights how power can be sought cooperatively, and how donors can be committed to issues of 'global public goods' in their actions (as opposed to only in words). The existing discourse of 'us-and-them' and North *vs.* South, expected by Structuralists, provides another piece to the puzzle. The combination of these elements from various IR theoretical backgrounds serves as an example of how 'analytic eclecticism' is a valuable strategy to link abstract concepts to better understanding complex 'real-life' decision making.

Still in the debate over how power is created, exerted, and increased, the decision to provide technical cooperation without conditionalities or ties expands the studies of various power-related concepts, particularly: 'soft power'; 'middle power'; 'middle power diplomacy'; 'niche diplomacy'; and the power of 'gift-giving'. Despite the difficulties involving their conceptual boundaries, both 'soft powers' and 'middle powers' have been helpful to understand and analyse certain behavioural elements of Brazil's foreign policy decision-making process. However, the research reiterates concerns over the use of two concepts given the contested nature of what they mean (or *should* mean). Brazil's choices certainly appear to be driven by a desire for soft power and its (possible) position as a middle power, yet other countries which also seek soft power and could easily be classified as middle powers have *not* chosen to give unconditional and untied technical cooperation. 'Middle power *diplomacy*' was found to be a relatively more manageable concept, and together with its strategy of 'niche diplomacy', they provided strong explanatory power, including helping to visualize a logic (curiously) connecting development assistance choices made by Brazil and Norway. Finally, the empirical case reiterates the importance of understanding the unwritten mechanisms at the base of reciprocity. Unless a gift is given in anonymity, the giver and the recipient are connected to the social dynamics of retribution, which can lead a variety of feelings such as gratitude and admiration, but also inferiority or resentment.

## Drivers of foreign policy variations: technical cooperation

To understand the variation in the use of development assistance (and technical cooperation) as a foreign policy tool, it is necessary to embrace the foreign policy decision-making as a process which incorporates both domestic and international elements. Three forces were deemed key in impacting Brazil's decision to provide unconditional and untied technical cooperation: ideational, institutional, and 'positional'. While each one by itself did not determine the outcome, the combination of these three vectors provides a solid reasoning for why diplomatic gains were prioritized over commercial gains. This same framework of analysis might be useful to understand variations in countries engaged in development assistance.

Ideational forces highlight the understanding that ideas matter for foreign policymaking. Following a constructivist approach, to understand each country's path towards achieving and maximizing self-interest one must acknowledge the social construction of identities and interests. Principled beliefs specify the criteria for distinguishing right from wrong, just from unjust. Hence, a donor's preference bears a strong connection to norms held by its foreign policymakers. Conditionalities or ties will be more likely to be placed if they are interpreted in a positive ('the-right-thing-to-do') or neutral light (i.e., 'the-normal-thing-to-do'). But because different actors (people, institutions, and communities) can have different viewpoints, and fight over which one will be dominant, ideas and beliefs alone might not necessarily determine policymakers' decisions. It also matters *whose* ideas and beliefs prevail. Therefore, it is important to consider a country's institutional structure for foreign policymaking.

Regarding foreign policy, government-based actors are typically the Head of the Executive government and its high-level Cabinet, especially those in charge of Foreign Affairs, Trade, and Defence (or its equivalents). It is possible to speculate that the propensity for development assistance to serve as an instrument of commercial gains seems to be higher when the control of development assistance is located inside or close to government institutions focused on trade and commerce, or private interests have strong access to policymakers in charge of development assistance. Conversely, if development assistance programmes are designed by bureaucracies insulated from trade interests, the greater the chance the final product will be untied.

Legal elements were also shown to matter in the context of institutional influences over foreign policymaking. A country's legal framework can have direct impact upon foreign policy decision-making through various ways: (1) it can limit options for policy engagement by setting legal constraints towards certain actions; (2) it makes change more onerous, as either the law has to change or the (illegal) action has to be made covert; and (3) it might determine who are the necessary actors for decision-making. For example, if a country's law determines that foreign policy must be guided by the principle of unconditionality, the option for conditional development assistance projects is severely curtailed. It would take another legal directive of equal or higher status to challenge the existing one, or a new (and valid) interpretation. Ultimately, laws can be changed, but overcoming the status quo is usually a laborious and time-consuming process. Unless a strong actor (or a collection of actors) actively pushes for change, the tendency is for the legal rules to remain setting boundaries to the institutional setting.

'Positional forces' was the final element to be observed: where do policymakers see their country 'positioned' in the international system? Where would they like to see their country 'positioned' in the future? If one of the main venues for country to gain power in the international system is taken as coming primarily from within cooperative structures – such as international organizations and regional groupings – the likelihood for prioritizing diplomatic gains increases. As previously stated, the concept of 'middle power diplomacy' is useful: it highlights countries who tend to favour multilateral approaches and concentrate their initiatives in areas that are believed to yield greater return, i.e., 'niche diplomacy'. 'Positional' forces also interact with issues of identity. If a country's strategy to gain prominence in the international or regional system relies on it being perceived as a legitimate voice in a specific matter or of leadership among a group, its foreign policy choices are likely to reflect this desire. For example, a country that chooses to gain power in the system as a provider of SSC must be aware its actions will be judged by recipients, i.e., does it 'walk the walk'? The higher the degree of hypocrisy perceived by these recipients, the lower the chances for the provider to accrue diplomatic gains through 'soft' power.

### *Variations in technical cooperation among emerging donors*

This analysis has theoretically and empirically demonstrated what should be a rather obvious point: it cannot be assumed that all 'emerging' donors seek the same gains from development assistance or technical cooperation agreements. Even if Brazil, China, India, and South Africa act according to their own self-interests and want more power, this does not mean they will pursue the same strategies.

In the case of emerging donors, the tradition of equating conditionalities to (unwelcomed) interference has been combined with the choice of reaffirming their position as still developing/'Southern' countries. These two drivers are strong reasons for not just Brazil's, but China, India, and South Africa's decision to provide unconditional technical assistance. As for institutional forces, it seems there are very few domestic actors inside these emerging donors demanding changes in the unconditional character; the exception being some concern brought up in Brazil and South Africa over the ethical nature of unconditional interaction with recipients known to be severe human rights abusers. In the Brazilian case, because its *Constitution* explicitly states that non-interference is a fundamental principle of the country's international relations, this 'locks-in' unconditionality and makes any change towards conditionality unlikely.

As for untied technical cooperation, the ideas and principles attached to SSC hinted some explanatory power, but a closer inspection revealed an obvious weakness: China and India both abide to SSC but do not refrain from placing commercial ties to their provision of technical cooperation. Their interpretation of 'mutual gains' is one which opens the door for commercial profit for the donor without breaching SSC principles. At the same time, just like Brazil, China and India also desire to undeniably position themselves as 'developing' countries. So, unless China and India are exceptions to a general rule, the provision of untied technical cooperation is not a necessary element for an emerging donor who seeks to reaffirm its 'Southern' identity. In tandem, other explanations for Brazil's untied approach are weakened when compared to China and India, as all these nations explicitly seek more power in international organizations, a universal presence, 'Southern' credibility, etc.

It is possible then that the variance in these countries' approach towards commercial ties is related to two points in particular. First, institutional/bureaucratic foreign policy arrangements where commercial and trade interests are closely connected to the formulation of development assistance are more likely to result in tied assistance. Conversely, if the domestic internal arrangement 'shields' development assistance from direct commercial forces (e.g., Ministry of Trade or equivalent, lobby groups, for-profit interests in general), there is a greater likelihood that agreements will be untied. The claim is not that the bureaucratic setting determines the presence or absence of commercial ties, but rather that it increases the odds for the provision of tied or untied assistance.

The second point is related to 'niche diplomacy'. Countries with (relatively) limited capacity for international engagement are assumed to be more likely to devote their attention to specific areas (niches) in which they can stand out. Attempting to reduce power asymmetries in negotiations and providing untied knowledge on global public goods seem like an adequate strategy for donors wishing to be seen not simply as 'development-assistance-donors' but as donors whose reputation is of committed to recipients' development. This logic can be a possible explanation for the apparently odd overlap between Brazil and Norway, briefly mentioned in Chapter 3. Both countries appear to be deeply invested in building a reputation of 'good' donors whose (primary) interest is not direct commercial gain – something which can only be achieved if there are no commercial ties to the assistance given.

Still, it is easy to make a case that recipients are more likely to perceive hypocrisy in the 'mutual benefits' justification if the donor – even if it is another developing country – is clearly more powerful (in relative terms). If a donor believes that its image and reputation as a trustworthy partner with the recipient – i.e., being a 'good international citizenship' – is more valuable than immediate commercial gains, the propensity to propose untied agreements will increase. Thus, while the 'middle power' label is difficult to work regarding behavioural expectations, the concept of 'middle power diplomacy' and its strategy of 'niche diplomacy' are better suited for the task. A country which wishes to promote a specific image of expertise and leadership in an area has more incentives to give its knowledge than to seek immediate profits from it.

## Implications and looking ahead

This research has shown that more attention needs to be given to technical cooperation in the context of development assistance. Because of its relative accessibility, technical cooperation is a foreign policy mechanism used in a much larger scale than it might appear to be. Few countries can give grants, loans, or forgive international debts, but almost *all* countries in the world have some knowledge to share. This scenario contributes to the growing literature that challenges the division of the world between donors and recipients, and reinforces the need to investigate the development assistance strategies of countries with (relatively) narrow foreign policy resources.

The analysis of technical cooperation agreements needs to be attentive to volume and time: while one single agreement is likely to produce very little immediate significance, a collection of agreements in a mid/long timeframe is certainly capable of producing meaningful impacts. This latter point is of great relevance for those interested in studies of how power can be established/increased (1) based upon knowledge and (2) through network dynamics. These findings also raise important questions about how countries might have different timeframes for their foreign policy strategies, thus feeling more at ease with the prospects of forfeiting immediate (but 'limited') gains and hedging their bets for reaping more significant gains down the road.

This book adds to the studies of SSC and 'emerging donors'. While there has been a visible surge in 'Northern' academic publications on these themes, the research done stands by Mawdsley's (2012) assessments the there is a need for more specific country based studies and that South-South development cooperation remains under-theorized and analysed (Mawdsley, 2012:257–261). One detail should be added: there *is* a significant level of analysis, awareness, and discussions of SSC and the foreign policies of most 'emerging' countries which is available in non-English-based academic publications from 'Southern' countries. This is clearly the case for Brazil, where the vast material, many times available only in Portuguese, has significant 'local' impact but due to the language barrier, sits outside of 'mainstream' academic literature.

SSC has a long and rich history, and the clear majority of non-DAC donors have embraced its discourse. The research reinforces the assertion that 'Southern' donors don't all act alike, even if they all follow the same broad principles. As the comparison of Brazil, China, India, and South Africa demonstrated, not only do some SSC principles (such as 'mutual benefit') have different meanings for different countries, but the same country might have had varied interpretations over time of what abiding to the SSC framework should mean in practice. This point provides yet another case for those highlighting the risks of reifying 'South' as a homogeneous category of analysis, such as Hochstetler's parallel finding that "recent patterns of South-South trade provide ample documentation for the unsurprising conclusion that *there is no single 'South' in recent global economic developments*" (Hochstetler, 2013:44; emphasis added). The findings therefore embrace authors who identify similarities among emerging donors, but also cautions against the risk of overlooking crucial differences among these countries' strategies. This dual dynamic was captured by Mawdsley's (2012:262) assertion that there are common aspects to 'Southern' donors' discursive positioning of development cooperation, even if these countries "are not unitary or uniform, but complex, contingent and sometimes contradictory assemblages of different actors, institutions and interests, engaged in dynamic and differentiated relationships with their different partners". For example, there is no reason to challenge Woods' (2008:1205) understanding that common to emerging donors "is a quest for energy security, enlarged trading opportunities and new economic partnerships, coupled with rapidly growing strength and size in the global economy". Yet, many countries fit this profile while approaching the provision of development assistance from different angles. Hurrell (2006) correctly highlighted the similarities in discourse and global interests of Brazil and India; but as the present research has shown, the countries approach their development assistance strategies in different ways.[2] Thus, the present research builds upon previous academic findings on similarities among 'emerging' donors to push towards uncovering their differences ('what') and the explanations for these differences ('why').

The comparisons of various countries' approaches to the provision of technical cooperation yielded many relevant findings, the next four in particular. First, as repeatedly stated, development assistance 'frameworks' (DAC *vs.* SSC) are very strong predictors for a country's propensity towards placing conditionalities or not, while being weak regarding decisions to attach commercial ties to agreements or not. Second, about their choice to frequently provide technical cooperation agreements with commercial ties, China and India appear to have more in common with most 'traditional' donors than with Brazil or South Africa. Third, because non-DAC donors each have their own understanding of what is accounted for as 'provision of development assistance', direct comparisons between DAC and non-DAC donors (as well as *between* non-DAC donors) are deeply problematic, and therefore should be either avoided or done only for categories with clearly similar methodological definitions (in many cases, a challenging process in itself). Fourth, there appears to be no link between the donor's democratic 'status' or ideological orientation and its decision to tie the assistance it provides.

This analysis has also shown that just as traditional donors, 'emerging' donors are also motivated by self-interest. The notion that the latter are moved mainly by an 'altruistic Southern solidarity' seems to be more of a myth (based on ideology) than a reality (based on actions). At the same time, this does not mean an element of camaraderie based on shared problems can't exist or be promoted among developing countries. In this case, such a feeling could very well drive agreements to reflect *both* the donor and recipient's self-interests. Power asymmetries among developing countries exist and are undeniable in many cases. Nonetheless, the study has shown there is some room for donors to (attempt to) mitigate the recipients' perceptions of power asymmetries through unconditional and untied agreements. The description of Brazil's image in Africa (written by a South African academic), just the year before the FAO election, is worth quoting:

> Brazil is building its interests on this very foundation by increasing development aid and technical cooperation alongside an array of strategic investments – all the while improving its image in Africa. This positive image or 'soft power' has become an important component of Brazil's Africa policy. (…) Brazilian leaders are very popular and regularly invited guests. (…) Brazil's nuanced approach to Africa is different to the former colonial masters and new players like China. There is a greater sense of mutual partnership and reciprocity in the relationship, which is not always the case with other established and emerging powers in Africa. This could be a defining trait of Brazil as a global emerging power and active player on the African continent, which will earn it much-needed support from the developing South.
>
> (White, 2010:239)

The empirical analysis of Brazil's provision of technical cooperation provides an opportunity to expand the existing literature on this country's foreign policy, whether by offering novel data and ideas or comparing the present findings with other authors' previous material. For example, the material found seems to corroborate with Burges' (2008) concept of 'consensual hegemony' as the "leadership strategy of an emerging middle power state" whereby influence is "sought by disseminating ideas or by attempting to create situations where it [becomes] implicitly too costly for other countries to deviate extensively from the Brazilian position" (Burges, 2008:66). It also supports Nina's (2006:21) analysis of President Lula's engagement in an international 'crusade' against hunger as coming closer to realist beliefs (than *idealist* ones), in the sense that it envisaged "the perceived distribution of capabilities in the international system as the main source of systemic incentives to Brazilian policy makers – seen through the perspective of an emerging middle-power constantly in search of power, prestige and recognition of its status". Giving knowledge with no-strings-attached fits the same logic where "standing in support of the development of other countries could be, under certain circumstances, an act of rational self-interest" (Nina, 2006:22). The present research also advances Puente's (2010) thorough historical description of Brazil's use of technical cooperation as a foreign policy tool by adding a theoretical layer of analysis to the same theme. There is ample agreement with many academics who have considered the broad motivations behind Brazil's 'donorship', with significant overlap to Inoue and Vaz's (2013) findings, and worth highlighting:

> The main finding of this article is that the empirical evidence does not fully support the official rhetoric that Brazil's external development assistance is beyond hierarchical international relations. The central argument is that it is accurate to classify Brazil as a 'Southern donor', which expresses both the novelty and tensions of simultaneously being a donor and a developing country. The underlying assumption is that the dual motivations of altruism and national interest are not necessarily mutually exclusive.
>
> (Inoue & Vaz, 2013:508)

### *Areas for further exploration*

This book opens the door for a variety of new questions and research possibilities among the topics here developed. The issues below provide only an initial guide for further venues of academic investigation.

#### *Expanding cases studies*

This research focused on Brazil's provision of technical cooperation, and provided the concise picture of what was done by other traditional and 'emerging' donors. While the actions of DAC donors have been the subject of ample inquiry, mainstream literature has only begun to scratch the surface of non-DAC donors' development assistance actions. Much advance has been made towards detailing and analysing China's donor profile, but the pace has been much slower for Brazil, India, and South Africa. The academic investigation (especially in English) for less 'prominent' net donors (i.e., countries both giving and receiving aid) is very scarce. To be fair, it can be argued this is a consequence of their limited impact upon the global governance of development assistance, the negligible amounts involved in their provisions, and/or the difficulty of obtaining basic data given that official numbers might not even exist. However, this reasoning obscures a myriad of constant foreign policy connections made by most countries in the world who are neither developed nor 'emerging' countries, once again reinforcing the need for a conscious promotion of deeper academic investigation of various nations' approaches to South-South cooperative actions. Also, to theorize over big questions – such as 'why do countries provide development assistance?' and 'why do countries give things (such as knowledge) without demanding anything back?' – the number of case studies available *must* be as wide as possible. To make all-encompassing claims about how donors act based upon data from a few countries, or (at max) DAC's member-countries, can (mis)lead to faulty conclusions.

### *'Emerging' and 'southern' donors*

The need for more in-depth case studies of 'South'-identifying donors is also necessary to tease out what is – and is not – unique about them vis-à-vis 'traditional' donors. To understand *how* and *how much* the SSC framework matters for 'Southern' countries, one cannot only rely on what is done by Brazil, China, India, and South Africa. As a matter of fact, one important next step is to evaluate if these countries (or some of them) constitute a separate category from or within those abiding to SSC. Are 'emerging' donors creating, even if unconsciously, a two-tier structure within South-South relationships? Are they (whether collectively or individually) in fact "eroding the distinction between donors and recipients, thus undermining the old system of donor-dictated, top-down aid" (*The Economist*, 2010)? Even if a more powerful country is fully committed to fostering a horizontal relationship with the less powerful one, will power asymmetries invariably "tilt the axis" to a vertical position (see Abdenur, 2002; also, Mawdsley, 2012)? This was a topic of great debate among Brazilian civil servants interviewed, with no agreement over if Brazil's quest to promote horizontality – which they all said they themselves were individually committed to in their direct contacts with recipients' counterparts – was *perceived* as such by the countries receiving the 'assistance'. Even if Brazil has a genuine desire to engage in horizontally with a country like Mozambique, for example, from this country's point of view the structure might be North-South by proxy, given the power asymmetry between the two. This discussion leads to research possibilities over how *recipients* perceive the approach from individual 'emerging' donors compared to other donors. The prime candidates for such an investigation are African nations, recipients to both 'emerging' and traditional donors.

### *'Emerging' donors, democracy, and transparency*

As previously stated, there appears to be no connection between donor's commitment to democracy and its decision to tie agreements or not. Also, the likelihood of a donor demanding conditionalities are strongly linked to whether it is a DAC-member or not. Yet, as the domestic and international visibility of 'emerging' donors' actions increases, it is possible to speculate that there will also be more scrutiny over unconditional assistance to recipients known for serious human rights violations. It is likely that, in the near future, democratic 'emerging' donors such as Brazil, India, and South Africa will eventually face a clash of principles: to maintain a policy of unconditionality based on the principles of non-interference and sovereignty, or to allow some flexibility and thereby attach pro-democracy/good-governance conditionalities to their development assistance. Either choice will lead valuable empirical cases for those interested in the drivers of foreign policymaking in democratic 'emerging' donors. Greater domestic visibility of giving without securing immediate commercial gains might also prompt some inside these countries to question the strategy, under the lines of 'they [recipients] are needy, but so are we'. In tandem, time can bring about a greater demand for accountability, such as "where is all the effort on cooperation going", and "what results are being achieved" (Andrade, 2009)?

### *Finding and explaining patterns*

The list of issues yet to be explored in this topic is substantial: as already signalled, not only does this involve understanding 'emerging' donors' similarities and differences (1) vis-à-vis 'traditional donors', but also (2) *among* each other. The analysis has indicated great similarities between Brazil and South Africa in their approach towards being development 'donors', and hinted some interesting parallels between Brazil and Norway – what explains these overlaps? The proposed framework of looking at ideas, institutions, and 'positional' forces pushing foreign policy decision-making seems to be a useful tool in helping describe, compare, and theorize about donors' underlying domestic foreign policymaking structures.

### *Definitional issues*

There is space for further refining many of the concepts used, starting with the adjective 'emerging' when referring to Brazil, China, India, South Africa, and other *net* providers of development assistance – what does (or should) *emerging* mean? How adequate is it to equate (for the sake of parsimony) 'non-DAC' to 'Southern' donors? Also, the analysis does leave room for questioning the difference between working with the concepts of 'middle power' and 'middle power diplomacy'. It was posited that the latter was relatively more successful than the former in the understanding of certain foreign policy choices made by Brazil – yet, there is certainly space for further academic scrutiny over the position taken.

***

For Brazil, as for all 'emerging' donors, the future is one of opportunity, expectations, and increasing domestic and international scrutiny over their actions. In the end, with great power comes great responsibility, evoking a millennia-old Biblical passage "from the one who has been entrusted with much, much more will be asked" (Luke 12:48).

## Notes

1 Classical Realism is not a sub-school of Realism: "it is the realist tradition in all its diversity as it unfolded prior to the publication of Waltz's *Theory of International Politics*", which then introduced the idea of *neo*realism (Wohlforth, 2008:136). *Neoclassical* Realists look at the "gritty details of foreign policy that marked classical realism while also benefiting from the rigorous theorizing that typified neorealism" (*idem*, 140).

2 Of course, neither Woods or Hurrell were investigating the specific use of technical cooperation by emerging donors, so it was not their responsibility to explain the variations among these actors.

## Bibliography

ABC – Agência Brasileira de Cooperação. (undated). *Orientação Básica para a Apresentação de Projetos de Cooperação Técnica entre Países em Desenvolvimento – CTPD*. www.abc.gov.br/Content/ABC/docs/PORTFORM-2002.doc.

Abdenur, A. (2002). Tilting the north-south axis: The legitimation of southern development knowledge and its implications for comparative education research. *Current Issues in Comparative Education, 4*(2), 57–69.

Albin, C. (2003). Negotiating international cooperation: Global public goods and fairness. *Review of International Studies, 29*(3), 365–385.

Andrade, M. (2009, February). Is the south ready for South-South Cooperation? *International Policy Centre for Inclusive Growth*, One Pager no. 77.

Baldwin, D. (1966). *Economic development and American foreign policy, 1943–1962*. Chicago, IL: University of Chicago Press.

Barbosa, P. H. (2011). *O Brasil e a EMBRAPA: o viés instrumental da cooperação técnica horizontal*. Brasília: Instituto Rio Branco.

Bermeo, S. B. (2010). Development and strategy: Aid allocation in an interdependent world. http://ssrn.com/abstract=1681104.

Bernal-Meza, R., (2010). International thought in the Lula era. *Revista Brasileira de Política Internacional, 53*(special edition), 193–213.

Burges, S. (2008). Consensual hegemony: Theorizing Brazilian foreign policy after the Cold War. *International Relations, 22*(1), 65–84.

Costa, A. C. (2011, June 25). *Um petista a caminho da FAO.* Veja. http://veja.abril.com.br/noticia/economia/um-petista-a-caminho-da-fao.

*Economist, The.* (2010, July 15). *Brazil's foreign-aid programme – Speak softly and carry a blank cheque.* www.economist.com/node/16592455.

FAO – Food and Agriculture Organization. (2012, February 21). *Brazil to fund food purchasing in five African countries.* www.fao.org/news/story/en/item/123551/icode/.

FAO – Food and Agriculture Organization. (2013, August 28). *FAO-EMBRAPA partnership gets under way.* www.fao.org/about/who-we-are/director-gen/faodg-news-archive/detail/en/c/195690/.

FAO – Food and Agriculture Organization. (2014, January 24). *Angola, Brazil and FAO sign South-South Cooperation agreement.* www.fao.org/news/story/en/item/212887/icode/.

Flemming, T. (2011, July 10). *Elections done right: The FAO.* http://globalmemo.org/2011/07/10/fao-election-the-real-thing/.

Hochstetler, K. (2013). South-south trade and the environment: A Brazilian case study. *Global Environmental Politics, 13*(1), 30–48.

Hook, S. W. (1995). *National interest and foreign aid.* Boulder, CO: L. Rienner Publishers.

Hurrell, A. (2006). Hegemony, liberalism and global order: What space for would-be great powers? *International Affairs, 82*(1), 1–19.

Inoue, C. Y. A., & Vaz, A. C. (2013). Brazil as 'southern donor': Beyond hierarchy and national interests in development cooperation? *Cambridge Review of International Affairs, 25*(4), 507–534.

IPEA – Instituto de Pesquisa Econômica Aplicada. (2013). *Cooperação brasileira para o desenvolvimento internacional: 2010.* Brasília: Instituto de Pesquisa Econômica Aplicada, Agência Brasileira de Cooperação.

Kennan, G. (1993). *Around the Cragged Hill: A personal and political philosophy.* New York: W. W. Norton and Company.

Mawdsley, E. (2012). The changing geographies of foreign aid and development cooperation: Contributions from gift theory. *Transactions of the Institute of British Geographers, 37*(2), 256–272.

*MRE – Ministério das Relações Exteriores.* (2010). Balanço de Política Externa 2003/2010. Brasilia.

Nina, A. (2006). *Action against hunger and poverty: Brazilian foreign policy in Lula's first term (2003–2006).* University of Oxford – Centre for Brazilian Studies, Working Paper No. CBS-83–07.

Oxfam International. (2011, June 24). *Election of new Director General must signal new era for FAO.* www.oxfam.org/en/grow/pressroom/pressrelease/2011-06-24/election-new-director-general-must-signal-new-era-fao#sthash.Em8vOnkm.dpuf.

Puente, C. A. I. (2010). *A cooperação técnica horizontal brasileira como instrumento de política externa: a evolução da cooperação técnica com países em desenvolvimento – CTPD– no período 1995–2005.* Brasília: FUNAG.

Schirm, S. (2012). Leaders in need of followers: Emerging powers in global governance. In E. Fels, J. F. Kremer, & K. Kronenberg (Eds.), *Power in the 21st century: International security and international political economy in a changing world* (pp. 211–236). Berlin: Springer.

Siqueira, A., & Aggege, S. (2011, July 01). A revolução "duplamente verde" de José Graziano. *Carta Capital*. www.cartacapital.com.br/politica/a-revolucao-duplamente-verde-de-jose-graziano

Tran, M. (2011, June 07). FAO's new leader lays out his plans. *The Guardian*. www.theguardian.com/global-development/2011/jun/27/fao-director-jose-graziano-da-silva

Waltz, K. (1993). The emerging structure of international politics. *International Security, 18*(2), 44–79.

Wendt, A. (1999). *Social theory of international politics*. Cambridge: Cambridge University Press.

White, L. (2010). Understanding Brazil's new drive for Africa. *South African Journal of International Affairs, 17*(2), 221–242.

Wohlforth, W. C. (2008). Realism. In C. Reus-Smit & D. Snidal (Eds.), *The Oxford handbook of international relations* (pp. 131–149). Oxford: Oxford University Press.

Woods, N. (2008). Whose aid? Whose influence? China, emerging donors and the silent revolution in development assistance. *International Affairs, 84*(6), 1205–1221.

# Index